Marketing Strategy

The Chartered Institute of Marketing/Butterworth-Heinemann Marketing Series is the most comprehensive, widely used and important collections of books in marketing and sales currently available worldwide.

As the CIM's official publisher Butterworth-Heinemann develops, produces and publishes the complete series in association with the CIM. We aim to provide definitive marketing books for both students and practitioners that promote excellence in marketing education and practice.

The series titles are written by CIM senior examiners and leading marketing educators for professionals, students and those studying the CIM's Certificate, Advanced Certificate and Postgraduate Diploma courses. Now firmly established, these titles provide practical study support to CIM and other marketing students and to practitioners at all levels.

The Chartered Institute of Marketing

Formed in 1911, The Chartered Institute of Marketing is now the largest professional marketing management body in the world with over 60,000 members located worldwide. Its primary objectives are focused on the development of awareness and understanding of marketing throughout UK industry and commerce and in the raising of standards of professionalism in the education, training and practice of this key business discipline.

W9-CNA-902

Books in the series

Forthcoming

Marketing Strategy

Second edition

Paul Fifield

Published in association with
The Chartered Institute of Marketing

BUTTERWORTH
HEINEMANN

OXFORD   AUCKLAND   BOSTON   JOHANNESBURG   MELBOURNE   NEW DELHI

Butterworth-Heinemann
Linacre House, Jordan Hill, Oxford OX2 8DP
225 Wildwood Avenue, Woburn, MA 01801-2041
A division of Reed Educational and Professional Publishing Ltd

 A member of the Reed Elsevier plc group

First published 1992
Paperback edition 1993
Reprinted 1994, 1995, 1997 (twice)
Second edition 1998
Reprinted 1998
Reprinted 1999

British Library Cataloguing in Publication Data
A catalogue record for this book is available from the British Library

ISBN 0 7506 3284 4

Composition by Scribe Design, Gillingham, Kent
Printed and bound in Great Britain by
Biddles Ltd, Guildford and King's Lynn

Contents

Preface to the second edition

The first edition of this book was written in 1990/1991 and was my very first foray into the world of books and writing on such a scale. Over the life of the first edition, the world – and our marketplace – has undergone a number of radical changes, some of which I have tried to capture in this revised edition. Working through the revisions I have been struck by the nature and scope of the changes that have affected marketing over the past six years. Driven by the fundamental changes in society which we have and continue to witness, marketing as it is practised is changing fast. The buoyant markets of the 1980s have given way to 1990s' markets which are much more competitive, focused and unforgiving of failure. Time to plan is a luxury of the past although, paradoxically, the need to plan and think strategically is more important than ever. The simultaneous need to think strategically and act tactically in today's business environment of fewer resources and shortening deadlines is working to separate the marketing 'sheep from the lambs'.

The pace of change in marketing is such that at the moment we are still in the process of working out how to solve today's problems. Knowing that yesterday's solutions no longer work is the first step, finding the answers we need is still a voyage of discovery. I had hoped that this second edition would be more illuminating in terms of answers than it has, in fact, turned out to be. But working with clients on a daily basis it is apparent that markets are moving at a speed that renders 'new' ideas redundant at a rate that makes them inappropriate for a book of this nature. Consequently, I have tried to concentrate on the mindset and attitudes required of the successful and practising marketer in the late 1990s. When there are no successful case histories to guide us only a return to the fundamentals of marketing make sense, from here we will have to create our own case histories.

Also, I stress again that this book is designed primarily for the use and guidance of the *practising marketer*. Since writing the first edition I have spent a number of years as senior examiner (Diploma) at the UK Chartered Institute of Marketing. This role has brought me (and this book) into contact with more academic writers and educators. The response of many to this book's approach to marketing worried me at the time and concerns me more as time goes on. My approach to marketing has remained largely unchanged over more than twenty years and is based on the constantly supported belief that:

1   Long-term profit is the name of the game, and
2   Only satisfied customers (who come back for more) will produce long-term profits.

This book is based on the belief that marketing is about achieving results, not manipulating theories, this is not always a precise or elegant process. Not an approach which some of my academic colleagues find to their taste, believing that technical knowledge and ability to manipulate theory is what should be taught and what should be done. I do not imagine that many academics of this mould will be lovers of this book but I remain unbowed by such criticism. This book was, and is still written for the practising marketer, not the academic. Marketers not driven to find practical and workable answers and to implement them will probably find other marketing texts more to their taste.

Finally I must thank the primary contributors to this edition. They say a writer must always write about what he knows. Working full time as an independent advisor/consultant with large organizations I am confronted by today's complex strategic marketing problems on a daily basis. The problems of declining resources, increasing competition and short-term targets are real for all my clients, both market leaders and pretenders. For all of them, the overwhelming challenge has been to find strategic solutions that can be implemented and then to implement the solutions which we have found. Achieving this has often necessitated rewriting the old tenets of marketing. Without the experience gained working with such clients, this edition could not have been written. It is a great pity they must remain anonymous.

Paul Fifield

Preface to the first edition

This book has been written with one clear goal in mind – to make the whole area of Marketing Strategy (and Strategic Marketing) accessible to the widest possible audience. I have tried to strip away all the jargon, the mystique and the confusion that tends to surround one of the most simple and common sense areas of modern business – marketing. Only response from you, the reader, will tell me whether I have succeeded.

Putting the theories, the science and the buzzwords to one side, there is really nothing at all complicated about marketing and marketing strategy. We and our organizations will continue to thrive as long as we make what our customers want. As soon as we deviate from this simple line we will start to founder. Obvious – yes. Common sense – yes. Then why do we all have so many problems? Because we are human beings and not machines.

Human nature is what, I hope, typifies this book. Marketers are people, customers are people, even organizations are simply collections of people. Marketing and strategy are about relationships – not organizations to markets but, in reality, people to people – it is this simple dimension that I have tried to bring into play all through discussions about financial objectives, competition, market segmentation, etc. Not that theories are completely absent, they have their place, but they cannot be used to hide behind.

This book is written above all for the practising marketer, whether in marketing, finance, engineering, personnel or sales, and at any level in the organization that is affected by the customer. The book follows what is, I hope, a logical framework but the most important lesson must be, *try it*. Try something, see how it works and then grow bolder. As Samuel Johnson said, it matters little which leg you put in the trousers first!

When you try – let me know what happens.

Paul Fifield

Acknowledgement

To Jane

Without whom subsequent editions would have been unthinkable.

Introduction

What is marketing?

'Consumption is the sole end and purpose of all production; and the interest of the producer ought to be attended to, only as far as it may be necessary for promoting that of the consumer. The maxim is so self-evident that it would be absurd to attempt to prove it. But in the mercantile system, the interest of the consumer is almost constantly sacrificed to that of the producer; and it seems to consider production, and not consumption, as the ultimate end and object of all industry and commerce.'

Adam Smith, 'Wealth of Nations', 1776

Definitions of marketing abound, from the lengthy and all-embracing academic versions to the short and snappy favoured by advertising executives. The concept is not new, it is not difficult to understand, it is not difficult to explain to the troops and our customers love it. Why then does it seem almost impossible to implement? Why, when we look at the quotation from Adam Smith, do we wonder whether we have made any progress at all over the past 200 years?

There are four distinct but interrelated aspects to the concept of marketing. It is at one and the same time:

- an attitude of mind;
- a way of organizing the business;
- a range of activities;
- the producer of profits.

The literature's apparent obsession with marketing as a range of activities, has tended to overshadow the first two, much more important, aspects. This is the first, but not the last, time that we will see how western society's preference for 'doing' rather than 'thinking' has too often made it more difficult for real businesses to make real profits.

Marketing as an attitude of mind

This is what is known as 'marketing orientation'. Marketing as a fundamental business philosophy is a state of mind which should permeate the entire organization. It states quite categorically that we recognize that our existence, and future survival and growth, depends on our ability to give our customers what they want. Internal considerations must be subservient to the wider needs of the marketplace.

These are of course fine words and unlikely to raise any serious objections. Nevertheless it must be apparent to all of us, whether consumers or producers, that this happy state of affairs is quite rare in the real world. Why?

We should all realize (but not necessarily use as an excuse) that looking outward and taking cues from the marketplace and the wider business environment is easier said than done. The larger the organization, the more the customer is excluded from the decision-making process. The organization becomes an entity in itself with self-sustaining systems that demand constant attention. The customer is out of sight and so, increasingly, out of mind. Employees are recruited and promoted for tending the system and worshipping at the altar of internal efficiency. Worse still, it is often the most able corporate politicians that gain promotion so signalling to everyone the skills that the organization really values. We can complain:

- we can say that it's all wrong;
- we can even say it won't happen in our company.

But, being realistic, we should recognize that this is in fact the normal state of affairs in any organization.

This 'internal orientation' is the very antithesis of market orientation and the two cannot co-exist. We can decry internal orientation as blinkered, petty and damaging but we cannot ignore its attraction. While we might know that without satisfied customers we do not have a business, we all spend our days on office and factory floors where customers are forbidden. Our working lives are effectively dominated by internal issues such as regular cost-cutting exercises, selecting a company car, who gets a private office and who sits in the open-plan area, who gets fitted carpets and a chair with arms or . . . . Human nature being what it is, we should not be surprised that customer interests are forced down the scale of priorities on a regular basis.

The marketing philosophy can be driven through any organization, but it will not be easy. We cannot expect the logic of the argument to succeed on its own. The principal problem is not one of introduction but of regression. Presented in the right way and from the right point (the top), marketing orientation has an inescapable logic and very few people will fail to espouse the cause. Getting there is not the problem – staying there is. Unless accompanied by appropriate changes in the systems and the organizational structure, internal issues will continue to distract attention away from the needs of the marketplace and marketing orientation will be yet another flavour-of-the-month exercise dreamed up by management that has nothing better to do. Regression is a real and constant threat. Maintaining a marketing attitude of mind will be a full-time job for all the organization's senior managers.

Here is your first management conflict, all this takes time, effort and money – how can we be sure that it is necessary and that it will pay off? Much will depend on the particular competitive position faced by your organization. If you are in a cosy market with no real head-to-head competition and no danger of easy substitution then you probably don't have to change – yet.

If you are in a more exposed and competitive environment, and making enough money, you have probably had to change already. Now comes the real test, can you keep on changing to retain the market position you have attained? This is not the time to rest on your laurels and watch the competition leap-frog you in their turn.

Marketing as a way of organizing the business

If we accept that the organization exists and will continue to exist only as long as it continues to satisfy the needs of its customers, we must ensure that the organization has a structure that will enable it to deliver. How many times have you, as a customer, tried to 'phone a large company to get some information or to register a complaint? While you are being passed from one person to another, from one department to another like an unwelcome guest you might get the impression that the organization had been designed for its own convenience rather than for you, the customer – you might be right.

Organizational structure and design are critically important to market-place success. No purpose is served by instilling and nurturing the marketing philosophy if the structure of the organization makes it impossible for the people to deliver on their promises. The traditional structure of larger organizations, the functional pyramid, is designed for internal efficiency but is relatively rigid in the face of a constantly changing marketplace. The temptation is always for this type of organization to attempt to mould the market to its own needs rather than adapting itself to the needs of its customers. Organizations of this type are typically long established and may have emerged from a protected or regulated environment. Often laden with older managers who lament the passing of the good old days when customers bought what 'they were damn well offered – and were grateful for it', these organizations do not always achieve a graceful transition to the new order. Many of the large and powerful organizations of the 1950s and 1960s found the internal friction too great to bear and have since been absorbed by more adaptive organizations or have disappeared altogether.

If the organization is to survive in today's fast changing environment, it must make itself more responsive to its customers. Typically this will mean:

- shorter chains of communication and command;
- fewer people employed in 'staff' or other non-customer related functions; and
- an overall structure that reflects the different needs of the marketplace rather than the technical specializations of employees.

Following privatization the UK's British Telecom embarked on a series of reorganizations. Operation 'Sovereign' at the end of the 1980s attempted to reduce numbers as well as levels/grades in the organization so that no employee was more than six steps distant from the chairman – no mean feat for an organization of (then) 240,000 people!

As any good industrial psychologist will tell us, structure gives behaviour. The appropriate organizational structure can play a major part in reinforcing the marketing attitude of mind over the longer term.

Marketing as a range of activities

Marketing is also a range of specific activities used by the marketing department to meet marketing and business objectives. Centred mainly around the concept of the marketing mix (traditionally accepted as including product, price, place and promotion), this is the technical 'how to' of the discipline.

Marketing as the producer of profits

It is generally accepted that marketing has the responsibility for producing profits. Indeed Peter Drucker went as far as to say that, only marketing and innovation produced profits for an organization, and all other areas should be regarded as costs. Profits are generated by markets. Profits are not generated by products, by efficiency, by management or by diligent workforces. It is only the customer's willingness to pay the right price for the right product or service which keeps us in business. Marketing, as the primary interface between the organization and the markets which it serves, is then the primary producer of the organization's profit stream.

But it is in the area of profit that we meet what is probably the most critical role of marketing. In almost every organization there is likely to be a stark conflict between the customer's need for value and the organization's need for profit and efficiency.

It is the role of marketing to search for and strike the elusive balance between these two demands. Hugh Davidson suggests a solution to this problem and while agreeing that marketers should always start by asking what is best for the customer the 'offensive marketer' should ask the other questions as well:

- given that there is more than one way of satisfying customer demand, which route is the most efficient from the organization cost point of view; and
- how can we best balance customer need for value against the organization's need to create and maintain a low-cost operation.

Profit is a function of the price which the customer is willing to pay and the cost of production. Successful and effective marketing (if measured in profit terms) must pay attention to both these areas. Marketing is definitely *not* about satisfying customers at any price. Marketing is about satisfying customers at a profit.

Non-marketing orientations

So far we have looked at the holy grail of business in the 1990s, the market-oriented organization. There are other forms of business philosophy or orientation. These are not only alive and well but are still in the majority although this fact should surprise nobody given the problems associated with achieving and retaining a marketing orientation. The next three styles of business are the most common.

Production orientation

The production-oriented organization's primary concern is to maintain a constant and uninterrupted flow of materials and product through the production process. This organization is in the business of finding any markets it can for what it happens to make. It is much more concerned with what it makes than what the market wants. On a day-to-day basis its primary concerns are with production efficiency and cost control. This organization relies heavily on sales orders to feed the production system but has little interest in where the product goes. Consequently there is a heavy emphasis on sales volume but little interest in sales direction.

Product orientation

The product-oriented organization's primary concern is to produce 'the best product'. It works to create an ever better mousetrap and then waits for the world to beat a path to its door. This organization firmly believes that the best product will sell itself (and always quotes Rolls-Royce as its model). Unfortunately, this organization is so wrapped up in the technical possibilities emerging from research and development that it is disconnected from the marketplace. It does not know what constitutes the 'best product' from the customer's point of view so continually improves and enhances the product with its own opinion of the needed features – and wonders why sales do not double overnight. This organization still relies heavily on sales volume to feed the production process but knows too little about marketplace demand to offer any useful direction to the sales effort.

Sales orientation

The sales-oriented organization, unlike the product-oriented organization, believes that fundamentally all products and/or services are the same. It therefore follows that success will come to the company that sells the hardest. This organization has little allegiance to the product or the production process and may even buy in product from outside suppliers. It believes that sales volume is the only measure of success and it is prepared to support the sales activity fully in terms of heavy promotional activity and price competition – anything to maintain sales levels and volume. Once again the sales activity is given little direction but targets are an integral part of the corporate culture.

How does the marketing-oriented organization approach differ from these three?

Marketing orientation

The marketing-oriented organization does not start the whole process with the product. The most important factor for this organization is the customer. It understands that it is not, in fact, selling products but that it is providing solutions to match identified customer needs or problems. This organization realizes that it can be dangerous to become too closely associated with the product it produces because customer demand may change forcing the organization into new or different technologies to retain its markets. It realizes that it will still have to produce and deliver efficiently, but that long term success will ultimately depend on its ability to listen to the marketplace.

When discussing the concepts of marketing and marketing orientation, the most common question I am asked is 'why should we bother to take all this on?' Being practical, it is not an easy question to answer. As we have seen, the road to marketing orientation is not easy, worse, once you have arrived you have to fight to stay there. As long as you are making enough money to keep your owners satisfied and to allow reinvestment in the fabric of the business then why bother? Why not continue just as we are? The answer to these and similar questions lies in the competitive nature of any particular business. If you have identified your organization as production, product or sales oriented and you still command a sizeable market share and are making reasonable profits, then the odds are that your competition is similar. As long as the competition stays that way you will not have a problem. Unfortunately as (among others) UK and US car producers discovered, competition doesn't always stay that way.

> 'If I had set out to write this book twenty years ago, or even ten years ago, my starting point would have been very different.
>
> Then I would have had to focus it on the reasons *why* I think every business should be customer driven. It may be hard to believe it now but only a short time ago that idea was off the wall.
>
> Every business has customers. Every business took them into account to some extent. But very, very few were genuinely customer driven.
>
> By customer driven I mean a company where *all* the key decisions are based on a overriding wish to serve the customer better. A company where everyone in it sees serving the customer as their *only* business.
>
> That's the principle on which I staked my supermarket business in 1960.
>
> I didn't do so because I believed in it as a theory. I did it because it came naturally to me, and because my very first business experience as a teenager convinced me of it.
>
> Once the company was up and running, I learnt two things very quickly. First, that the customer-driven approach pays off. Second, I also found that the customer-driven approach that came naturally to me was incredibly rare. I say "incredibly" because I find it hard to believe that people could so often ignore something that was at the root of their profitability.'
>
> Feargal Quinn (1990), *Crowning the Customer*. O'Brien Press, Dublin.

The future as always is unclear but forecasters appear united on a few important aspects. There is general agreement that competition is becoming, and will continue to be, more international in the 1990s/2000s.

Protected markets will be eroded and more organizations will be exposed to stronger and determined competition.

Consumers too have changed in the 1990s, in some countries more than others. The 1980s saw increased disposable income in Europe and North America matched by increased consumer spending and debt. The recessions of the early 1990s have had a profound effect on British consumers and less effect on other countries – as yet. While the fundamental change in British society created by economic conditions of the first part of the decade have still to be fully understood there are signs that as income continues to rise people's perceptions of security, confidence and therefore 'need' have changed significantly. Consumption in the UK (mirrored to a greater or lesser extent in other countries) has and will continue to move towards higher quality, more individualistic products and services.

As consumers buy less often, but products that they expect to last, organizations will have to work harder to satisfy their needs. Given the explosion of products and services on offer the consumer of the 1990s/2000s will award no points for trying – only succeeding.

What is strategy?

'Thus it is in war the victorious strategist only seeks battle after the victory has been won, whereas he who is destined to defeat first fights and afterwards looks for victory.

'In warfare, first lay plans which will ensure victory, and then lead your army to battle; if you will not begin with stratagem but rely on brute strength alone, victory will no longer be assured.'

Sun Tzu, 500 BC

The word 'strategy' has become one of the most common and badly used words in business writing. Everywhere we look we see terms such as business strategy, corporate strategy, marketing strategy, strategic marketing, product strategy, pricing strategy, advertising strategy and even discount strategy. We are not helped by the original, flexible use of the Greek word *strategos* from which our word strategy derives. In its original form it meant the art of the General or Commander-of-the-armies. The first time the word 'strategy' was used in a business context was by William Newman, in a book published as recently as 1951. Now the word strategy is almost synonymous with 'important'.

Overworking the word in this way helps nobody. It simply serves to confuse. Strategy in its strictest sense refers to means and not ends. Strategy is all about how an organization will achieve its objectives. Best described as **business strategy**, the original meaning concentrated on how the key decision making unit of the organization or the board was going to marshall its resources in order to achieve its stated **business objective**. The use of the word strategy in the business literature arose when it became apparent to management researchers that, in sharp contrast to economic models of perfect competition, companies engaged in the same activity and using the same technology often performed differently. Closer inspection suggested that firms in the same industry adopted different approaches to products, distribution and organizational structures. These differences, within similar market environments, came to be known as 'strategies'. The concept was readily absorbed into Harvard Business School's Business Policy curriculum in the 1950s and 1960s. This concept will be explored in more detail in Part Two.

At this point, however, we need to highlight the most significant aspects of strategy. This should help to dispel some of the major misconceptions which have sometimes been encouraged by sections of the marketing literature.

Strategy is longer term

Since strategy is about marshalling the gross resources of the organization to match the needs of the marketplace and achieve the business objective, this cannot be a short-term activity. Every organization is complex and any change takes time to accomplish. Strategic decisions like the general choosing his battle ground, will have long-term implications. Strategic decisions, such as which business area to enter, cannot be reversed at a moment's notice – momentum has to be built over a planned period.

Strategy is not changed every Friday

Constant change produces uncertainty, confusion, misdirection and wastage – not results. Tactics are designed to change on a weekly or even a daily basis in response to changes in the marketplace caused by customer needs or competitive response. Tactical change causes no problems of uncertainty since the strategy, the broad overall direction of the organization, remains constant.

Strategy is not another word for important tactics

Tactics can be likened to manoeuvres on the field of battle and can be changed as often as required in response to the changing situation faced by the organization in its markets. No matter how important or critical the tactic under review, this does not make it a strategy. For the want of a nail the horseshoe, the horse, the knight, the battle and the war were lost – I agree, but once 1000 soldiers have found a nail each they should all know that the reason why they are there is to win the war – not to search for nails.

Strategy is not top management's secret

Strategy is undoubtedly top management's responsibility to define and agree but not to keep as one of the organization's most closely guarded secrets. Top management can decide the strategy on their own (it is normally safer by far that they involve others in the process too) but they cannot implement it alone. Strategy is most effective when those that have to implement it not only understand it but also believe it and can see their own role in carrying it out. As Mintzberg (1996) states: 'Every failure of implementation is, by definition, also a failure of formulation.' The only reason for formulating strategy is to create some profitable activity in the marketplace. If people are to implement they must know what, how and why. Despite management's traditional reluctance, communication and active involvement will often be the key to success.

Strategy is not just a public relations exercise

One of the first rules of strategy formulation, as we shall see in Part Two, is that it must be capable of implementation. Hence the British military strategy in the first years of the Second World War was, despite the fine words and propaganda, not aimed at beating the German armies – Britain simply did not have the resource to do so. Rather the strategy was one of containment of Hitler's ambitions while trying to assemble the resources needed to defeat the enemy. Strategy is about action not words. It is about implementation not just planning.

Strategy is based on analysis, not straws in the wind

While tactics are properly based on short-term market developments, they can be either active or re-active in nature. Effective tactics often depend on a rapid summing up of the market situation followed by fast implementation. Strategy, on the other hand, is about the long term. Rapid summings up and reaction are unlikely, of themselves, to be sufficient to build a robust strategy. To build a sound strategy for the future we will need a deeper degree of analysis – at least beginning to understand why things are happening as well as just knowing what is happening. An analysis of the macro and market environments is essential even for the more 'emergent' strategic routes that the organization may favour.

Strategy is essential to an organization's survival

If you don't know where you are going, then any road will take you there. A well thought out strategy will allow managers to test actions and propose tactics against that strategy and the overall business objective to ensure the consistency which is essential to continued success. Without a clear guiding strategy, managers will continue to spend time and money agonizing over decisions that could be made in minutes if only they knew what their organization was trying to do. Worse, managers will take decisions that look reasonable given the tactical information available but which will have to be undone at a later stage because of conflict either with other tactical decisions made elsewhere in the organization or with top management's privately held view of the future direction. A well-communicated and understood strategy brings the organization together and provides a common purpose. It, like marketing orientation, involves everyone in the organization and challenges them to relate what they do to what the whole organization is trying to achieve. If people and departments are not all looking in the same direction, they cannot help but be working against each other. In the more competitive days ahead, it is less and less reasonable to expect customers to pay for our inefficiency.

Of course, some commentators state that organizations should not continually seek to survive. That a regular flow of business failures is necessary to unlock human and physical resources to 'refresh the genepool' – but that's another story.

What is marketing strategy?

'Those who want to make sure of succeeding in their battles and assaults, must seize the favourable moments when they come and not shrink on occasion from heroic measures; that is to say, they must resort to such means of attack as fire, water and the like. What they must not do, and what will prove fatal, is to sit still and simply hold on to the advantages they have got.'

Sun Tzu, 500 BC

Anyone brave enough (or reckless enough) to have consulted more than one of the wide range of books or articles on the subject of marketing strategy will have discovered that every author seems to start from his or her own premise and lays down a new set of parameters and definitions before starting to write. It is worthwhile reproducing here a selection of some of the better known definitions of marketing strategy, for example:

'The (marketing) strategy concept can be encapsulated into two core elements: the product-market investment decision which encompasses the product-market scope of the business strategy, its investment intensity and the resource allocation in a multiple business context.

'The development of a sustainable competitive advantage to compete in those markets. This core concept encompasses underlying distinctive competences or assets, appropriate objectives, functional area politics and the creation of synergy.'

Aaker

'Marketing strategy (is) a process of strategically analysing environmental, competitive and business factors affecting business units and forecasting future trends in business areas of interest to the enterprise. Participating in setting business objectives and formulating corporate and business unit strategy. Selecting target market strategies for: the product-markets in each business unit, establishing marketing objectives, and developing, implementing and managing program positioning strategies for meeting target market needs.'

Cravens

'Marketing strategy: This section of the marketing plan indicates how each element of the marketing mix and each subdivision of the elements will be used to achieve marketing objectives. The detailed provisions of this part of the plan enable specific operations to be carried out by designated personnel in a definite time span.

Foxall

'Marketing strategy (can be specified) as being composed of five component parts, . . . market positioning, product positioning, the marketing mix, . . . market entry and timing.

'The rationale for finalizing marketing strategy as being composed of these five components is that they represent the central issues of the marketing operation.'

Greenley

'Strategic marketing management is the analytical process of seeking differential advantage through (1) the analysis and choice of the firm's product-market relationships with a view toward developing the best yield configuration in terms of financial performance: and (2) the formulation of management strategies that create and support viable product-market relationships consistent with the enterprise capabilities and objectives.'

Kerrin and Peterson

'A master marketing strategy provides the linkage between the strategic plan and specific marketing programs. On the one hand, it should be consistent with, and contribute to the achievement of the objectives specified in the strategic plan. Simultaneously, it should provide an integrative focus and direction for all marketing activities.

'After market targets have been selected, it is useful to spell out, in general terms, the marketing strategy that will be used to penetrate them. As used here, marketing strategy refers to the general procedure and central concept upon which the firm's entire approach to the market hinges.'

Kollatt, Blackwell and Robeson

'Marketing strategy is the marketing logic by which the business unit expects to achieve its marketing objectives. Marketing strategy consists of making decisions on the business's marketing expenditures, marketing mix, and marketing allocations in relation to expected environmental and competitive conditions.'

Kotler

'Marketing strategy reflects the company's best opinion as to how it can most profitably apply its skills and resources to the marketplace. It is inevitably broad in scope. The plan which stems from it will spell out action and timings and will contain the detailed contribution expected from each department.

'Marketing strategies are the means by which marketing objectives will be achieved and are generally concerned with the four major elements of the marketing mix, as follows: Product, Price, Place, Promotion.

'Formulating marketing strategies is one of the most critical and difficult parts of the entire marketing process. It sets the limit of success. Communicated to all management levels, it indicates what strengths are to be developed, what weaknesses are to be remedied, and in what manner. Marketing strategies enable operating decisions to bring the company into the right relationship with the emerging pattern of market opportunities which previous analysis has shown to offer the highest prospect of success.'

McDonald

'Marketing strategy (is) an approach, a process and a set of skills, for examining business situations and a "marketing strategy statement" (is) the output of applying this approach.'

Wensley

'A marketing strategy encompasses selecting and analysing a target market (a group of people whom the organisation wants to reach) and creating and maintaining an appropriate Marketing Mix (product, distribution, promotion and price) that will satisfy those people. A marketing strategy articulates a plan for the best use of the organisation's resources and tactics to meet its objectives.'

Dibb, Simkin, Pride and Ferrell

'A marketing strategy is the means by which a marketing objective is achieved.'

McDonald and Payne

These definitions are by no means exhaustive. There are many, many more for the interested reader to discover. The major problem for the practitioner, the manager who would actually like to do something about the organization's marketing strategy, is where to start. The one thing the many definitions do is to confuse. We are left with burning questions: What is marketing strategy? What is included in marketing strategy? Where does marketing strategy start and finish?

The main reason for this apparent confusion is the writers' attempts to try and force every possible situation into a generalized blueprint concept. Marketing is littered with attempts to force theories out of observed 'good practice' and thus make the teacher's and the consultant's job that much easier. We should once and for all accept that this scientific approach just doesn't work in areas like marketing. Marketing success depends on customer acceptance and this is just not predictable in any scientific sense within scientific limits of accuracy.

Also, within the different definitions, we see a whole range of modern marketing terms. Many of these we think we know, at least we have heard of them at some time, although we may not feel completely at ease about what to do with them. Terms such as:

Environmental factors	Target market needs
Business factors	Sustainable competitive advantage
Business units	Marketing programmes
Target market strategies	The marketing mix (The four P's)
Product markets	Market positioning
Marketing objectives	Product positioning
Program positioning strategies	Market entry

Given enough time, we should all be able to understand what these concepts mean in isolation. What is not forthcoming from the literature, however, is how to use these ideas practicably. How to apply these concepts in a real business environment, which ones to pursue, which ones to ignore, what order to apply them and how they interrelate – if at all. Unfortunately, and here we really must be fair to the writers, it is not easy to give prescriptive help that is applicable to every organization. Each situation is different and each organization will have to respond to its own particular market circumstances.

Marketing strategy then, will mean different things to different organizations. It will fulfil different needs both within the organization and in the marketplace. Organizations differ in a number of respects:

- the variety and nature of markets served;
- the variety and complexity of products and/or services marketed;
- the diverse nature of technology and operating processes used;
- the 'sophistication' of existing planning procedures;
- the characters and capabilities of the individuals involved in the strategy formulation and planning process;
- the norms and values of the organization;
- the nature of the business environment within which the organization must operate;
- the nature of competition; and
- the nature and demands of the stakeholders and so on.

Having now looked at what other writers have done and criticized everything, I am going to avoid the issue of definition completely. Rather than attempt an all-encompassing string of words that cannot fail to be misleading for the practitioner, we shall leave the question of what marketing strategy is until later in the book. More importantly we will look at what marketing strategy does. After all, it is only through practical application that marketing strategies have any meaning for, or effect on, the business.

Marketing strategy is the process by which the organization translates its business objective and business strategy into market activity.

This critical link between business strategy and marketing strategy is invariably lost in the literature since business or corporate strategy is deemed a different discipline from marketing. While this split is reinforced by the business schools and the management gurus who may have different skills and who certainly come from different business backgrounds, the artificial split between these two areas is absurd and potentially dangerous for two very clear reasons.

First, the marketing director, vice-president or person in charge of the marketing function in an organization is simply incapable of developing a clear marketing objective and practical marketing strategy without a deep and thorough understanding of the organization's business objective and its business strategy over the longer term. If we do not have a clear idea of what the organization is doing, where it is going and quite precisely where it wants to be in three, five or ten years time, then our marketing can be nothing more than a reactive day-to-day function in the organization. In effect there will not be a marketing strategy – or worse it will exist in name alone.

Second, the practical success of the organization's business objective and strategy will depend on the quality of the marketing input right at the top. In too many organizations strategic planning is seen as top management sitting down and transferring to paper their ambitions or wishes of where they would like the organization to be or how they would like the organization to behave. While satisfying and even productive, in terms of producing a written document of some sort, this is unlikely of itself to produce success. Documents such as this (and I have seen plenty) tend to be inward looking and often fail to take proper account of external competitive and market factors. As we have seen, profits are produced only by customers and an organization's success will depend on its ability to continue to satisfy customer needs and wants over the longer term. Setting the business objective and developing the business strategy then, will depend on a good understanding of the organization's competitive position and the present and most likely future trends in customer demand. In other words there is a critical marketing input right at the very beginning of the business or corporate planning stage.

To put it bluntly, a business plan that is not securely rooted in the market place will be irrelevant. Any plan is only as good as its implementation. The 1970s saw a proliferation of strategic planning departments – in organizations that are no longer with us today. The reason for this is simple – the growing availability of computer power and statistical modelling techniques blinded managers to one important fact. If the business objective and strategy are not based on a realistic assessment of the organization's present position and likely market opportunities – then the plan is not worth the paper it is written on.

Since the two areas of business planning and marketing planning are so intricately intertwined the next section of this book will look as briefly as possible at the whole area of business planning with a special emphasis on the marketing input to the business objective and business strategy before looking in somewhat more depth at the whole, presently quite confused, area of marketing strategy – both what it is and what it does.

To start then – at the beginning

'Now the general who wins a battle makes many calculations in his temple ere the battle is fought. The general who loses a battle makes but few calculations beforehand. Thus do many calculations lead to victory, and few calculations to defeat: how much more no calculations at all! It is by attention to this point that I can foresee who is likely to win or lose.'

Sun Tzu, 500 BC

Having been lulled into a sense of security so far by (I hope) everything seeming to make some sense, we arrive at a figure. The good news is that the whole strategic process can be represented in one flow chart, the bad news is that it is more than a little complicated and we will need the whole of the rest of the book to go through it! A firm believer in the need to get all the pain out of the way at the outset so that we can fully enjoy the recuperation, I have laid out the full plan in all its malevolence as seen in Figure 1.

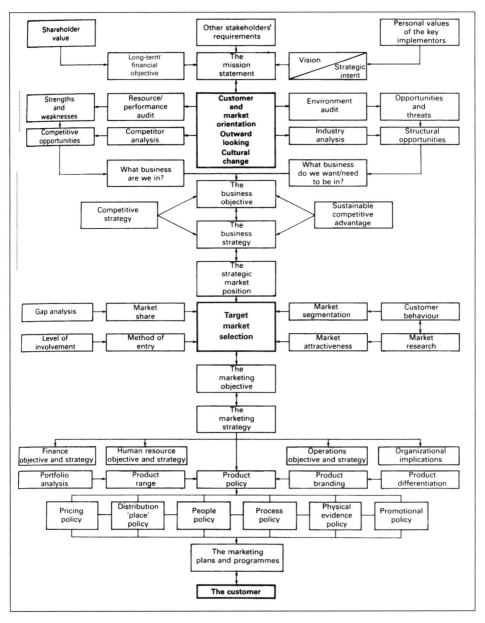

Figure I   A flow chart for evolving marketing strategy

Assuming that your eyes are still focusing, a few points should be made at this stage:

- This chart is intended to show the *approximate relationships* between the various aspects, analyses and decisions that go to make up the business and marketing strategy formulation process.
- The arrows are intended to show one possible route for logical thought through the process. However, as we shall see later, this is one but not the only route.
- Since every organization faces different competitive and market conditions, then no single strategic process can possibly be proposed to suit all needs. This chart should not be viewed as a blueprint.
- Practitioners should feel perfectly free to adapt and amend the diagram to meet their own needs. Certainly some sections might be jumped and others emphasized to meet specific requirements.
- Before you skip or downgrade a stage in the process, make sure you fully understand what it is you are leaving out!

In the same way that an ant may eat an elephant, we will have to break the complete figure down to bite-size pieces before we can hope to put any of this into practice. To do this it is probably easier to see the whole diagram as an explosion of the traditional three steps in strategy development. The four key questions are:

1   Where are we now?
2   Where do we want to be?
3   How do we get there?
4   How do we make it happen?

The approach of this book

This book is aimed primarily at marketing practitioners. People who have to implement marketing ideas for a profit. With such an audience in mind I have decided to break down the strategy approach according to what seems logical from a practitioner's point of view. Readers approaching the subject from a more academic point of view may find some of the process misleading and to them I make my apologies. I may apologize but I remain unrepentant – implementation not formulation is the key to profitable marketing strategy and to get the ideas 'on to the street' sometimes some rules just have to be bent a little.

To make the approach of this book as practical and as accessible as possible it will follow the four-step approach to strategy described above.

Part One will look at the detailed analysis that is essential to the development of any robust, practical marketing strategy. Part Two looks in more depth at the specific question of how to develop and plan marketing strategy. Part Three separates marketing strategy from marketing tactics and considers how strategy is implemented.

Part One – Where are we now?

Before the marketer can hope to develop even the most rudimentary strategic decisions, a degree of analysis is required. Marketing may be more art than science but working on gut feeling is not the same thing as working by the seat of the pants. We should never forget that the quality of gut feeling or intuition improves with the amount of painstaking research that goes before. The groundwork stage can be put into three steps.

The internal business drivers

Too many marketers try to bluster their way through life with a 'holier-than-thou' attitude towards the business's customers. Customers are important, more important than they are treated in most organizations, true – but the customer is not all. There are essential forces alive in every organization that cannot just be ignored (see Figure 2). Taking an ostrich-like approach to those forces will not solve the problem.

The owners and key managers of the organization are human beings and they have needs, wants and demands that your organization must

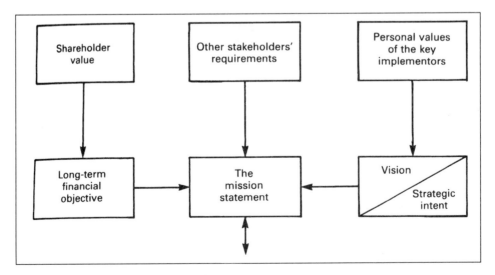

Figure 2 The internal business drivers

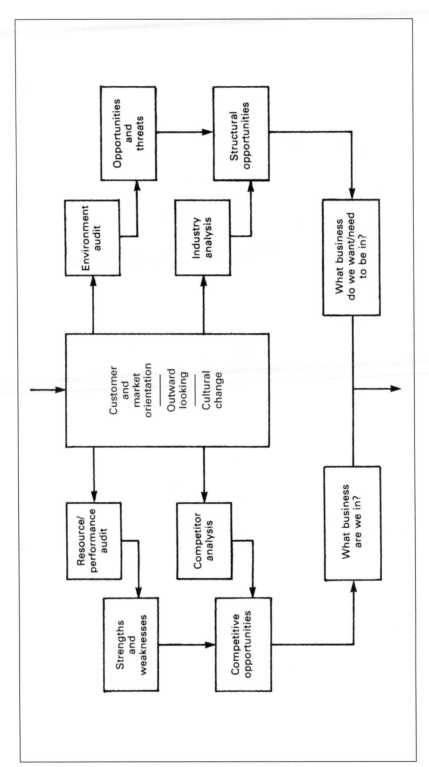

Figure 3 The external environment

satisfy. The marketer must understand these important forces as many of them can run directly counter to the needs of the customer. It will be the marketer's delicate task to manage these often opposing demands so as to satisfy as many people as possible inside the organization while creating unbeatable value for the customer.

The external environment

No man (or organization) is an island – clichéd but true. No organization in the 1990s/2000s, regardless of size and market power, can pursue its goals in disregard of the business environment within which it operates (see Figure 3). We will look, in some detail, at this process of analysis. At what can be learned from the environment.

More important (when dealing with matters strategic rather than the detailed, tactical aspects of marketing) is the way in which this analysis is carried out.

Have you ever wondered why, when the same facts exist to be uncovered by all, some organizations are successful in the marketplace while others are not. The secret lies not in the quality of the information itself, but rather in the way that it is perceived and interpreted.

Customer and market orientation is the key. Investigating and analysing (often for far too long) the external environment from a basic understanding of what the organization needs rather than what the customer needs will only produce a long series of product-led answers. The secret, as we shall see, is not what to look for – but how to look.

Developing the business strategy

The whole area of business strategy has experienced something of a hype during the 1980s, mostly produced by the thoughts and writings of Michael Porter. While Porter's books adorn countless thousands of influential bookshelves, developing business strategy now seems to be no easier than it ever was.

We shall look at the problems encountered in developing a long-term business strategy (see Figure 4) as well as the essential (but not developed by Porter) link between the marketing orientation of the organization, business strategy and marketing strategy.

Part Two – Where do we want to be?

This, the main part of the book, covers the various elements of marketing strategy. I have been careful to separate marketing strategy from marketing tactics, a common fault in many writings on the subject, and have concentrated on the critical influence of the market on the organi-

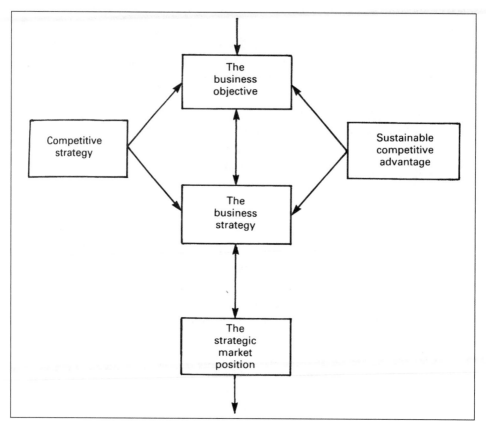

Figure 4   Developing the business strategy

zation's activity. Many of the headings in this part will be familiar to most practising marketers although how they fit together may not! (See Figure 5.)

Part Three – How do we get there?

The third part deals with the subject area which is probably most familiar to readers of marketing text books. I shall not deal with the area of marketing tactics in any depth – this job has been very successfully accomplished in a number of other publications and you, like me, probably have your favourites.

The main aim of this part is to demonstrate the relationship between marketing strategy and marketing tactics. More importantly we will look at the whole area of strategic implementation, an area far too often

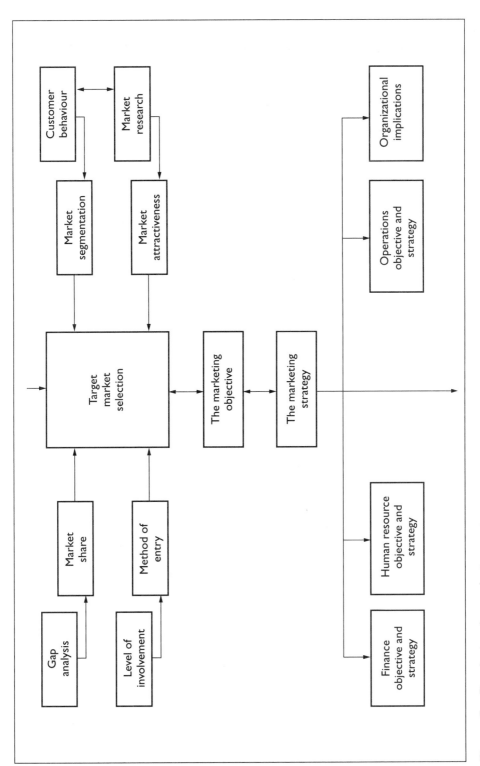

Figure 5 Developing the marketing strategy

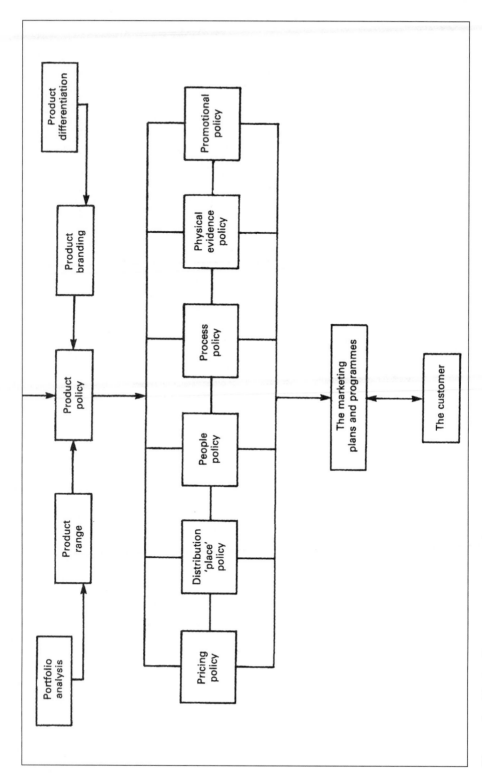

Figure 6 Moving from strategy to tactics

ignored by strategic writing that seems to favour the comeback to the practical (see Figure 6).

Part Four – How do we make it happen?

This part will look at the seemingly endless list of barriers to the implementation of marketing strategy and what can be done about them. It will also look at using 'the system' to help support and implement the sometimes radical ideas that marketing strategy represents.

Part Five – Where next?

This final part should be approached only by the more advanced, secure reader who is happy to have questions raised for which there are no obvious ready-made answers.

The world is changing ever more rapidly and we are all being forced to confront, to a greater or lesser extent, situations which are unfamiliar. Situations which have not appeared in the past and for which our experience has few solutions to offer.

Pundits, futurologists and prophets have labelled the phenomena but cannot agree on where it will all end. The only common prediction they make is for more and greater uncertainty.

Strategy and planning can deal with a degree of uncertainty but there are limits. How then do we set marketing strategy for a series of unknown and unfamiliar situations? Do we have to question the whole basis of our current thinking as we approach the end of the century?

A lot of questions and, I'm afraid at the moment, not too many answers.

Further reading

Davidson H., *Even More Offensive Marketing*, Harmondsworth (Penguin, 1997).

Oliver G., *Marketing Today* 3rd edition, Englewood Cliffs, N.J. (Prentice Hall, 1990).

Townsend R., *Up The Organization* expanded edition, London (Coronet, 1975).

Tzu S. (Clavell J., ed.) *The Art of War*, London (Hodder & Stoughton, 1981).

Part One

Where are we now?

Chapter 1

Before we start – what are we trying to do?

'The purpose of war is peace.'

Sun Tzu, 500 BC

Any building is only as good as its foundations. The same holds true for any attempt to develop a practical marketing strategy. To add a touch of realism, unless you live in an earthquake belt (and most of us don't) there is no reason why you should dig down as far below ground as you are going to build on top. Resources are scarce and should be used judiciously. Analysis is important but 'analysis paralysis' can be deadly and can produce a moribund organization. Balance – as in all things – is essential.

One of the most common questions I am asked is how much research and analysis should we do before we are ready to start taking decisions. This question is almost impossible to answer since it depends on so many different variables. Too little analysis and the organization can end up flying by the seat of its pants, producing products and services it knows nothing about and venturing into markets where it has no right to be. Not that this approach is always disastrous – far from it – there are a number of well-documented success stories of whole business empires based on one person's inspiration. The problem is, there are as many case histories of the same organizations falling away from a market that has changed because they did not know the reason for that change. Disaster comes when an organization is more concerned with its own flair than the needs of the marketplace.

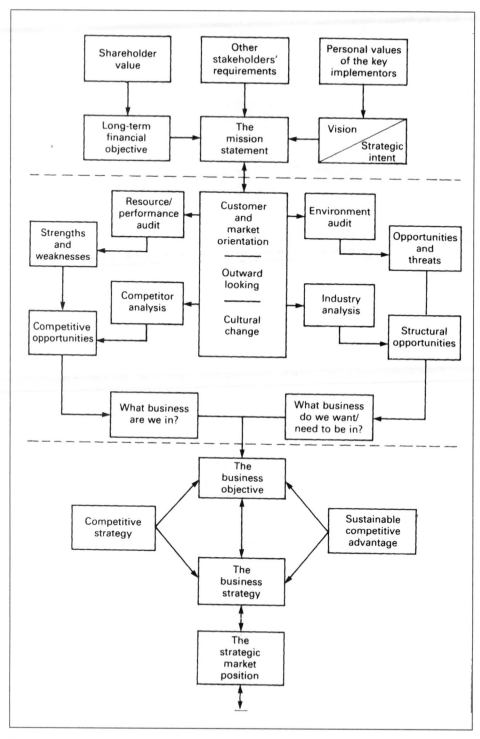

Figure 7 The essential groundwork

No, the key to information and analysis is knowing, before you start the collection process, exactly what you are going to do with the data. Since data collection is a means to an end, not an end in itself then the data collection and analysis process should be driven by strategy, not the other way around. In this case the answer to the question: 'How much research and analysis should we do?', depends upon the strategic process that you are going to undertake.

Those of you who have purchased every book written by Michael Porter, have worked through all the various chapters and studied hard to understand and apply competitive strategy in your organization – well I've got some bad news. Depending on which argument you follow, not only might Porter's work be wrong, depending upon your organization and your marketplace, trying to follow Porter's work may even be doing your organization more harm than good! In case you were too busy fighting through the recession to notice it, I should point out that the first part of the 1990s has been taken up with . . .

The great strategy debate

As soon as someone pioneers a new product or service and then opens up a market which did not hitherto exist, the pioneer is rapidly followed by a series of me-too copies, sad imitations and higher quality offerings. This has certainly been the case in the strategy business – for business it certainly is.

Michael Porter's work on competitive strategy created one of the biggest leaps from academic thinking to business practice seen since the Second World War. His books were conceived in the 1970s, published in the 1980s and applied in the 1990s, not an unreasonable lead time for new ideas. But why was Porter successful where many other writers have singly failed to place their books on the corporate bookshelf? Whatever you happen to think of Porter (I know at the moment you are sure the man can do no wrong and you are starting to wonder what heresy is about to leap from these pages) his timing proved to be impeccable. The 1980s was a trying time for many, many businesses. The post-war growth and stability of the 1960s and the 1970s was starting to fall away, international competition, especially from the Far East, was becoming a serious irritant, and markets started to behave in a less than rational manner. In short, many managers felt that they were losing control of the situation. Porter's thinking, based on understandable economic theory, showed managers that there was something they could do about the terrible situation they found themselves in. By a systematic process of analysis and decision making, they could once again assert their control over the turbulent marketplace and order would rise out of chaos. Given that this was just the message that most managers wanted to hear, Porter acquired dedicated followers at an astonishing rate.

In the 1990s two things then happened. First, it started to be apparent that Porter's ideas didn't always work in every situation. Once again dashing hopes of discovering the universal panacea to all our business problems! Second, since Porter had brought the strategy debate into the world of practising business, the door was open for all sorts of academics and business gurus to parade their own strategic hypotheses in front of a hungry marketplace.

This is neither the time nor the place to investigate and analyse the streams of consciousness that have flowed through the academic and business literature over the past decade, the interested reader can start with the references at the end of this section and wallow in *Harvard Business Review* papers after that. We will, however, try to distil the essence of the argument in the great strategy debate. This is important in as much as it helps you to decide the most appropriate process for formulating strategy within your organization, and hence the level and quality of data you will need to collect in order to make that strategy practical and capable of implementation.

Michael Porter has encountered a lot of competition over the past ten years and the fight, it seems, is still far from over. The one competitor who appears to be gaining the largest share of the competitive voice is Henry Mintzberg, an academic but this time from a Canadian university, McGill. Mintzberg's main argument (although to attempt to paraphrase five books and countless articles does seem to be rather foolhardy) is that Porter and people like him who propose a systematic approach to strategy formulation have simply got it wrong. He argues that while managers and planners might like the idea of intense data collection followed by rigorous intellectual analysis, the world just isn't like that and it won't stand still long enough for you to get your plans into operation. In the 1970s Mintzberg was proposing what he called emergent strategy as a complete alternative to the Porter-type deliberately planned approach to strategy. Now in the 1990s Mintzberg is somewhat more pragmatic and declares that while the Porter-style approach is a good first step it is not, of itself, enough.

The argument in a nutshell, between the 'deliberate' strategy schools and the 'emergent' strategy schools is as follows. The proponents of deliberate strategy believe that managers and planners can stand back from business and, through a rigorous analysis of the market and the environment in which the operation works, can devise a logical and structured plan to achieve the business objectives. The proponents of emergent strategy say that this is completely unrealistic essentially because the marketplace is unpredictable. The emergent strategists say that managers and planners should come out of their ivory towers and should experiment on a grand scale. The business should launch a number of initiatives onto the marketplace and, like a market gardener, ruthlessly cull the weeds while hothousing the apparent successes. In this way a pattern of success emerges and a strategy appears.

As if this wasn't enough Mintzberg also goes back into history and looks at all the various schools of thought in the area of strategy formation. The schools he identifies are many and various and just to give a flavour of how complicated the question can become if you decide to research it further, the schools of thought that Mintzberg identifies are as follows:

- the design school;
- the planning school;
- the positioning school;
- the cognitive school;
- the entrepreneurial school;
- the learning school;
- the political school;
- the cultural school;
- the environmental school;
- the configurational school.

Before we leave Mintzberg (for the moment) it is certainly worth saying that he is a man to watch in the future. If past experience is anything to go by organizations should be starting to come to grips with Mintzberg's ideas on emergent strategy about the beginning of the next century.

When it comes to making practical sense of the great strategy debate we can gain a greater insight if we turn to Whittington (1993). It would appear, in fact, that there are four generic approaches to strategy formulation. These four approaches are:

1   the classical approach;
2   the evolutionary approach;
3   the processual approach;
4   the systemic approach.

It is worth while briefly considering these four generic approaches to strategy, not because such knowledge will make you more impressive in dealings with your colleagues (which, of course, it will) but because the strategic route chosen by your organization will have a fundamental effect upon the formulation and implementation of a practical marketing strategy. What then are the basic ideas behind these four generic approaches to developing business strategy?

I The classical approach

The classical approach to strategy formulation is probably the oldest strategy approach, it certainly gets the lion's share of space in most business textbooks. The big names associated with this approach include Igor Ansoff, Alfred Sloan and Michael Porter.

The principal driving philosophy behind this school of strategic thought is economic theory. The proponents of this approach believe that profit maximization is the key objective of an organization and the job of the strategist is then to position the organization into those markets where most profit can be made. The underlying belief is that strategy is best created through a rational and intellectual analysis, often carried out in isolation from the normal ups and downs of any marketplace.

Adherents to the classical approach to strategy development believe strongly that high quality planning is what is needed to take control over both internal and external environments. Strategy, based on objective analysis and 'rational economic man' theory will make the difference between success and failure in the long term. The classical school also treats strategy formulation and strategy implementation as quite separate phases in the strategy process. It is almost a case of formulate the best strategy and it will implement itself.

2 The evolutionary approach

This approach is less evident in the strategy and marketing literature but is slowly starting to make an appearance. The most important thinkers behind this approach to strategy include Henderson (Boston Consulting Group), Friedman, Williamson and to some extent Tom Peters.

Proponents of the evolutionary approach to strategy believe, like the members of the classical school, that the primary objective of an organization is to maximize profits. Where they differ from the classicists, however, is that they argue that an organization should not take one single route but should keep its options open. The main thrust of the evolutionary argument is that the organization cannot control the environment in which it operates – markets are more powerful than the company. Since large organizations tend to be slow to react or respond to change, the power of an all-embracing strategy may be overrated. They even argue that investing in a long-term strategy could be counterproductive for the organization. Since best results will always be achieved by matching the needs of the environment now, the organization investing in the long term can always be undercut by the organization focusing on short-term cost-reduction processes. Some commentators, including Tom Peters, go even further and say that while short-term focus tends to stimulate the number of organizational liquidations over time this is a good thing since it ensures that the 'gene pool' is constantly refreshed as talent is released from dying organizations. So now even survival may be an unsound objective.

Moving away from some of the more extreme views in this approach the general thrust of the ideas seems to be that top managers don't make profits, markets do. In a competitive marketplace (in uncompetitive marketplaces, of course, none of these ideas hold up) the organization should launch as many small initiatives as possible and see what works. The competitive processes inherent in the marketplace should then allow the best initiatives to flourish and an overall strategy should begin to emerge as a pattern from the marketplace. In this way we can see that the idea is that the market dictates the strategy not the manager, the strategist, the planner or even the marketer!

3 The processual approach

This school of thought is starting to make an appearance in the literature and, while it does not count too many adherents as yet, the ones that are behind the idea are certainly the heaviest hitters of the 1990s. The two most noteworthy names associated with this approach are Henry Mintzberg and Gary Hamel.

Proponents of this approach are similar to those of the evolutionary school and argue that an effective and practical strategy will only emerge from close involvement in everyday operations of the organization. They believe that the environment is too strong for it to be overcome through intellectual analysis alone, but on the other hand seem to be less sure that the marketplace is efficient enough to ensure profit-maximizing results. They state (quite reasonably I think) that every organization is a coalition of individuals with their own personal objectives and ambitions, and corporate goals are therefore the result of a bargaining process driven by profit and non-profit motivated values.

Adherents of this approach believe firmly that planning which is not followed by implementation is an exercise in futility, what is the point then, they muse, of classical school corporate planning departments continuing to design elaborate strategic plans that the organization has no intention of implementing? Mintzberg especially argues that strategy is a craft rather than a science (or at the very best it might be seen as the science of muddling through) and a business strategy is best created by a series of small steps that slowly emerge into a pattern. He and others also argue that without the right competences in place in an organization many strategic plans can't be implemented anyway. Therefore the whole process should be one of slow development, construction and consolidation.

4 The systemic approach

The arguments behind the systemic approach have been a long time coming to the surface. Writings in this area are still quite rare and often originate in areas other than straightforward business strategy so are not always easy to find. Some of the main proponents to watch for include Richard Whittington and Knights and Morgan.

The main thrust of the argument behind the systemic approach is that while these theorists do believe in the ability of organizations to plan forward and act effectively within their market environments they argue that both the ends and the means of strategy depend on, and are deeply embedded in, particular social systems. What this means is that we should not view strategists as cool, calculation professionals but normal human beings (radical thinking this!) who are simply part of the social system or culture from which they operate. Factors such as the family, the state, professional and educational backgrounds, religion and even ethnic origin determine what is acceptable behaviour for their members and therefore acceptable objectives for the organization in which they work. This is obviously an important aspect for international and multi-national organizations who embrace a variety of cultures in one company. It is equally important, if not as easily identified, within a particular country, culture or industry. As Whittington points out, Western business works within a culture that respects profit, values, scientific method and sees the free market as an article of faith. In this context, any individual organization or leader who rejects the classical form of strategy making, places his or her reputation at stake. Perhaps this explains the reason why so many organizations insist on developing one logical, analytical strategy after another while consistently failing to implement anything.

The principal message then behind the systemic approach is that there is no such thing as a single strategy model that is applicable to all organizations. The objectives and the strategy process will depend upon the social/cultural background of the strategists and the social context within which they operate and these must be accounted for before an organization can plan forward. A pluralistic society creates a potential range of unique and creative strategies. Adherents of this approach also believe that implementation is critical and warn us that strategy must be sensitive to the sociology of the organization if it is to be successful.

Conclusions

For all the good it does talking about theories it might be just a question of 'you pays your money – you makes your choice', but then again maybe there is more to it than that! Whittington, who has really identified these four main schools of strategic thought, does bring in an interesting question of timing. He sees the classical school as the child of the 1960s, the processual school as the 1970s, the evolutionary school as the 1980s and gives the 1990s to the systemic approach. While this seems intuitively right to me it's certainly not what I see in most of the organizations that I talk to. Maybe we all have a lot of catching up to do. The four different approaches to strategy offer four very different views on how strategy ought to be, or even can be, formulated by the organization. Each, of course, is backed up by irreproachable theory and unassailable evidence. So what is the practising manager to do? The classical approach is the way that we have always been taught (from an extremely early age) that things ought to work. The last ten years' experience in most markets also suggests that the evolutionists have a very strong point to make. Our everyday experience of dealing with people in organizations also leaves us convinced that the processualists are edging closer to reality as we live it. Finally, basic intuition says there is a lot more to the systemic approach than anyone has admitted so far – although whether we can do anything about it is another matter altogether!

Given that trying to take on all four approaches at the same time will probably leave us in a worse mess than we are in at the moment the strategist is faced with a problem – what to do? The answer, as you will find on a number of occasions through this book, is – it depends. Remembering that implementation is key and that planning is only a means to an end, ask yourself the following questions. Your answers should lead you towards the obvious choice of the most appropriate strategic planning route for your organization.

1 Do you have access to sufficient information to make depth analysis feasible?
2 Is the organization large, stable and controlled?
3 Does the organization operate in a reasonably stable economic end-market environment?

4 Is competition in your industry quite restrained and 'gentlemanly'?
5 Do you have just a small number of obvious competitors?
6 Are barriers to entry high?
7 Are customer needs considered to be easily understood and relatively slow to change?
8 Is your company/division at the launch stage or decline stage of the business life cycle?

If the answer to most of these eight questions is 'yes' you are probably best advised to look at the classical approach.

9 Is the environment you operate in unpredictable and fluid?
10 Is the market you operate in highly competitive?
11 Are entry/exit barriers low?
12 Is the sales function one of the most important reasons for your success?
13 Is your organization in a period of rapid growth?
14 Are you in a 'new' industry?

If the answer to most of these six questions is 'yes', then you are probably best advised to follow the evolutionary approach.

15 Are the markets you operate in typified by pockets of ruthless competition and pockets of relative stability?
16 Is the environment relatively tolerant of underachieving organizations?
17 Is your business driven by brands, activity, sales promotion and media marketing?
18 Can you (and your customers) easily identify your immediate competitors?
19 Are the entry barriers reasonably high?
20 Is 'size' important in your marketplace?
21 Is your organization/division what would be considered a 'mature' business?

If the answer to most of these seven questions is 'yes', then probably the processual approach will work best in your organization.

If none of the above questions appear to make any sense or have any relevance for you then there are probably other factors at play here. The systemic approach is probably the one you should begin to investigate, it may shed some interesting light on past successes and failures, the reasons for which have so far remained a mystery.

The first step

Whatever strategic route you decide the organization is on, or the organization ought to be on, the first step is to start to acquire the information needed to take the process further. Even the evolutionists don't suggest that we fly completely blind in turbulent marketplaces, we must have some idea of what we think is going on if just in order to build a hypothesis before we launch off the myriad of small initiatives. If you are casting bread on the water you need at least some of it to come back cake!

The level and depth of data, the quality of data and the sources of data will depend on the nature of the strategic approach employed by the organization. Whatever the strategic approach, we will start as always, at the beginning, with the internal data.

Marketer's note

What on earth is all this about? It's taken me years to read Porter and now I have managed to condense it down to four overhead slides to explain it to the troops, it's taken me three years to free up enough space in my annual diary to spend some time on planning and now .... I know, I know but then I don't see it as my job to come up with the answers (this isn't an airport bookshop product) I would rather try and help you think through some of the alternatives for yourself.

We shall look in much more depth at what these various strategic approaches mean for marketing strategy later on. In the meantime you ought to recognize that as a marketer, implementation of strategic plans probably ends up at your doorstep before anybody else's. Not only that but the organization should rely on marketing to input the all-important customer information into the plans at early stages. So let's think through some of the implications here.

If your organization is devoting any time or energy to strategy formulation odds on it is employing the classical approach. If the answer to the first three questions above were not, in your opinion, 'yes', then there's also a good chance that no implementation worth talking about ever results from the plans. What can you do about this problem? Apart from taking the blame (yes, I know it's unfair isn't it) you can look at trying to modify the strategic approach to one that best fits the environment or structure of the organization. Alternatively you can look at employing a more relevant approach to the marketing strategy while making what links are possible back to the classical approach employed by the corporate planners.

If the organization is employing the evolutionary or the processual approaches then marketing will soon rise in importance in the organization. Neither of these approaches mean that you can now wallow in hand-to-hand combat with the competition and relegate all activity to short-term market share objectives. It means that you will need to hone your skills in recognizing patterns in the marketplace that could emerge as major strategies for future success.

If the systemic approach is the main method of strategy formulation in you organization – and I suspect it is essential that HR acquire the necessary strategic skills to help the organization. You would be advised to build a strategic alliance with this function and work together to define those activities and behaviours which are, at the same time, demanded by the marketplace and acceptable to the culture of the organization. There, you see there is some relevance in all this to the marketer, but it does need thinking through quite carefully.

Chapter 2

The internal business drivers

'Now the general is the bulwark of the State: if the bulwark is complete at all points, the State will be strong; if the bulwark is defective, the State will be weak.'

Sun Tzu, 500 BC

How strong is your general? How good is his or her vision? Morale might be good for the troops but there comes a time when honesty, certainly among the most senior lieutenants, is the most appropriate policy.

Marketing and business strategy, if they are to be practical, must be based on an assessment of reality not on hopes or wishful thinking. The successful marketer is one whose plans work in the only arena that counts – the marketplace. Plans that are based on hopes, inaccurate analysis, or worse, no analysis at all of the factors which drive the business cannot hope to withstand the onslaught of determined competition.

The common thread that binds all these business drivers together is people. Apart from the (all-important) customer, there are other people who also have demands on the business. Like customers, these people expect their needs to be met. Failure to do so may mean the failure of the business but will certainly mean the failure of the marketing strategy.

The 'people' concerned in this section fall into three categories:

- the 'key implementors';
- the shareholders; and
- the other stakeholders in the business.

We will consider these groups in more detail.

Personal values of the key implementors

This is a heading which may come as something of a surprise to people who thought they knew what strategy was all about. The main reason for its omission from a number of texts is that, while critically important in any successful business strategy, it is also one of the infamous 'soft' areas of a business organization. Soft aspects of the business such as these which are concerned with what people want, how people think and what motivates people to work are more often than not impossible to quantify and therefore to reduce to numbers. Thus their inclusion in flowcharts and neat, packaged diagrams is fraught with danger. The work of the systemic school of strategy is slowly gaining some momentum but it will still be a long time before the ideas that it proposes are properly accepted in most organizations.

The term 'key implementors' refers to that select body in an organization who actually make the decisions and who are central to what the organization does both in its thinking and in its actions. A special note – the key implementors may or may not include the board in its entirety. It may mean the board, it may mean the board plus a number of very senior managers, it may just mean the managing director and a special friend, it may mean the chairman and part of the board. In any event these are the people who really count.

By searching out the key implementors in an organization, often looking behind the titles, we can start to discover which eventual solutions might be acceptable and which patently unacceptable. The key implementors, individually or probably as a group, will have a very clear idea of what type of organization they wish to work for, what type of organization they wish to create, the types of products they wish to market and the types of businesses they wish to be in. At the same time they will also have a very clear idea of what businesses and activities they and their organization will not be involved in. It is, if you like, a kind of moral and ethical personal ambition blueprint against which all possible strategic alternatives will first be compared. If a possible route contravenes the personal values of this group it will of course be countered with non-emotional arguments based on good business practice – but it will be countered, and strongly.

We have already seen from the previous chapter that this is again edging towards the ideas proposed by the systemic school. The effects of any social system are, however, both strong and often invisible. The key implementors in an organization normally have an important role beyond that of developing strategy – they are custodians of corporate culture. They are normally the embodiment of what every manager has to be to progress in the organization. No strategy can be implemented that is counter culture. On the other hand a lot of time and effort can be wasted by pursuing the classical approach to strategy formulation just because that is what good business practice calls for!

The lesson is clear – even when the strategy and the strategic approach seems to be 'by the book', talk to and understand the key implementors and the social system to which they belong. Implementation is important, not the plans. Implementation has to fit what the organization is. Some organizations (and key implementors) would rather die than change what they are and what they believe in – this is human nature and we should accept it.

The vision

A lot has been written about 'the vision thing' in recent years, some good and some laughable. Apart from the evolutionists with their particular brand of commercial Darwinism, all schools see the vision as central to any form of strategy. Again it centres around the key implementors.

The personal values of this central group, once combined, create the vision driving the organization and hence what we might call the strategic intent behind the group (see Figure 8). This vision, sometimes written, more often than not implicit and mutually understood, needs to be clarified and defined before taking the process any further. The vision is often central to the organization's success. Mintzberg (*Observer*, London 12 June 1994) has been quoted as saying 'many of the great strategies are simply great visions. Visions can be a lot more inspirational and effective than the most carefully constructed plan. Only when we recognise our fantasies can we begin to appreciate the wonders of reality.'

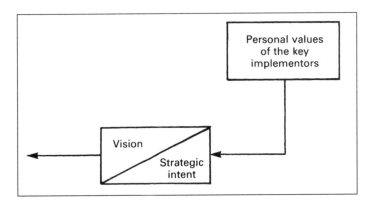

Figure 8 Personal values

The vision is not the same as an objective, it is not normally quantified. Rather it is a picture of what the future of the organization looks like. Vision enables the organization to set a broad strategic direction and leaves the details of its implementation to be worked out later. It has been argued (by Mintzberg) that the visionary approach is a more flexible way to deal with an uncertain world. In other words the general vision/direction can be 'deliberate' while the implementation and details of the strategy can be 'emergent'.

'Strategic intent' was first described as a concept by Hamel and Prahalad (*Harvard Business Review*, May/June 1989) and, like vision, fits into the case argued by the supporters of the emergent strategy schools. In short, what vision is to objectives, strategic intent is to strategy. Hamel and Prahalad argue that companies who have risen to global leadership in recent years have set ambitious goals such as 'Encircle Caterpillar' (Kamatsu), 'Beat Xerox' (Canon) and 'Become a second Ford' (Honda), and then used a dynamic management process that 'focuses the organization's attention on the essence of winning'. Importantly, details of implementation are left vague to allow for operational change as market and economic conditions change in time and geography – the emergent approach again.

While, in my experience, it is quite difficult to identify the personal values of the key implementors and the collective vision/strategic intent which these people hold, the costs of ignoring these often emotional aspects of how an organization is directed and managed may be devastatingly high. No matter how scientific, logical, rational and elegant the eventual plan, if it conflicts with the personal values of the key team, the business objective will not be achieved. The key implementors may ignore the plan, they might sabotage the plan or even just leave the organization. Far better a compromise that works to an ideal that doesn't.

In the absence of a clear vision (articulated or not) the organization will probably be in trouble. Without some light to guide it the organization will flounder aimlessly. A vision is categorically not the same thing as a financial target (see below) and everybody needs more than 'to maximize profits' to give them a sense of direction, purpose and worth. Having said this, organizations without a vision are really quite rare. The vision may be unclear, ragged around the edges, or even rather too emotional for senior managers to admit to – but it is normally there. It is often better to dig deep to find what makes people come into work in the mornings than to go through the (often pointless) exercise of trying to create a vision from scratch, what people are happy to put down on paper may not be what they are really willing to fight for.

Marketer's note

You always thought it was like that, just you never read it in a book before – oh well ...

Human nature is like that. And there's no way that we are going to change human nature. The most profitable route for you and the organization is not to beat them but to join them. Some marketing influence within the key implementors can do nothing but good.

How? I hear you ask. Well, the first thing to do is to start sharing your experience and insights with others. Show how marketing is just really common sense, it's not black magic nor does it have to be a threat to any of the longer established functions in the organization. Most importantly of all, try to show them that customers are important to the vision thing. If the key implementors hold fast to a vision that's great. If customers could share that vision just imagine what we could do together. You will need their help anyway if you are to get your marketing strategy on the road – who knows, you might even win a few converts.

Shareholder value and the long-term financial objective

By the long-term financial objective we do not mean the plethora of annual, quarterly or monthly financial targets which abound in any sizeable organization and act primarily as control systems against planned targets. The long-term financial objective is that requirement placed on the organization, specifically on the board of directors, by the individuals and institutions who have invested in the organization in the expectation of a financial return (see Figure 9).

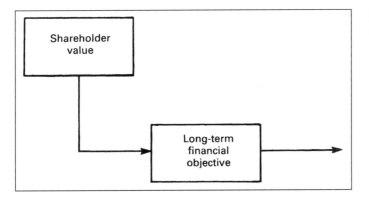

Figure 9
Shareholder value

In theory, the relationship here is very simple. The investors in the organization invest in anticipation of a return on their capital, they are in fact the owners of the business. As owners the investors employ the board to manage the business on their behalf and should the returns not meet their expectations, the investors, as owners, have the power to remove part or all of the board and replace it with other directors.

In fact, the relationship here is far more complicated in practice; there are investors and investors. For example, in a publicly quoted company the stockholders may be institutions such as insurance companies or pension funds, there may be private individuals and there may also be other publicly quoted companies holding stock. Furthermore stockholders may be primarily national or international in nature. It then follows that different investors may have different needs. Some may be investing for the long term, some for the short term. Some may require no income and be seeking a long-term increase in the capital value of their stockholding, others may be far less interested in capital growth but more concerned to secure a regular income stream from the investment, normally in the form of dividends. Yet others may require some mixture of both capital growth and income.

The organization may indeed be a smaller part of a larger organization – in this instance there is but one owner. In the case of the private company the director or directors may also be the owners, then the returns required may be for a steady or rising income stream over the longer term or for shorter term capital accumulation.

The concept of shareholder value can also be applied to organizations in the public sector. In this case, the government is the single (or possibly majority) shareholder and hence the effective owner of the business. In the case of public sector organizations, it will be important to identify the precise needs of this major shareholder and to ensure that any resulting business or marketing strategy does not run counter to the government's expectations. Such expectations may include a return on capital invested, employment, global market shares among others and, of course, are likely to change with political climates and changes in government or government policy over time.

This, however, is hardly the place for an in-depth evaluation of company law, much less a detailed analysis of the rights and wrongs of ownership and the capitalist system. The important thing here for the director trying to direct or the manager trying to manage is to understand the makeup of the ownership structure of the organization and, as precisely as possible, the returns required by those investing the capital. I have not attempted to provide an in-depth analysis of all the issues which underlie the setting of financial objectives, these are quite complex and the interested reader is referred to one of the specialist texts on the subject. For our purposes, it is sufficient to state that the director will only be allowed freedom to direct as long as the investor is getting what he or she wants.

Now, we might very well complain about modern trends towards short-termism, the rise of speculation and the harm this has on business which needs desperately to invest in the long term. We may also complain bitterly about the effects that this short-term mentality has on international competitiveness, comparing the UK, the USA or Europe, with their increasingly short-term financial requirements, to the traditional Japanese long-term view and wonder how on earth we can hope to compete over the next ten to twenty years. We may even be using this argument as a convenient excuse for our relatively low performance in a number of other areas. This aside – and I have as many firm views on the subject as everybody else – we all have to realize that we either meet our owners' financial requirements or we will be forced to give way to someone else better able to do so.

Apart from the share or stock capital there is also long-term debt financing normally provided by major institutions such as banks. The various banks are also the products of their own internal organizational culture as well as the national culture from which the organization operates. The different banks' views will also differ as to what is long and what is short term.

So far the question of long-term financial objective has been all fairly mechanical and straightforward. We must understand who the investors in the organization are, understand what they want, deliver what they want and we are all left free to run the business. In short the financial objective is a hurdle to be overcome. By translating business performance into numbers we have a convenient means by which the investors/owners who have no day-to-day involvement in the running of the organization may understand how their appointed managers have performed over the past period. While it also gives us a fairly good indication of what we must achieve in future periods, it provides absolutely no indication of how to achieve these future results or how to run the business. Profits are not only important, they are vital. At the same time, however, the pursuit of profits for their own sake can destroy an otherwise successful business over the longer term.

When talking to directors and managers of medium and large organizations about what they see as their business objective, probably the most common response is couched in financial terms. Answers such as 'to achieve a fifteen per cent return on capital employed' and 'to achieve a twenty per cent increase in sales with a ten per cent increase in net profit' are quite common. Smaller organizations might respond with 'to make enough money today to survive into tomorrow', which probably amounts to the same thing. Expressions such as these are financial objectives (more often short than long!) which, when cascaded down the organization in this form, give the managers who actually have to produce the results little or no indication of exactly how they should organize themselves, their departments or the resources at their disposal to achieve these objectives. Three managers given the same objective of increasing profit by five or ten per cent will find three different ways of doing it. The inevitable result, unless controlled in other ways from the top, an increasingly fragmented organization, lack of synergy and misallocation of resource certainly over the longer term. As we will see later, the business objective in its proper form is a far more powerful instrument, both for directing the organization and for developing long-term success in the marketplace.

The long-term financial objective acts extremely well – as a financial objective. Being a narrow measure it cannot be used as a surrogate business objective as it lacks the breadth to be an efficient driver of the business.

'It's all very well him saying that', I hear you say, 'but who's going to convince the finance director?' Yes – I know exactly what you mean. Two things may help. First a quote from Levitt who puts things much better than I possibly can. In 1986 (*The Marketing Imagination*) he stated:

'Eating is a requisite, not a purpose of life. Without eating, life stops. Profits are a requisite of business. Without profits, business stops. Like food for the body, profit for the business must be defined as the excess of what comes in over what goes out. In business it's called positive cash flow. It has to be positive, because the process of sustaining life is a process of destroying life. To sustain life, a business must produce goods and services that people in sufficient numbers will want to buy at adequate prices. Since production wears out the machinery that produces and the people who run and manage the machines, to keep the business going there's got to be enough left over to replace what's being worn out. That "enough" is profit. That's why profit is a requisite, not a purpose of business.

Besides all that, to say that profit is a purpose of business is, simply, morally shallow. Who, with a palpable heartbeat and minimal sensibilities, will go to the mat for the right of somebody to earn a profit for its own sake? If no greater purpose can be discerned or justified, business cannot morally justify its existence. It's a repugnant idea, an idea whose time has gone.

Finally, it's an empty idea. Profits can be made in lots of devious and transient ways. For people of affairs, a statement of purpose should provide guidance to the management of their affairs. To say that they should attract and hold customers forces facing the necessity of figuring out what people really want and value, and then catering to those wants and values. It provides specific guidance and has moral merit.'

Elegant, I think you'll agree.

If this still doesn't cut any ice with the finance-minded leaders then I suggest you get hold of an excellent piece of research carried out by the RSA (Royal Society for the encouragement of Arts, Manufacturers and Commerce, London WC2N 6EZ) entitled 'Tomorrow's Company'. Based on research carried out in 1993 among key business leaders and opinion formers in the UK, the RSA concluded that this country has a long trail of underperforming companies and that too many companies are not as good as they think they are. We shall be looking at this research again later but the RSA identified a key reason for under performance. They state:

> 'Yesterday's companies do not see the need to have a distinctive purpose or values, and often confuse purpose with measures of success.'

There we have the problem in a nutshell. According to Levitt (paraphrased by Drucker and others) the purpose of a business is clear, it is to 'create and keep a customer'. An (possibly the most) important measure of how well an organization does this is profitability or bottom line. Financial measures then are a measure of success – not the purpose of the organization. As far as I am concerned (and, of course, the RSA) if organizations do not manage to shake free from the obsession with bottom-line measures they will progressively fall behind more customer-focused competitors – and will have less revenues and profits to count!

Marketer's note

Now I realize that most marketers went into marketing because they hated dealing with numbers but this phobia just can't be allowed to continue unchallenged. Accountants and financiers are just like us, insecure and so forced to protect their turf with jargon and rituals. We have the product life cycle and the Ansoff matrix – they have the trial balance and DCF.

Someone has to take the first step to bridge the gap between the two areas, it may as well be you – you need to understand the basic mechanics of the financial system that operates in your organization. At the end of the day you are going to be measured against it anyway.

Why not buy a book? Even better, talk to a numbers man – he'll appreciate it.

Other stakeholders requirements

So far we have considered who are the groups influencing an organization's activities and future. Namely, the shareholders or the suppliers of long-term equity capital and secondly, the key implementers, however this team is described within the particular organization. Beyond these two important groups there are other groups of people who also have expectations from the organization (see Figure 10).

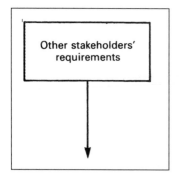

Figure 10   Other stakeholders' requirements

Apart from the shareholders and the key management team, there are other employees, there are the customers of the organization, the suppliers to the organization, and, of course, the community in the wider sense. All these groups have needs and will rightly expect a degree of service and satisfaction from the organization.

The RSA study (cited above) also draws this aspect of the organization's activity into stark relief. The research discovered that UK society generally no longer 'defers' to business activity and organizations need to actively maintain public confidence in company operations and business contact if they are to maintain a 'licence to operate'. The RSA concludes that, in the future, successful organizations will 'value reciprocal relationships and work actively to build them with customers, suppliers and other key stakeholders through a partnership approach and, by focusing on, and learning from, all those who contribute to the business, will be best able to improve returns to shareholders.

How unlike many companies today who prefer adversarial relationships with stakeholders. These organizations still firmly believe that shareholders would have to be the losers if employees, suppliers, customers or the country were made more important.

Now the concept of the 'stakeholder economy' has started to reach a broader audience through the political debate too. This is unfortunate since, being raised by one side of politics it will automatically be rubbished by the other side – but for political not necessarily business reasons. Important work has been carried out in the USA (Bevin 1996) which shows that profits really do come from retained customers. Their argument that, on average, a two per cent increase in customer retention is equivalent to a ten per cent reduction in overheads has even started to convince financial people that it might be worth investing in customers!

In short the argument runs as follows. Profits come from satisfied customers who come back. Satisfied customers are created by:

- offering value-added products and services that meet their needs;
- service offered by committed and motivated staff.

These offerings are made by companies who:

- understand their customers;
- build alliances with their staff, communities and suppliers.

These companies are created by investors who take a long-term interest in what the organization is trying to achieve – not only short-term financial returns.

The stakeholder concept term is not just a 'good thing'. It is a highly 'profitable thing'. The days of viewing stakeholders as just innocent bystanders is probably gone. For an organization concerned with implementing its strategy rather than simply formulating it, stakeholders hold the key to success.

The corporate mission

Why have a mission statement?

It is the organization's mission statement which should bring together the apparently diverse groups that we have discussed above (see Figure 11), but what is a mission statement? At its simplest level, the mission is a statement of the core corporate values and as such is a framework within which employees and individual business units, divisions or activities prepare their plans. It should be constructed in such a way that it satisfies and can be subscribed to by the most important groups of people who have expectations from the organization. The mission statement is not the same thing as a business objective and it cannot be treated as such, they have been described as long on rhetoric and short on numbers. Missions are, by their nature, non-specific and are difficult to achieve cleanly on their own. A business objective, by contrast, should be both

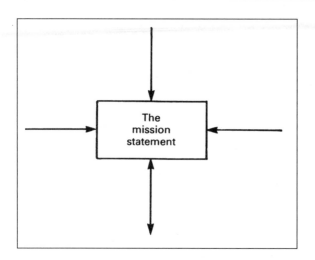

Figure 11   The mission
statement

measurable and achievable and is therefore normally expressed in quantitative terms. A mission is essentially qualitative in nature and should be
expressed in these terms.

What then should the organization think of including in its mission
statement? There is no set lay-out or structure to a mission statement.
They tend to be quite personal to the organization and while some
missions can be contained in a handful of words, other mission statements can easily run to one or two closely typed pages. Ideally, the
organization's mission statement will be a reflection of the corporate
values and ethics that prevail in the organization. It will probably include
very broad goals as well as fundamental beliefs about the right ways to
behave. It may contain more detailed information and include views
about the organization vis-à-vis its competition, the technology within
which it operates, its product quality, its role in society, or the particular
style of ownership of the organization. This is quite a long list but every
organization will have what it knows and understands as being its few
'guiding principles', which are particularly important to its sense of unity
and its individual character. These are, at the very least, the issues which
should be included in a mission statement.

A more important question is what does the mission statement actually
do? This will influence what the organization should include within its
mission statement. Above all else, the mission statement should do as its
name implies, it should give the organization a clear mission or purpose.
It should give all people connected with the organization, primarily the
organization's personnel, but also the other interested parties, a clear
sense of where the organization is headed. If the mission statement is
sufficiently motivating in this regard, then everybody should have a sense
of shared direction, shared opportunities, shared significance and

ultimately a sense of shared achievement. A good mission statement will give your organization a much greater sense of cohesion – it will improve morale in the organization. It has been known to improve the speed of response of the organization's people to external demands. Of course all this does no harm at all to the organization's external reputation.

Mission or vision?

What a good question! Look at most of the books and you will tend to find either one or the other in the index – not often both. Are they the same thing? Does it matter? Strictly speaking the mission is about corporate values and how the organization will behave – important. The vision is about what the organization is going to become – very important. The organization obviously needs both but probably it is best to say that it doesn't really matter what we call it as long as it does the right job. Organizations tend to love either one or the other but rarely both – I've never understood why this should be but such is life.

Since a properly thought out and well-constructed mission/vision statement becomes the source and focus of the organization's complete energy for the next five, ten, or fifteen years, it is obviously not something which you should look to adapt or even misguidedly improve on a year-by-year basis. The mission/vision statement should be both broad and qualitative, and while it will highlight the preferred values and ethics of the organization, it should allow enough latitude for more precise objectives and more detailed tactics to be developed and changed as the prevailing circumstances dictate.

Marketer's note

Putting together the mission/vision statement is quite a lengthy process of discussion within the organization. Indeed, practical experience in a number of organizations has shown us that when missions/visions simply emerge like a brand new car model from behind the locked doors of the senior management group, they do not tend to be anywhere near as effective as if discussions have been carried out with the personnel and the other stakeholders which affect the organization.

So we are faced with the inevitable long discussion period which will produce a multitude of views, feelings and beliefs from all sectors. Unfortunately, this lengthy discussion period is also likely to generate a mission statement which runs to not one but maybe two or more closely typed pages. A good meaty document may make people feel better but its not necessarily the most effective way of communicating a message. If we have to keep, preserve and enshrine the full blown version for official use in the annual report and accounts, then so be it. This needn't necessarily stop us from modifying the basic text into something which is more appropriate for passing down through the organization.

The Declaration of Independence is a beautifully manicured document but the general needs something more pithy for the troops to shout as they go over the top!

Chapter 3

The external environment

'If you know the enemy and know yourself you need not fear the result of a hundred battles. If you know yourself but not the enemy, for every victory gained you will also suffer a defeat. If you know neither the enemy nor yourself, you will succumb in every battle.

'To secure ourselves against defeat lies in our own hands, but the opportunity of defeating the enemy is provided by the enemy himself.

'Knowing the enemy enables you to take the offensive, knowing yourself enables you to stand on the defensive. Attack is the secret of defence; defence is the planning of an attack.'

Sun Tzu, 500 BC

In the previous chapter we have tried to uncover the most important internal drivers of the business. If the organization has a mission statement or a clearly articulated vision this will help us focus our attention on the more important aspects of the external environment which we must analyse next.

Attempting to lay any sort of plans for the future without first gathering enough information is not only foolish, it also demonstrates dangerous tendencies towards complacency and arrogance. Knowing that information must be gathered is one thing, knowing how much and what to gather is quite another. But before we step out into this particular minefield, it is worthwhile looking at another of those dreaded 'soft' areas of the business, the basic state of mind or context within which information is gathered.

Customer and market orientation – the culture

Even the two great bestselling strategy books of the 1980s, *Competitive Strategy* and *Competitive Advantage* by Michael Porter both require (although this is not explicitly stated) that the organization be market oriented for the strategic approach to be beneficial. Porter's whole approach is based on the importance of looking outward to the environment and the competitive marketplace rather than basing our future on purely internal considerations. Unfortunately Porter doesn't then pay enough attention to the power of markets and their ability to derail the most eloquent of strategic plans. Mintzberg fares a little better in his respect for customers and markets, stressing, as he does, the need to be more flexible when crafting strategic plans. When it comes to the customer/market orientation of the business Mintzberg is as myopic as other writers, concentrating for the most part on how strategic planners do, or should do, their job.

We have already seen what marketing and a market orientation means for the organization and its future in an ever more competitive marketplace. Marketing orientation is necessary but difficult to achieve and retain . . . but I don't want to start labouring the point all over again. Suffice it to say, that during this important information gathering stage, the emphasis must be securely based on what is happening outside the organization and not what the most important factors appear to be within the organization (see Figure 12).

A state of mind which is inward looking rather than outward looking not only chooses to uncover the wrong data from the environment, but is also most likely to misinterpret the data which is collected. This emphasis will become clear as we go through the various sections of information collection and analysis process. It is the very important task of the

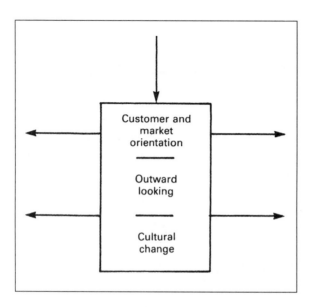

Figure 12 Customer and market orientation

marketer, whether his title be marketing director, business development director, vice president, marketing manager, managing director, or whatever, to create and to maintain this outward looking mentality within the top management team as they start to approach the whole question of business strategy.

The environment audit

Auditing the environment in which the organization must operate is arguably the most important and most significant data gathering activity that any business, firm, service, or even government department, can undertake (see Figure 13). Ten or twenty years ago, managers could turn round, with some degree of justification, and say that they had the market tied up. The very large 'mega' organizations or cartels tended to dominate completely certain market sectors and in the 1960s and the 1970s were effectively able to control both competition in the marketplace and determine what customers would buy. When, during this period, chief executives would turn round and say 'well, we know exactly what the customers want, it's what we give them', this remark has some degree of validity. Customers did, indeed, keep buying the company's products or services. They may not have been completely satisfied but more often than not they had no real choice in the matter. More dangerously, some chief executives are still saying the same thing today. Furthermore they will

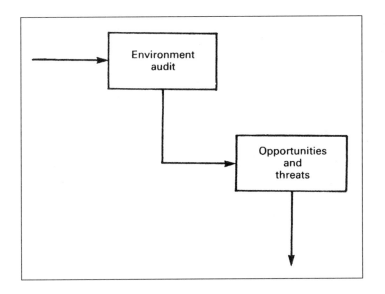

Figure 13
Environment audit

probably remain absolutely convinced that they know precisely what their customers want as they watch their organization slide from dominance to obscurity in the more competitive markets which are today's reality.

In the UK and the USA and the majority of the western world, the 1960s and 1970s was the era of the large corporation. Size and economies of scale were everything during this period. With size naturally enough came power to control. Size gave corporations the ear of government always concerned with balance of payments, international trade and, of course, employment. It also followed that, compared with these issues, the satisfaction of the individual consumer was considered relatively unimportant. The net result was that the larger corporations had a degree of real control over the environment in which they operated.

The 1980s saw the beginning of a shift in power away from the producer towards the customer. In the 1990s this trend has accelerated. Generally international trade has become more liberal and the barriers to international competition have been dismantled as more governments seek actively to promote competition in national marketplaces. What the early consumerist movement started has now produced a much greater degree of choice for the customer and in many instances a reduction in the absolute market share of the larger corporations. With the wider range of products and services in the market, customers have had to learn how to evaluate and choose among the competing offerings and as a result have become more sophisticated in the exercise of choice. While there still remain examples of markets where free choice really does not yet operate (British and European banking, telecommunications and public utilities, among others, still have a long way to go), generally organizations in the 1990s do not and will not be able to control the environment in which they operate. The environment will inevitably control them.

It is therefore only by achieving a much better understanding of its environment that the organization can possibly hope to establish its market position and survive over the longer term. So what do we mean by the word 'environment'? – it is another of those words which, of course, mean everything and nothing. We must break it down into its most important constituent parts or we will once again get lost in a morass of detail. While some commentators seem to take the word 'environment' to mean everything outside the factory gates, this 'catch-all' term is unlikely to be very useful when it comes to laying specific plans for future activity.

Remember that at this stage we are still concerned with the overall problem of finding what is going on in the broad business and social environment within which the organization must operate. We need to understand how we should position the organization relative to its competition and likely future shifts in marketplace demand. The more

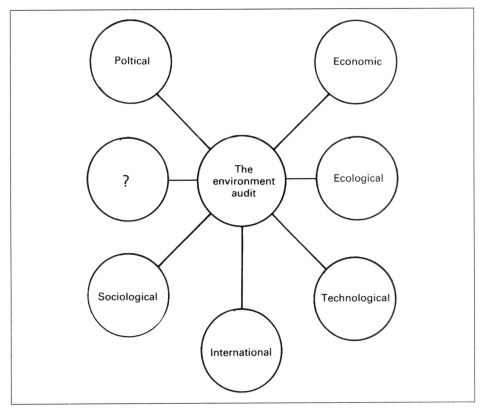

Figure 14   Constituent parts of the environment audit

detailed analysis of specific target markets is not pertinent at this point. This will be considered in more depth in Part Two.

Two other more detailed areas are often included under the 'environment' heading. These relate to the question of competition and the specific analysis of the industry within which the organization operates. These two sub-headings are indeed important, so much so that they should have a separate place in the information gathering phase. We will deal with these two subjects later.

After removing the more detailed aspects of the external environment we are left with the question of how to identify the most important macro elements of the environment which may impinge on the organization in the future. Traditionally the environment audit is broken down into four constituent parts. To these four I have added a fifth and a sixth (see Figure 14).

Although these classifications are traditional, they are not absolute and some degree of overlap is quite normal. The four sub-divisions, or headings, are: political, economic, sociological and technological aspects (known as

PEST). To these four traditional classifications I have added additional headings. While, twenty years ago, an organization might justifiably have maintained a purely domestic and non-environmental stance, the nature of competition and customer demand have forced us all to look beyond our traditional frontiers. We will consider the various elements in turn.

Political

Under the political heading we are concerned with the motives and the actions of governments and the way that, via legislation, regulation and the legal/political system, they impact on business. All too often, especially in the West, managers tend to take the role of government and the influence of political ideology on business as a given situation that we just have to live with. Apart from the regular overreaction of stock markets when national elections are in the air, we don't normally expect or plan for any radical shift in political direction. In some respects this slow, gradual change can be a disadvantage to the organization since gradual change often goes unnoticed. Such gradual, cumulative change can be treacherous. The organization can easily find itself at a competitive disadvantage without knowing how it got there.

It is supremely important that the organization understands the role of government in the marketplace, be it regulator or participator. We must understand the true impact that government policy can have on business. We must also understand which of the vast array of legislation impacts on our organization and our marketing activities.

Commercial activity is regulated, to a greater or lesser extent, in every country in the world. Government control extends from the way we structure and organize our business, how we deal with our employees, how we remunerate and motivate the people who work for us, and even the degree of profits which we can make. We are also regulated, overtly or covertly, in terms of what we can sell, how we sell and who we can sell to. Often we are controlled in terms of the prices we can charge, the distribution channels we can use, the promotion activities which we can employ. Very little business and marketing activity is free from the laws and acts of government.

Our first efforts must be directed at trying to understand exactly what effects these measures have on how we run our business. Try, for example, to imagine what we would be doing differently if these rules and regulations did not exist. Secondly, we need to try and grasp the reasoning behind the legislative and legal regulation. What is the political ideology which forms the basis of the regulation? Does the government wish to control and create an atmosphere in which enterprise can flourish or does it feel obliged to control business enterprise for the social good? Are its measures aimed at raising income taxation or are they aimed at maintaining maximum levels of employment? – the list continues. It is only by understanding why governments act the way they do that we will have any chance of predicting the most likely future changes in legislation. If we can predict future moves then we can plan for them.

Quick check list – political factors
- role of government, regulator or participator
- political ideology
- political motivations
- rate of change of political direction
- political stability over time
- political attitudes to:
    competition
    social responsibility
    environmental matters
    customer protection
- legislative effects on:
    organizational structure
    organizational behaviour
    employment
    salaries and payment levels
    profits (taxation/repatriation etc.)
    permitted markets
    product policy
    pricing policy
    distribution policy
    promotional policy

Economic

Under this heading we should be considering such things as the current and likely future rate of inflation. We should be looking at the current and future positions of exchange rates, especially if we are deeply involved in international markets or alternatively, we require high levels of foreign content to our product or service.

Taxation can also appear under the economic heading as well as the political heading. Over the longer term we should also be concerned with the current state of the economy, whether we are in a recession or a boom, whether the economy is largely stable and, importantly, the likely future direction of the economy over the next three to five years.

A new dimension that needs attention in the maturing Western markets is the 'real' rate of inflation facing our customers. While inflation rates (as quoted in government statistics) seem to be under greater control than in the past, what these figures don't take into account are the additional family and individual expenses caused by the gradual withdrawal of the welfare state. Most European governments have now recognized that they cannot continue with the welfare payments of the past forty years, confronted as they are with ageing populations and declining workforces. As citizens now have to pay for what was offered by the state in the past (health, schooling, university education, pensions) while still paying full taxes, disposable income is effectively declining. These 'new essentials' can seriously affect how often customers renew their cars or take holidays.

Probably the most tangible facet of the economic factors is the disposible income of our customer base. The future prosperity of any organization will depend on its ability to win and keep customers who are both prepared and able to pay the prices which we need. If our potential customers can't afford what we provide then we just don't have a business.

Quick check list – economic factors
- gross domestic product (GDP):
    per head
    social/private
    distribution
    regional disparity
- government policy:
    fiscal
    monetary
- industrial:
    structure
    growth
    labour rates
- income:
    current
    growth
    distribution
    relation with population groups
- wealth:
    distribution
    effect on buying power
- employment:
    structure
    full-time/part-time
    male/female
    regional disparity

Sociological

This aspect of the environment is probably the most difficult to understand, quantify and predict, dealing as it does with people and human behaviour.

Basically we are dealing with people's motivations, needs, wants and perceptions and, more broadly, how society or culture is changing over time. The most difficult problem is not in acquiring the basic data – this is reasonably freely available, certainly in Europe, the USA and the more advanced markets of the world where governments pride themselves on collecting and maintaining information on their citizens. The problem comes in the interpretation.

There is normally quite an amount of data on local, regional, national preference and consumption patterns, on changes in society, marriage rates, size and growth of households and so on. Past trends are fairly evident and any number of combinations are available, projecting forward ten, twenty or even thirty years, to show where society is likely to be. The skill however, as with any form of market or marketing research, is to understand exactly what these trends mean for our organization and our future.

The essence of good marketing is to anticipate and identify what our customers want and then be in the right place at the right time to be able to offer it to them. Sounds simple but the anticipation is the difficult part. The longer the production lead times required for your product or service, the more interest your organization should be showing in trying to unravel the likely future shape of its markets.

Quick check list – sociological factors
- cultural/sub-cultural groups:
    characteristics
    growth/decline
- demographics:
    socioeconomic groupings
    home ownership
    geography
    family structure and influence
    family life stages
    usage patterns
- natural segments:
    characteristics
    differentiators
    growth/decline/change

- psychographics:
    preferences
    benefits
    attitudes and belief systems
- social trends:
    changes in personal value systems
    changes in the structure of society
    changes in moral and ethical positions
    changes in belief systems

Technological

The rate of change of technology has been one of the most visible under-currents of society of the past twenty years. Under this heading we are concerned with factors like information technology in the use of computers and computerization. We are concerned with the effect on the cost base of increased IT and automation. We should also be concerned with the likely changes that this may have on the types of materials that we use, the components that we use and the general resource base available to the organization.

There is an important relationship here with the previous section and that is the reaction of our customers to the increased use of computerization and automation. While many managers welcome the advances made in IT and the increased efficiency and cost savings which IT can produce, too many organizations, especially in the service sector, forget that their customers are by nature technophobic. This means that while cost savings and increased efficiency may be possible in 'back office' operations it is often less easy and less acceptable to bring automation through into the 'front office' in full view of the customer. While automation may be an aid to it, it is very rarely an alternative for personal service.

When considering the technological perspective and drawing scenarios of tomorrow's world we should be careful not to create scenarios of the world as we would like it to be but rather as we think it will be. So many of the pictures of the IT-dominated world of the 1990s have simply failed to happen. Apart from the innovators and early adopters in IT, many people have remained unimpressed by the PC except where they have been forced to change – in the workplace. I still keep seeing extrapolations for home-based PCs by the end of the century and strategic plans based on this assumption. Most innovations take at least twenty years to go 'mainstream', why should IT be different?

Quick check list – technological factors
- rate of technological change:

- organization's ability to keep up
  customer acceptance
- research and development:
  cost of investment
  matching customer needs
  control
- production technology:
  costs versus savings
  internal skill base
- protection of technology:
  patents
  copyrights
  impact on investment
- universal availability of technology:
  the rat race to technological edge
  product differentiation possibilities

International

As industry and commerce becomes more international in nature so more and more organizations are having to deal with an international environment audit. There are, of course, some organizations which are still purely domestic in nature, these need go no further than considering the environment of their domestic market. However, the number of organizations which have no international markets, no international suppliers for various components or raw materials and no international competition in the domestic market are becoming fewer and fewer every year.

Broadening the environment audit then to an international basis for the organization that has overseas markets it will have to consider the political, economic, sociological and technological aspects of each different market in which it intends to operate paying special attention to the ever present critical social and cultural differences which lie submerged in foreign markets ready to trap the unwary.

Ecological

Ecology too has entered the mainstream. All types of organization are now faced with issues that they could ignore just a decade ago. Serious environmentalists are still in the minority but those of us who like to bathe our consumption in a 'light green wash' are now the majority.

Finally, be prepared for the future. Nothing remains fixed in time and space, not even the trusty 'PEST' analysis. As always, much depends on your organization and your market, but beware of over simplistic models. What does '?' mean for your business?

Marketer's note

While these environmental classifications are 'standards' it is important that each organization decide which of the six classifications given above have the most severe impact on its activities and its profits. Obviously this is where the attention needs to be directed.

Since change is the order of the day in the business environment, the environment audit is not an exercise that can be completed and then forgotten. Nor is it an exercise that can be safely carried out on an annual basis – there is too much important change. Ideally the organization should create a tracking mechanism that will show up the most important changes as they occur. Time is of the essence in competitive markets.

Opportunities and threats

Having looked briefly at the environment audit and done our best to make sense of what is going on in the wider business scene we need now to turn this information into action. Specifically we need to search through the environment for the specific opportunities which appear to

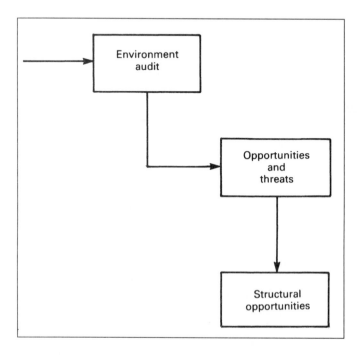

Figure 15
Opportunities and threats

be open to our organization (see Figure 15). It takes time to develop new products and new services and to develop and open new markets. If we are given a hint from the environment audit that new market possibilities are likely to open then we should plan our time accordingly and be ready when the market is just appearing. Arriving six to nine months late along with the bulk of the competition is hardly the best way to win a market reputation.

As well as identifying the opportunities in tomorrow's market place it is also important that we clearly identify the threats which may appear in the business environment, especially those which might seriously hinder our development and continued prosperity as an organization. In my experience managers have few problems in identifying threats in the future environment. Indeed, the list of threats is often twice or three times longer than that of opportunities. I must admit I am never quite sure whether this is because the environment really is tough out there or because a pessimistic nature is a prerequisite for the modern manager. Be this as it may, the important thing is not just to identify the threats but to be able to do something about them. As long as they are spotted early enough most threats can either be negated or avoided by the organization – or even turned into opportunities. Unfortunately for every example of an organization which has, perhaps, successfully lobbied government to avoid certain regulations being brought into force or has diversified out of its original core industry into other newer more secure market sectors, there are three or four examples of organizations that have seen the abyss and then promptly walked straight into it.

Marketer's note

Unfortunately, it is not just tomorrow's threats and opportunities that can be unearthed by a solid environment audit. If your organization is about to start an audit for the first time you are likely to discover an interesting bunch of threats and opportunities sitting right underneath you now – you just didn't know they were there!

Foregoing opportunities is one thing, not knowing about a threat until a few years of declining profits makes it too late to do anything about it is quite another.

This may sound like an overly pessimistic note but I know many firms in this situation. By the time that the pain gets bad enough to make management do something about the problems, it might just be too late.

Industry analysis

I have looked at the broad macro elements of the environment which will impact the organization. These macro elements could be considered the standard factors which will be analysed by all organizations regardless of the type of business they are in. Now, dropping down a level from the general to the more specific, we must look at the first of two very important areas of the external environments which the organization will need to analyse and understand thoroughly in order to be able to set out its objective and strategy for the future. We will start with the question of industry analysis.

In order to survive and flourish an organization will not only have to learn to live with and profit from the constraints placed on it by its political, economic, sociological or technological environment, it will also have to learn how to deal with the specific rules, regulations and constraints placed on its activity by its membership of a specific industry (see Figure 16). Michael Porter in his book *Competitive Strategy* considers that competitors' strategy must grow out of a sophisticated understanding of the rules and competition that determine an industry's attractiveness. He goes on to describe five distinct competitive forces which will collectively determine the profitability of any industry – industry competitors, potential entrants, suppliers, buyers and substitutes. He suggests that, together, they influence at the same time the prices which the organization can charge, the costs which the organization is likely to incur and also the required investments of the organization if it wishes to remain in that industry (see Figure 17).

While this view is, to my mind, overly economics led (there are good examples of companies breaking away from industry-driven pricing by offering genuinely unique value to customers), his description of competitive forces is a good one. We can use Porter's classification as a convenient

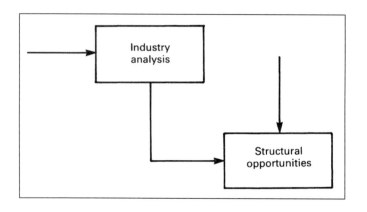

Figure 16
Industry analysis

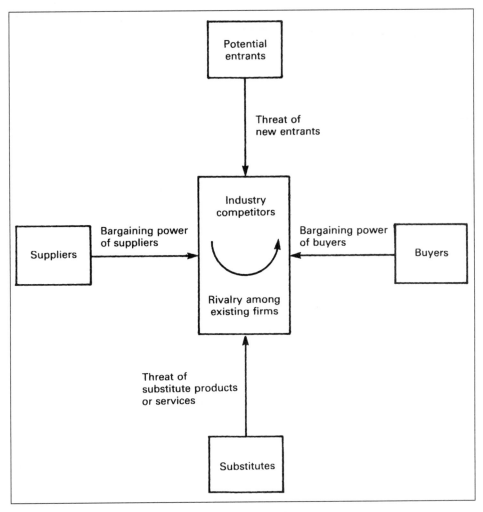

Figure 17   The five competitive forces that determine industry profitability. *Source:* Porter M.E., *Competitive Advantage of Nations* (Free Press, New York, 1990).

guide to understanding how to analyse the industry background of an organization.

Industry competitors

Before we consider industry analysis, a point should be made. How does the organization determine what industry (or business) that it is in – not as easy as it sounds. This point will be covered in more depth at the end of this environment section.

An analysis of the actual competitors within a given industry is often as far as many, superficial analyses would take an organization. While it is important to understand who are the organization's direct competitors in an industry, it is not the only component to an industry and its profitability over the long term. Specifically, as far as industry competitors are concerned we should be specially concerned with the degree of rivalry which exists between them. Factors such as the rate of growth of the industry, the amount of capacity which is considered 'spare' within the industry, its general maturity in terms of image, brand identity and differentiation among competitors and, very importantly, the exit barriers (the costs needed to exit an industry can often be very, very high). These factors, among others, will determine how much rivalry exists in the industry, the degree of competition and so the amount of time, money and effort which have to be invested by the organization in competing with its direct industry rivals. Competition is expensive and can only be financed through profit. The degree of rivalry in an industry will determine the profit levels and the organization must then decide for itself whether there is sufficient profit potential in the existing industry to meet the needs of its shareholders.

New entrants

While we need to understand the capacities and the abilities of our direct competitors in the industry it is also very important (although too often overlooked) to look into the future and to try and see who might possibly want to or try to enter the industry as a new competitor. The key to an understanding of the new entrant threat to an industry will ultimately depend on our ability to assess realistically the barriers which exist to entry from outside. For example, have existing competitors established significant economies of scale in production, in marketing, in advertising and so forth that would form an effective barrier to a new entrant? Are there specific strengths in brand awareness and brand loyalty in the marketplace? Do we have control over access to distribution? Do we, because of our existing position as an organization in the industry, have real cost advantages over new entrants?

In any discussion about entry barriers the emphasis must always be on the words 'realistic assessment'. An effective barrier to entry does not exist purely and simply because we wish it to exist. Secondly, entry barriers are not always effective over the very long term.

Breaking down the barriers

1 Retail banking in the UK

For very many years (up to the mid-1980s) the existence of an extensive and expensive retail branch banking network was considered to be a sufficient barrier to competitive entry. This enabled the major players to dictate their own terms to customers. Since the late 1980s the big players have been facing competition from two directions. First the Building Societies (who already had their own network of retail branches) are allowed to compete with banks through legislative changes. Second, companies are offering selective banking products through different (new) channels such as the telephone, by post, through automatic teller machines (ATMs) and through supermarket checkouts – so gradually removing the need for a high street presence. Are the banks seeing the high street branch network still as a barrier to competitive entry or as a millstone around their necks?

2 Telecommunications

For many years the national telecommunications organizations (PTTs) have been able to force their will on their markets through the direct control of the copper wire network and trunking systems that carried all the calls. Even local competition was forced to use existing systems or dig up all the roads! Modern technology now threatens this high barrier to entry with personal communications networks based on radio, microwave and eventually satellite links. Will this make the huge investment in fixed networks redundant?

Too often new entrants can cause damage to an organization simply because of the surprise factor. A history of operating in one sector can make managers believe that there is only one way of doing things and that only they can do it – bad mistake!

Substitutes

The whole question of substitute threat is a very difficult one for the organization to grasp if it is not truly market oriented. There are really two areas in which substitutes become a threat. The first is what we could call product substitutes, often driven by changes in cost structures or technological advance whereby the product or service itself is improved but not essentially changed in nature. Examples of these substitutes may be, the progress from real ground coffee to instant coffee, the development of the electric carving knife or the move from black and white to colour TVs. The potential threat of these substitute products are normally quite easy to plot and depends largely on the relative price and performance of substitutes compared to the existing products and services offered as well as the buyers' willingness to change to the substitute offer.

The more difficult category of substitute to see, unless the organization (or at the very least the marketing director/vice president) is in very close contact with the marketplace, is based on the concept that the market does not buy product or service features. What it buys is a package of benefits or specific solutions to a problem which it has. Naturally enough there is more than one way of solving any solution. So we can see what in marketing terms are very straightforward and logical shifts to substitutes but often in product terms are complete illogical shifts so far as the production minded manager is concerned.

Substituting Detroit

While IBM managed to move from electric typewriters to computers other organizations have not been so adept. The US car industry is a fine case in point. Despite many warnings (and even after an offer to Ford to take over the Volkswagen plant for free after the war) the VW Beetle proved the undoing of Detroit.

> 'In 1950, 330 VWs sold in America; in 1955, 30,000; in 1957, 79,000. The VW Bug and van, virtually unchanged year after year and bolstered by a brilliant, honest, low-key advertising campaign, thrived for more than a decade. Detroit's refusal or inability to respond in a meaningful way to the VW challenge opened the door to other low-cost quality imports, culminating in the near take-over of the American car market by the Japanese in the 1980s.'

Jack Mingo, *How the Cadillac got its Fins*. Harper Collins, New York, 1994.

Examples of the second form of substitutes would be the move from railroads and shipping to airlines for long-distance travel or the shift from carbon paper and stencils to electronic photocopying machines. In cases such as these, the basic customer need remains constant and is still being satisfied by the marketplace. However, the technology being used is often so fundamentally different that organizations wedded to the old technology either find themselves repositioning into a new industry or disappearing. More aware companies such as Rolex watches and Waterman pens have successfully re-positioned themselves and now operate in the luxury gift market.

Suppliers

Another important aspect of an industry which will determine its attractiveness to the organization is the bargaining power of suppliers to that industry. Here we need to know, who are the key suppliers? How concentrated is supply? Are there hundreds of organizations supplying to the industry or are there just two? How important are the volumes of the supplies to the industry, both in volume and intrinsic value to the eventual output of the industry itself? How much of the total cost structure in the industry is represented by suppliers' margins?

These sorts of question should enable us to understand the strength of the suppliers and the bargaining power which they hold over the industry as a whole. Naturally the stronger the power of the suppliers, the greater the threat of forward integration. In other words, the greater the threat of the suppliers entering the industry as an additional competitor possibly with significant competitive advantage if they have direct access to limited raw supplies. An additional threat is that the more concentrated the supply aspect of the industry then the greater the risk that one or more of the competitive organizations in the industry might decide to involve itself in backward integration, in other words buying back into the supply source which feeds the industry. This could place the organization at a competitive disadvantage and might influence its view on the long-term attractiveness of the industry itself.

Buyers

There are two separate aspects which determine the degree of buyer power in any industry. The first aspect concerns the actual direct power of the buyers themselves and is most normally typified by situations where there are either relatively few buyers or where a fairly small number of the buyers tend to purchase a very large volume of the industry's output. This might typically be the case in many industrial situations. More frequently nowadays this situation is evident in the distribution of packaged consumer goods, grocery distribution in the UK is highly concentrated into a small number of very large organizations. In such circumstances the industry is obviously at a certain degree of disadvantage vis-à-vis buyer power although the eventual exercising of that power will depend on a number of factors such as how important the industry's output (products or services) is to the actual buying unit. How easy it would be to switch from buying products from one industry to buying from another industry or indeed the availability and cost of substitute products and services.

Of course, intermediary buyer power has its limitations especially if it is not considered by the end consumer as delivering the benefits required. A number of successful business have been started by dissatisfied consumers who, unable to find what they wanted, started their own business in competition. Such is (at least the stated) reason for the beginnings of The Gap, The Body Shop and Virgin Financial Services.

The second aspect of buyer power concerns the degree of price sensitivity which exists in the marketplace. This is what economists call elasticity of demand. In other words the freedom which the industry has to increase its prices and the effect any price increase will have on demand and, ultimately, sales. The economist's concept of a straightforward price/quantity/demand relationship is, although effectively correct, much too simplistic for today's modern marketing environment. The relationship between price and quantity demanded can easily be distorted by elements such as brand loyalty, product differences and differentiation, and customers' perception of quality versus performance and price. However, although elements such as brand loyalty and product differentiation can increase potential profits for the industry, these do require significant investment to establish in the marketplace.

Conclusions

As Porter points out, the strength of the five competitive forces described above can vary from industry to industry and indeed they can change as an industry evolves over time. The net result is that all industries are not alike as far as profitability and hence attractiveness are concerned. There will be some industries where all of the forces could be considered favourable. In these conditions all or most of the organizations within the industry will be flourishing and will be attracting average or above average returns on their investment. At the same time there will be other industries where all or most of the forces will be unfavourable and in these instances, despite the very best endeavours of management, profitability for organizations will not be that good in absolute terms.

Most importantly, managers must realize that even if all the forces are favourable at the moment, the future is in no way guaranteed and the direction and influence of these forces can and will change over time.

Also, if we are currently looking at an industry where all the forces are negative (or at least appear to be so) this does not mean that industry itself has no future. Indeed, unlike the previous question of the broad macro environment audit which we have considered, where the organization has little or no control over the environmental factors in the industry environment, the organization will be able to exercise some long-term control and influence over the direction of the five factors. The degree to which it is able to influence these forces will, of course, depend on its size and its influence within the industry. But we will now go on to look at exactly what the organization can or cannot do.

Structural opportunities

As we have already seen, industries will vary from one to another in the different strengths of these five competitive forces. The reason why the various forces will be different from industry to industry is largely because of the different marketing–economic and production–technical characteristics which underlie each different industry. These important characteristics are known as the industry structure.

It is important to understand at this point that the organization has the power, through the business strategies which it chooses, to influence the structure of the industry within which it operates. In certain instances this influence can be a double-edged sword, so care must be taken (see Figure 18).

Since every industry is different then the relative importance of the five forces will also be different from industry to industry. So an organization

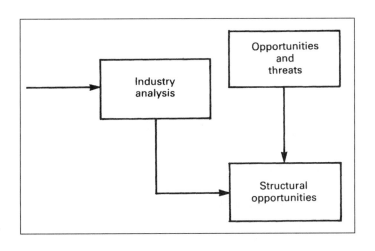

Figure 18
Structural
opportunities

need not necessarily worry about influencing each and every force but may decide to concentrate its effort on one or two to maximize its effect. It would be difficult here to explore in depth all of the possible structural opportunities open to the organization but a few examples may serve to illustrate the point.

Regarding the question of industry competitors and intensive competition there are a number of instances where competing organizations have grouped together and mounted collaborative generic advertising and promotional campaigns with the aim of expanding the total market size. Increased market size obviously reduces the intensity of competition since there is a larger market to fight over. On the down side of course there is the question of a larger market acting as a magnet for outside organizations unless entry barriers are high. If new entrants appear, the intensity of competition is back to where it was. Collaboration is a tactic which has been used in Europe for such diverse industries as insurance, shock absorbers and beef.

If the threat of new entrants is a key force in your industry then the emphasis should be on building significant entry barriers which will be durable over the longer term. Marketing barriers in terms of brand loyalty and product differentiation can be effective but tend to take time to construct and are also quite expensive in terms of investment. Other methods include lobbying government for protection of industry or, perhaps through increased specialization, driving down the unit cost of production to a level which inhibits new entrants. Again, any barrier needs to be robust over the long term and technical barriers are often at the mercy of large quantum technical leaps – which overnight can make a very expensive barrier obsolete. (Just imagine how the lowest cost producer of radio valves must have felt when the transistor came along.)

There are obvious possibilities in the area of substitution. However, as we have seen in the introductory section, it is not easy either to become or to remain a truly market-oriented organization. This being said, there are very significant rewards to be reaped from keeping in very close contact with our customers. Substitutes need not necessarily be a threat to the industry or our position as long as we are the organization marketing the substitute.

There are also structural opportunities for the organization in terms of suppliers. If this is a key factor in your industry there are two ways of dealing with the problem. One, attempting to negate the power of certain suppliers by locating alternative sources of supply. These may not be the most economic in the short run but, of course, we should also be looking for the long term when devising our strategy. The second route is to take advantage of the possibly concentrated supply situation by integrating backwards into the supply end of the industry.

Structural opportunities too in the area of buyer power fall into two broad categories. As we have seen above, the first area of buyer power is in terms of the concentrated power which comes from either a small number of buyers or a smaller number of very large volume buyers. One solution here might be to further concentrate the purchase activity of the industry to these buyers to create equal strength. Alternatively, the product or service scope could be broadened to encourage new buyers into the industry and thereby reduce the power of the primary buyers. In terms of the second area of buyer power, that of price sensitivity, the most obvious solution is to build strength on brand awareness, product differentiation and loyalty in the marketplace. This, of course, can cost money over a fairly long period but is naturally aimed at improving the price levels and hence the profit margin. Just one example in this area, there are relatively few producing companies in the UK packaged food/grocery industry that have equal or superior power to the major supermarket chains. Heinz is one of these companies which, through continued support of its major brands to the end consumer, has more power and consequently more say in the setting of its final market prices.

So we can see that if the organization is able to change and mould the structure of the industry in which it operates this can then change the fundamental attractiveness of the industry for better – and for worse. What is happening is that the organization or organizations are actually changing the rules of competition within the industry. Unfortunately organizations have been known to make strategic choices of this kind without due consideration of the long-term consequences for the industry structure. Any action, as the law of physics tells us, will elicit a reaction. An organization which makes a strategic choice and approaches what it sees to be a structural opportunity considering only its own potential gain in the short to medium term may generate competitive reaction of such a nature that the whole structure of the industry is altered over the longer term to make competition even harsher and profits even more scarce. In fact this chain of action–reaction may even produce an industry where everybody is worse off at the end of the day. Nothing causes quite as much devastation as a misguided organization starting a price war without thinking of the consequences. Competitive reaction is an immensely potent force and one which we will consider later.

The resource/performance audit

A resource audit is another of those grand titles which serves to disguise the existence of a very simple question – what are the capabilities of the organization? (See Figure 19.)

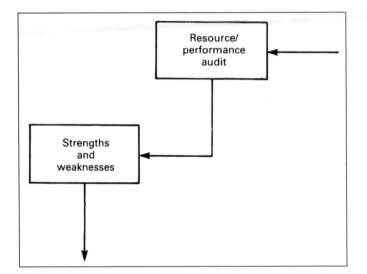

Figure 19
The resource/
performance audit

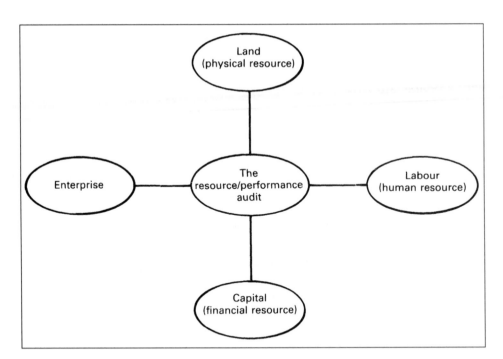

Figure 20   Four traditional headings of the resource audit

A practical strategy is one which is essentially achievable. While an organization may wish to achieve certain goals, wishing on its own is unlikely to be enough. The organization must have the resources and the capability to achieve those objectives. For example, the Principality of

Monaco may wish to be a leader in satellite communications technology. it may even do their economy some good, but it is patently clear that with the resources apparently at their disposal this is likely to remain a wish and is not a realistic objective.

When we are considering the resource audit, the simplest approach is for the organization to break down its resources under the four traditional headings – land, labour, capital and enterprise (see Figure 20).

Land (physical resource)

Under this heading the organization should consider its resources in terms of production facilities and capacity if it is a manufacturing business, in other words, factories, locations output capacities, flexibility of production lines and methodologies, the age of the plant, recent levels of investment and so on. For service organizations we will be concerned with office space and flexibility of use, possibly the number of retail or other outlets, access points for customers, delivery trucks, rolling stock, mechanized plant and equipment and so on. It is very important that, right at the outset, we should have a clear understanding of exactly what the organization can deliver to the marketplace and precisely what delivery levels would be impractical, at least in the short to medium term. In the medium term, of course, constraints can be overcome by building up resources or by buying in temporary resources. Strategic alliances to support key strengths can also be considered.

Labour (human resource)

Labour is another simplified term which we would use to cover all forms of human resource open to the organization. Under this heading we are concerned with both manual and mental labour (if such a distinction is still valid today). The organization needs to know how flexible is its human resource to meet the new challenges which the strategy may place on it. We would need to consider aspects such as industrial relations, training and management development, skills base, internal communications and organization and morale.

There are also specific questions which the organization should be asking about its top and middle management capabilities. Specifically, how good are they, how responsive is management to change and how competitive in nature. The more competitive nature of the business environment since the 1980s, has exposed certain deficiencies in top management both in Europe and North America. If your top and senior middle management structure is made up of people who have 'come up through the ranks' these may not be the best people to see you into even more turbulent times. Managers who have risen due to their ability to manage organizations in a stable environment have very little expertise or experience running organizations in more turbulent periods. It is simply not true that no decision is better than a bad decision. The markets of the 1990s/2000s will demand managers able to make quick decisions under ever-increasing pressure. The organization that does not have, or cannot groom, managers such as these may soon be at a severe competitive disadvantage.

Although we will be dealing with the subject in more depth later on, the whole vexed question of organization structure and design falls into this category too. At this stage it is probably sufficient to note that an organization's structure (including its systems, reward mechanisms and administrative processes) will have a major effect on what actions it can take in the marketplace. In too many cases organizations are unable to survive simply because the structure is too rigid and change resistant to allow managers and staff to deliver on its customers' needs. So the genepool gets refreshed!

Capital (financial resource)

This category refers to the financial muscle called for in a strategy. Whether the strategy eventually calls for consolidation, redirection, head-to-head competition or the erection of barriers to entry to your market-place, the costs are already high and are getting higher. Financial strength is no guarantee of long-term survival, but it helps. Naturally, the eventual strategy for the organization must be formulated within the confines of the finances which the organization either has or is able to access.

Strategic decisions call for strategic capital. It is as important that the organization attracts the right kind of finance – not just enough. Banks and capital markets always have enough money but it comes with strings attached, financial support from promiscuous investors can put the wrong kinds of pressure on an organization. Short-term returns can always be provided by an organization but one of the other stakeholders will have to bear the cost. If the costs are not equally shared over the long term, strategy cannot be implemented.

Enterprise

This last category covers the whole area of creativity and business acumen needed to survive in competitive marketplaces. Although marketing typifies the enterprise concept, it has no monopoly over the area. In simple terms, enterprise is the collection of ideas, new thoughts and drive required by an organization if it is going to continue to grow and flourish in the years ahead.

We will be looking at this question in more detail when we consider the implementation of marketing strategy in Part 4, but at this point it is worth noting that the behaviour of individuals inside an organization is very largely dictated by the organization structure. The structure of the organization, its layout, reporting systems, reward systems, implicit and explicit culture and its communications processes all serve to spell out to people what behaviours are valued and will guarantee progress within the system. These structures and systems have often evolved, over time, to meet the needs of the organization itself rather than its customers. Generally, customer needs tend to evolve faster than organizations' ability to keep up and an organization may find itself unable to serve its customers as well as it did in the past. Creating the degree of internal change necessary to continue to meet customer needs is never easy – the organization will actively resist it, preferring the life it knows and a falling order book to an unknown future.

Once the organization has considered all these four areas individually, it is important that the four areas be put together and a suitable balance found across all four aspects of the resource audit. All four elements are required if the organization is to have a future. We can all think of good examples of organizations that have been perhaps flush with money but have had, as far as they were concerned, no good ideas into which to invest (GEC–UK would be a good example of this). There are also the young thrusting organizations full of new ideas and revolutionary thoughts but with little or no capital to back them up. These are soon snapped up by the larger organizations where the enthusiasm of the young is injected like monkey glands into tired old veins in the hope of some form of corporate rejuvenation. More worryingly, there are scores of examples where the creative west has generated ideas which in the absence of sufficient, patient capital have gone to Japan and the east where they have been successfully modified and marketed.

Strengths and weaknesses

Falling straight out of the resource audit in the previous section, the organization should now be in a situation to identify its particular strengths and its potential weaknesses. The idea being, of course, that the eventual strategy will be one which exploits the organization's strengths and protects its weaknesses (see Figure 21).

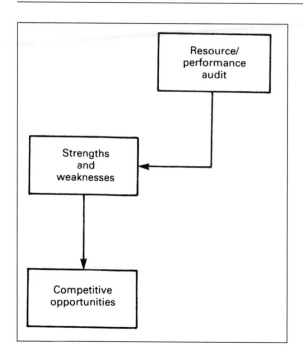

Figure 21   Strengths and weaknesses

It is, of course, inevitable that an organization will start looking at its strengths and weaknesses through internally focused eyes, that is essentially what the resource audit is all about. Nevertheless it is important for managers to realize that a strength is really only a strength if the marketplace perceives it to be so. This fact is probably best demonstrated through an example. If we look at the organization Slazenger in the 1980s, their strengths may very well have been considered at that time to have been engineering and chemical in nature, rubber and synthetic technology and so forth. However, they managed to launch, quite successfully, a range of specialist toiletries aimed at sportsmen and sportswomen. Initially these were a gentle shampoo for frequent application and a stronger than normal deodorant. Both products were successful – but how could this be, since they appear to have little or no relationship with what might be considered to be the primary strengths of the organization. In fact, what happened, was that Slazenger's customers, the sporting people, believed that Slazenger as an organization understood their needs in a sporting context. Hence the move from racquets and shoes to toiletries would appear to be quite consistent in a sporting context. The fact that Slazenger had little or no production experience in the mixing and fabrication of toiletries, as far as the marketplace was concerned, was irrelevant.

So long as the organization has identified what it believes to be its strengths it is imperative that this profile is researched in the marketplace to find out, very clearly, whether the marketplace agrees that these are the strengths of the organization. If not, what are the strengths of the organization as perceived from the outside? These are the ones on which the organization should build, all others are simply an illusion. It is the market's view of the organization's strengths that provide the best source of competitive advantage.

Marketer's note

When you help to put together the strengths and weaknesses analysis for your organization you should remember one thing – it pays to be honest no matter whose feelings you might hurt. The organization may not be able to deal with an honest assessment of its strengths and weaknesses but a simple re-statement of conventional wisdom does no good.

Restrict circulation of the analysis to preserve morale if you must – but be honest with yourselves. A practical strategy demands it.

Competitor analysis

It is a truism to say that we all need to understand our competitors better than we do at the moment. But before you nod sagely and add yet another mental note to the pile of things that you really ought to do as soon as you get time let's try and understand exactly why it is so important to understand what our competitors are trying to do in the marketplace. We must look at the whole problem from the customer's point of view (revolutionary I know but maybe we ought to try and get into the habit of doing this more often). (See Figure 22.)

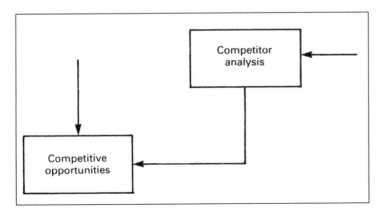

Figure 22
Competitor analysis

Regardless of what your organization produces, as soon as you make an offering to the marketplace what's the first thing the customer is going to do? As much as we would like to believe that our customer is an intensely logical, rational, decision-making being, potential buyers, industrial as well as consumer, are simply not used to making decisions in absolute terms. In order to judge the benefits of your products or services and the claims which you make, their first step is always going to be to compare your offering to an alternative offering made by one of your competitors. Although we all know this to be the case it's surprising the number of organizations that operate as if in a vacuum and as if they were the only possible choice in the marketplace. We also know that nothing galvanizes our organization into action better than something new being marketed by an active competitor. Would that it were otherwise, but the bulk of innovation in industry and commerce is in fact stimulated by competitor activity rather than carefully identified needs stemming from the marketplace.

One word of warning before we look in slightly more detail about the best way of getting to understand your competitors and trying to predict how they would like you to react in any given circumstances. We can all agree that competitor analysis is a 'good thing', but you can in these instances have too much of a good thing. Competitor analysis is the main area where all of the comparisons between marketing and military warfare (the 1980s have seen a spate of such books) start to fall down. In the military analogy the objective of the opposing forces is to overcome the enemy, in marketing terms the objective is to capture as many of the customers (perhaps in the military analogy these would be the innocent bystanders), at the expense of the competition. While few organizations really have enough information and understanding of how their competitors operate it would be difficult to justify additional resources to this area if they were to be at the expense of acquiring a deeper understanding of our target customers.

'When elephants fight it is the grass that suffers.'

African proverb

This being said, how can we go about developing an understanding of our competitors and then use this in developing our strategic approach? Most organizations have a database of sorts on competitors' capabilities and activities. Although this information tends to be gathered in an ad-hoc manner from meetings, from secondhand sources such as customers and intermediaries, or perhaps from the sales force, very few organizations collect data in a systematic manner. It is, of course, the systematic process carried out over a longer period of time which tends to develop a better understanding of our competitor's ambitions and capabilities. The entire competitor analysis process should be designed to build a 'response model' for each competitor which we face. This 'response model' is very important in the development of our business and marketing strategy because it will enable us to assess any considered change in policy or strategic direction for the likely competitive response it will provoke. Hence we concentrate on the ultimate effects of our policy or strategic change in the marketplace where it really matters.

There are two separate aspects to competitor analysis. The first is data which are easier to collect, the second is information which is more useful to developing an understanding of our competitors. The first area of analysis concerns what the competitor is currently doing and what in our opinion the competitor is able to do. There are three questions to be answered here (again for each competitor).

- What is the competitor's current strategy?
- How is the competitor currently competing with our organization?
- What are the competitor's capabilities?

The first two questions are necessarily interlinked and intelligent observation of the competitor's activity in the marketplace is often enough, especially if linked with published material such as annual reports, press commentaries and so forth, to work out the competitor's most likely strategy in its approach to its markets. The last question, that of the competitor's capabilities, is deceptively simple. As we have seen already from looking at our own strengths and weaknesses, the important questions are not what we may believe our competitors' strengths and weaknesses to be but more importantly what the customers believe the competitors' strengths and weaknesses to be. Hence there may be two aspects to this information gathering. One, our observation of the competitors and two, some form of market research among our common customers.

The second important area of competitor analysis is concerned with what actually drives the organization, in other words, what has in the past motivated it to act the way it has and what do we believe to be the motivations behind the organization which may influence its activities in the future. There are two important questions in this section. Both equally difficult to answer. The first is, what are the future goals of the competitor and of its management? The second question is, what are the assumptions which the competitor and its management hold about themselves and the industry in which they operate? While these questions are undoubtedly more difficult to answer than the previous ones it is, of course, the motivational aspects of the competitor which will provide us with a far better key to understanding a competitor's most likely behaviour in the future.

As I have already said, competitor analysis is not just about rushing out and beavering away for the next three to four months acquiring some information and then leaving it at that. It is a question of developing a systematic approach to the gathering of information over a longer period of time. It is unlikely that anything as complex as an organization of managers and individuals is going to be satisfactorily assessed within a short period of time. We need a slow, gradual build up over time to develop a clearer picture with each successive piece of paper joining the rest and building up into more of a workable profile of the competitive organization and its key managers.

A final note. If you have worked through this section with only your direct competition in mind then you have left yourself and your organization open and vulnerable. In the previous section we considered the nature of competition and the 'five forces' of competition described by Porter. Any competitor information system worth the investment must take into account the full array of competition facing the business. After all, it's no use creating an entire department to tell you what your biggest direct competitor is planning to do next year if your market share can be halved by the entry of a substitute product or service that slipped in unseen.

Competitive opportunities

Once we have managed to create and maintain a regular data gathering system which adds successive pieces of data and builds up a fuller and fuller profile of the major competitors, what should we be looking to do with it? More precisely, what competitive opportunities are there for our organization? (See Figure 23.)

So far in this section of information gathering we've looked at the resource and performance audit of the organization, the environment audit, the analysis of the industry and structural opportunities which may exist for our organization. Finally we are considering the competitive situation. None of these elements on their own are sufficient to construct a strategy for the organization but taken together a picture slowly should start to appear of the range of strategic opportunities open to us. Now, bearing in mind our own internal capabilities and the broad macro environment in which we operate and also depending on the structural opportunities which exist within the five competitive force framework of the industry we must look closely at our competition before attempting to decide what is possible and what is not.

Once the database has started to build we should be able to answer a

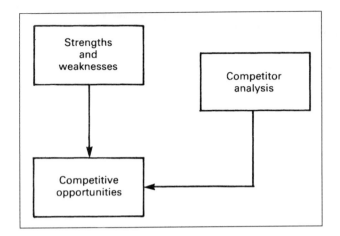

Figure 23
Competitive
opportunities

number of questions which are important inputs for our strategic decision-making. For example, it should start to become clear in time whether a given competitor appears to be satisfied with its current position in the industry and in the marketplace. If the competitor appears to be satisfied then we can expect that it will be looking to maintain its position rather than aggressively grow. However, we can expect that it might mass its resources against any likely threat of activity within the industry to reduce its power. Retaliation could be quite a major threat in this case.

A better understanding of our competitors will also enable us to understand what likely moves they will make in the industry. What segments they are particularly interested in and where they see their future and the types of market they would like to penetrate.

We would also expect to build up a picture of where a competitor is particularly vulnerable to any attack, not, of course, that this means that we would instantly pile in with a major frontal attack on this vulnerable position, rather this information would need to be aggregated with our better understanding of the industry and its likely stability and structural make-up. It is very important to control any 'action-man' managers at this point since hasty action could result in a net loss of market and profits over the longer term.

Last, but no less important, the competitor analysis would enable us to identify what action by us would provoke the greatest, the most effective reaction from any given competitor. Here I come back to one of my opening statements that the primary aim for any organization must be to win and to keep profitable customers. Straightforward, bloody head-to-head battles with major competitors is not the aim of the organization (or rather it shouldn't be). While competition itself may bring certain benefits to the customer, for the organization it is an extremely wasteful exercise. An understanding of likely retaliation points by various competitors will allow us to sift through strategic alternatives and to choose those activities which will, at the end of the day, produce the maximum positive effect in the marketplace. The alternative to proper competitor analysis in this instance may very well be in the design of an extremely elegant strategy aimed to make maximum penetration into a new marketplace which results only in massive retaliation from one or more competitor. The entire marketing thrust can be transformed into a fruitless exercise of organization to organization competition with no guarantee of marketplace advance for any player.

Marketer's note

A quick word on the SWOT analysis. Everybody does it but then, everybody seems to either put it away in a drawer or consign it to the appendix of a plan and forget about it. The SWOT, if it is properly done, is worth more than that — certainly to the marketer.

The well-constructed SWOT is not an easy thing to put together so should be used to promote change in the organization. A SWOT that simply collects internally focused beliefs should be buried, of course, but that's not what we are talking about here! While it is not subtle in its approach (like mental arithmetic helps us check the final result generated by calculator), the SWOT should provide us with the first clues to the content of the business and the marketing strategies. Knowing what our customers consider our strengths and weaknesses to be and knowing where our threats and opportunities probably lie we should end up with a simple grid with (only the most important please) factors listed as shown in Figure 24.

But we can do something with this! By adding three important arrows we can create a rough-and-ready check on the final strategic proposals (Figure 25).

Do the proposals, at the least, show us how to:

1 Turn weaknesses into strengths.
2 Turn threats into opportunities.
3 Use our strengths to profit from our opportunities.

Don't tell me, you always knew there was more to the SWOT analysis than filling in boxes.

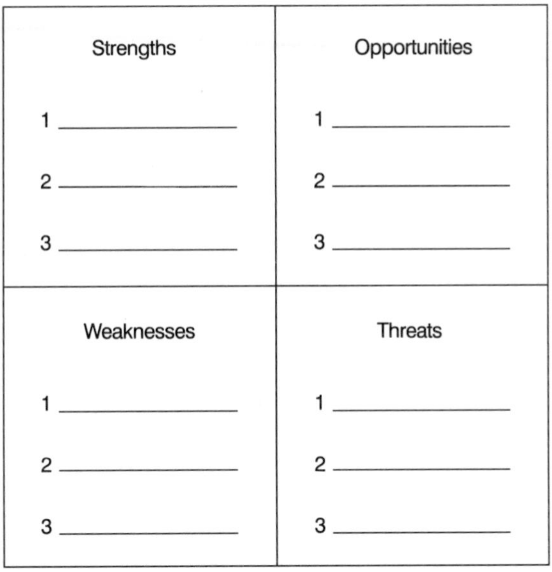

Strengths
Opportunities
1
2
3
1
2
3
Weaknesses
Threats
1
2
3
1
2
3

Figure 24 A SWOT analysis

Strengths
Opportunities
Weaknesses
Threats

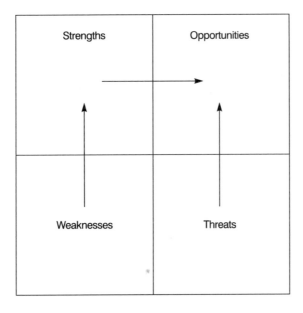

Figure 25 Adding to the SWOT analysis

Assessing our current position – a conclusion

I am always conscious of the fact that quietly gathering data and compiling facts is somehow not as satisfying as actually designing a new product or developing a new advertising campaign or even entering a virgin market. Nevertheless, just because it's not as interesting doesn't mean it is any less critical to the overall success of the organization's plans. Remember that you have to know where you are as well as where you want to be before you can plot the route between the two.

In working through the whole range of data gathering exercises that the organization should be considering I have tried to break down the operation into the major component parts. At the same time I have tried to explain the various reasons why each piece of data is going to be important for the eventual strategy/direction of the organization.

In this data gathering exercise, as with any form of data collection or research, we should bear in mind that data gathering is a means and not an end in itself. Before embarking on the process the organization must clearly understand exactly what it needs to know, and more importantly, precisely what it is going to do with the results of the analysis once they are available. To use some jargon here, the entire approach must be 'output oriented'. In short, the organization needs to develop a long term business objective, a business strategy and a robust marketing strategy which will guarantee its future over the medium to long term. Whether the strategy is tight, scientific and planned or whether it is loose and flexible depends on the nature of the organization and its marketplace. In any event, there must be, at the very least, a sense of direction.

The nature and complexity of decisions which we have to make will depend on the nature and complexity of the organization, its markets, its industry and the specific competitive situation which it faces. We need to understand what these factors are, how important they are and how they impinge on the organization if we are to establish our existing position and so have the vaguest idea of how to set forward from here. The strategic analyst should be as ruthless in his rejection of unnecessary data as he or she will be in the collection of vital information.

When putting together an outline of the entire data gathering process as I have tried to do above, I have been very aware that not all the elements explained will be of equal importance to every organization since every organization is different and every competitive situation is unique. Your organization will need to decide for itself which are the most important factors to consider and which are relatively less important. The route above is only a guide and it is not a blueprint that should be followed slavishly in every situation.

So what about the results? Once the data has been collected it needs to be transformed into information. In other words it needs to communicate something useful to an audience of people who will have to make decisions based on it. By definition, and specifically in the area of strategy, information is not communicated in reports of an inch thick or more. If the entire purpose of the exercise is to facilitate decision making then the important aspects should be communicated in the minimum of space. Although it is little more than a rule of thumb, I always suggest that the outputs of this process should be reduced down to approximately one side of paper for each of the following – the resource/performance audit, environment audit, the industry analysis and one side of paper for each individual competitor analysis. At the end of every sheet there should be a clear section which highlights precise implications for our own organization. This is what I call the 'so what factor'. You might very well find that rendering down a mountain of data into one sheet becomes the most challenging aspect of the whole process. But remember, if you can manage to get the whole complicated problem down to half a dozen or so key bullet points then you might just have a chance of properly explaining it to others.

I would make one final point on this important stage in the evolution of the organization's strategy, and that is that this whole exercise should not be viewed as either a one-off exercise or even an annual ritual. We and all of our organizations have to live in a dynamic environment. Nothing stands still and the only constant that we can count on is change. Also, no model which hopes to predict the future can ever be right. The only thing we attempt to do through the effort spent on predicting is to minimize the error between what we expect and what will actually happen. For these two reasons the data gathering activity as described above (and, of course, this is only one way of approaching the problem) should really be viewed as the start of a complete management information system. In other words, this should be a constant and regular activity to be carried out on behalf of the organization. Someone, at least, should be in charge of constantly monitoring the industry, constantly monitoring the environment and constantly monitoring our most important competitors and likely future players in the marketplace. Regular data gathering and regular reporting to the decision makers, even if the reports show no change against forecast activity, will itself be an addition to the knowledge held by those managers responsible for plotting the future course of the organization and adds further weight to the plans that they devise.

One final warning for that small minority of you who actually found this preceding section not only important but even exciting. I reiterate my warning about research generally being about ends not means. There is always the risk, especially in larger organizations, of the whole research function starting to take on a life of its own. As soon as this happens an extra resource is brought in to play. With a self-standing research facility collection and, even worse, analysis starts to take place which is not needed for the strategy but to justify the continued existence of the research function itself. This situation is extremely dangerous and should be rooted out as soon as possible.

We move to the next stage of the problem which is analysis. By its very nature the type of data gathering with which we have been concerned will be very subjective in nature. It will be heavily dependent on a relatively small number of 'expert' opinions and views on the structure of the industry, the likely forward progression of various competitors and assessments of strengths and weaknesses both ours and the competitors. This type of inherently biased and basically subjective information will not warrant too much analysis. Qualitative data of this nature will not support quantitative and analytical techniques and the spurious accuracy that such techniques can bring.

The nature of the business

Having now gained a better idea of where the organization stands relative to its environment we need to decide and clearly state the business in which the organization will operate in the future (see Figure 26). This is a very important decision for the organization (and one which is rarely arrived at without a degree of soul searching). This decision effectively draws the lines around the organization's arena of activities. Naturally it is important that the lines are neither too narrow, the organization must have enough market to approach and also that they are not too broad so that the organization is directionless.

Traditionally there are three ways in which the business might be defined by the organization.

1   The customer groups that will be approached.
2   The customer needs that the organization will satisfy.
3   The technology that the organization will use to satisfy the needs.

Let's take for example here a medium-size organization operating internationally which makes fire hose. This company then could define the business that it is in a variety of ways. It could define its business as hose technology. This would then naturally send the organization seeking opportunities in a variety of markets where there was a need for this type

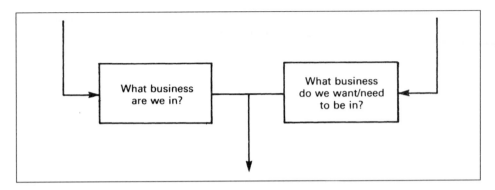

Figure 26   The nature of the business

of technology. This might include using hose technology to reline gas and oil pipelines as an alternative to pipe replacement. Alternatively it could define itself as being in the fire business. In this case should the organization wish to expand it might start looking at alternative products and services to deliver to the fire industry as a whole. This thinking might take the organization into electronic fire detection and safety areas. Or thirdly it could define its business as the fluid transfer business. It would then, should it wish to expand, be seeking opportunities in which perhaps fire industry would remain a large but just one segment within a market needing to transfer various fluids from one point to another. Examples here might include entering the pipeline business or managing a fleet of tanker lorries for flight refuelling.

It should now be readily apparent the importance and indeed the power the business definition has on the way the organization sees itself, the way the organization sees its markets, and most importantly, the way in which the organization sees its future. In the many dealings I have had with organizations who have been wrestling with this difficult question I have always found that a business definition based on customer needs, while it often appears overly esoteric in its definition, has a much stronger effect on the organization and is more easily communicated to the marketplace than definitions based either on customer grouping or technology. This is, in fact, the point made by Levitt who argues that a business should always be viewed rather as something which delivers customer satisfactions not which simply produces goods. He then goes on to make the classic argument in his article 'Marketing myopia' that had the US railroads defined their business in terms of customer needs (that they were people and goods movers) rather than in production terms (that they were in the business of running a railroad), they would not have suffered the enormous competitive onslaught of the airlines. Rather they themselves might today be running the airlines.

Levitt's work has, naturally enough, not been without its critics. As Mintzberg comments: 'Why should a few clever words on a piece of paper enable a railroad company to fly aeroplanes, or for that matter, run taxicabs? ... Nothing, of course, except the limitations of its own distinctive competencies' (p. 280). Obviously there is a world of difference between being able to identify a need and the ability to deliver a sound product or service to meet that need. Nevertheless, there is much to be said for focusing on customer needs and allowing them to direct the future of the business rather than just getting better and better at producing things that customers don't want!

Another reason for preferring the business definition to be based on customer needs rather than any other criteria is that it is the only base which will fully support the cultural change in the organization from a production to a market orientation. This, of course, was the key cultural shift required at the primary stage of information gathering. Also, it helps to define more clearly the competition facing the organization. Remembering back to the discussion on industry analysis and the five competitive forces, only by defining the business in terms of customer needs will we be able to include those competitors which offer substitute products to our own but which may be operating outside of our current technological base.

Last, the customer needs-based definition of the business also has proven to be more robust over time than the other bases used to define the business. While basic customer needs such as personal mobility and transportation; communication; nutrition; and the need for status and individualism all tend to be relatively stable over the longer period, the products and services which people buy to satisfy these needs have changed quite dramatically over the past twenty to thirty years. As have the technology bases used to produce these goods.

The next question facing the organization is how broad should the definition of the business be.

One last note on the question of the breadth or the narrowness of the business definition. There is a relationship between the decision made on the business within which the organization will operate and the competitive strategy which the organization will choose for its operations. If the organization were to use a fairly narrow definition of the business, one in which they would operate in all sectors of the business, then that would give them a fairly broad range approach to their competitive strategy. If for example they had a much broader definition of the business they were in and they were only operating in one part of it that would, by definition, make them a segment player rather than an overall market player. We will come back to this problem in more detail when we deal with competitive strategy but the point needs to

The leisure business?

Consider, for example, the case of a specialist company producing fillers, wallpaper adhesive, paint stripper and paint brush cleaning products for the non-professional home decorating market. Since the bulk of the company's products were used by people in their non-work/leisure time and also because the majority of the people using their products saw this as a constructive use of leisure time, the organization defined itself as being in the leisure business. This then led the organization to develop a range of paper toys for the children's market and a range of polystyrene dinghies for the leisure sailing market. Neither of these ventures was a great success. The market simply did not understand the use of the quite powerful brand name in one market sector being applied to these new product ideas. The organization then re-defined its business as the decorating ancillaries business which led them to strengthen their range of decorating products. A few years later this business definition was again extended to the home improvement business which led the organization logically from decorating products to home security products. In this instance the move was accepted by the marketplace and the organization experienced much greater success.

be made at this juncture since we can meet problems of definition later on.

I would like to make one final distinction, you will see from the flow chart that there are two boxes in this section rather than just one. There are, in fact, two questions to be answered by the organization and they are:

- What business are we actually in at the moment?
- What business do we want, or maybe better put, do we need to be in for the future?

In my experience these questions need to be asked separately and the first one needs to be answered with some degree of honesty. If you truly believe that your organization is a market-oriented organization and its primary concerns are with satisfying customer needs then you need not worry about answering the first question. If (and this relates to practically every single company I have ever encountered) you feel that you have marketing aspirations but your organization is primarily dominated by production and technical factors then you need to ask yourself what business you are actually in at the moment.

Number please ...

By way of an example let us consider the operator services division of a large national telephone company. Working through this process with the senior management team of this division it was readily agreed that the business they were actually in was managing the telephone operators' function. All their management skill and effort went towards this end and, of course, they were constantly required to take on a variety of different assignments from other divisions in the company for activities which needed to be carried out by an operator or similar person. After some, not inconsiderable, discussion it was agreed that the business this division needed to be in was that of 'call facilitation'. This was the core benefit which they needed to deliver to their customer base. This decision had two quite profound effects. First, the division could look quite freely at technologies other than people behind telephone consoles that might equally facilitate the call for the subscriber. Second, it enabled the division to differentiate quite clearly between those services required of it that fell into the category of what it should be doing and those services which had traditionally been provided by operators, such as early morning wake-up calls, which fell outside of the business which this division was in and therefore which they could remove from their much too lengthy product range.

Drawing a fine distinction between the business we are currently in and the business that we want or need to be in again fixes two points on an axis and therefore allows the organization to calculate a route between the current situation and the future required position.

'Till death us do part ...

A company providing pensions and other related financial services products decided to research its customer base to find what business its customers thought it was in. Not surprisingly (from a marketing viewpoint) the company had done the communications job well and its customers saw a marked difference between the money they invested or saved for general purposes and that which they invested for the specific purpose of providing for their retirement. They classified the company as a member of the 'retirement business' rather than in 'financial services'. Further research uncovered a wide range of opportunities for the company, outside traditional financial services but within what the market said was the retirement business.

Simply spotting the opportunities doesn't make them real. A lengthy history in the financial services business does not necessarily equip a company to take on business that falls outside what it thought was its core expertise. The company is now in the process of acquiring the competencies necessary to be successful when it enters the new markets.

Business definition is all in the mind. Consider the major motoring associations, technically they are in the financial services business. They take regular premiums from customers (membership fees) and they pay out when they receive a claim. The only difference is that rather than sending the member money after a breakdown, they convert the settlement into the service the customer really needs – a man in a van with the skills to get you going again!

Marketer's note

The whole question of defining the business is one which requires a very firm marketing control and a very strong marketing input. If the definition of the business is couched and agreed in marketing rather than production or technological terms then the entire process of developing a robust and effective marketing strategy becomes immeasurably easier. If, however, you are forced to accept a business definition based on technology or even customer groups it will be extremely difficult to put together a marketing strategy which is both consistent in market terms and which is effective given the quite normal resource constraints. The inevitable result of a non-market-based business definition will be that you will be trying to develop a marketing and competitive position for your organization in a number of different markets. These markets may appear superficially to be linked, i.e. via the technology which they use but will most likely be quite different in terms of the customers which they attract and the customer needs which the organization is attempting to satisfy.

If you were looking for a point in the process where you should dig your heels in firmly this is it.

Chapter 4

The business strategy

'In the practical art of war, the best thing of all is to take the enemy's country whole and intact; to shatter and destroy it is not so good. So, too, it is better to capture an army entire than to destroy it, to capture a regiment, a detachment or a company entire than to destroy them.

'Hence to fight and conquer in all your battles is not supreme excellence; supreme excellence consists in breaking the enemy's resistance without fighting.

'Thus the highest form of generalship is to baulk the enemy's plans; the next best is to prevent the junction of the enemy's forces; the next in order is to attack the enemy's army in the field; and the worst policy of all is to besiege walled cities'

Sun Tzu, 500 BC

We have spent some time considering what the organization is able to do, what opportunities exist for the organization in the industry and marketplace and what threats are apparent in the environment. We have also looked at what the organization must do in terms of its long-term financial objective. We have also considered the personal ambitions and values of the key implementors or the most senior management team in the organization. So far, we have even made one decision and that is, what business we want/need to be in.

We are still in the 'Where are we now' part of the book which means for the marketer, business/corporate strategy is a given that is required for the development of marketing strategy. Lest there be any confusion, business/corporate strategy and marketing strategy are not the same thing. Therefore, before we launch straight into a discussion about business strategy, a word about the emphasis of this book. The primary thrust of this work is to strip away some of the misconceptions about marketing strategy, that is, after all, why you bought it in the first place. It is not intended to be a book on business strategy. To be honest, I start this chapter with a degree of trepidation – business/corporate strategy is a vast and complicated area and everyone in the organization wants to be involved. The debate was started by Ansoff, popularized by Porter and widened by Mintzberg and many others. A book on practical marketing strategy is not the place to add fuel to the these particular fires so we will try to understand business/corporate strategy as far as it is able to help us in the marketing area.

Business strategy is important in that it provides the key to the development of the marketing strategy. In that the marketer must understand the business strategy concepts and their effects on the marketing process we will look at Porter's ideas and how they have influenced business in the 1980s. It goes without saying that anybody seriously interested in strategy has already read Porter, so the following sections will be little more than a reminder of the key points, but from a marketing point of view.

With the benefit of hindsight we will also look at some more recent ideas of business/corporate strategy and what these promise for the future.

Before we can begin to discuss marketing strategy proper we need certain minimum data on which to build our plans. As we have seen, there is a good argument for the involvement of marketing in these decisions but technically these areas are not the responsibility of the organization's marketing function. To develop the marketing strategy we need:

- a review of the environment within which we must operate;
- a definition of what business the organization is in;
- a definition of what business the organization wants/needs to be in (if different);
- the organization's business/corporate objective;
- the organization's business/corporate strategy;
- a definition of the organization's target strategic market position.

Definitions may be in order at this point.

The business/corporate objective

This is the goal, the aim to which all activities of the organization will be directed. This is the purpose of the organization and should not be confused with a simple financial target (such as profit) which is properly defined as a measure of the organization's success in achieving its objective.

Wherever possible the organization should be driven by a single objective. This takes time to agree and may involve senior managers in long, heated and emotional discussion. The alternative, for the management teams unwilling or unable to decide on a single objective, is to agree on the hierarchy of the objectives set or (least effective) to resign themselves to constant arguments when objectives conflict.

The business/corporate strategy

This is the means by which the objective will be achieved. The simple test of good strategy is that it should be both necessary and sufficient to achieve the objective.

The strategic market position

This is the unique (and differentiated) position that the organization aims to hold in the mind of its customers.

Sometimes the marketer will be faced with the job of creating a marketing strategy without the guidance of clear business objective or strategy – yes even in the competitive 1990s! In this situation there is little choice but to develop it for ourselves. In this case the marketer should not be attempting to take on the entire business strategy role, this might not go down too well with other functions, but a 'hypothesis' needs to be developed upon which the marketing strategy can be based. When looking at the question of business/corporate strategy, there are a number of issues that we should consider, we will deal with these in order.

Competitive strategy

Before we launch straight into a discussion about the alternative forms of competitive strategy which might be open to the organization, it's worth stopping for a moment to consider the nature of competition itself. Now, competition does a lot of very good and worthwhile things in the marketplace, it has been known to improve efficiency, it has been known to reduce absolute cost levels as far as the customer is concerned, it has also been known to improve customer choice. However, as far as the organization is concerned, we should all realize that in a free market competition works constantly and continually to erode profits. Since profit is effectively the name of the game, competition is not always a welcome visitor on the commercial and industrial scene (see Figure 27).

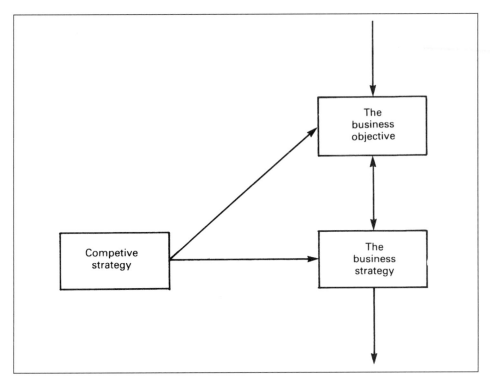

Figure 27   Competitive strategy

In short the situation is as follows – the heavier the competition the higher the cost of fighting that competition and the lower the profits. What then can an organization do about this? If your organization wants to achieve above average profits and even a superior return on investment you need to take action to control or at least manage the level of competition in the marketplace. Management needs to recognize that the competitive force is something that has to be dealt with and contained. The organization must seek and establish what can only be described as a defensible position against competition.

In other words competition should be avoided at all costs. The secret then is to build barriers around the organization in its marketplace and reduce the competition. This action should reduce costs and improve profits. According to Porter there are three generic strategic alternatives open to the organization. There is, in fact, a fourth which although it is not to be recommended does appear to be very popular with large sectors of industry. According to Porter, the organization which decides and then consistently follows one of these three prime strategic strategies successfully, will achieve good profits and above

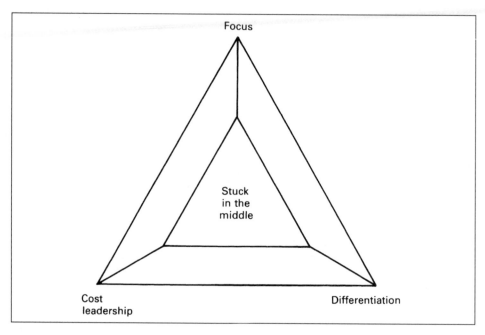

Figure 28 The three generic strategies. *Source:* Porter M.E., *Competitive Strategy* (Free Press, New York, 1983).

average returns on its investment. The three strategies which Porter describes are cost leadership, differentiation and focus. Porter has come under some criticism for the apparent simplicity of this approach, but then there is always somebody willing to complicate life, nevertheless as long as we recognize that these alternatives are broad orientations rather than fixed points to be occupied it is worthwhile here spending a little time looking at these three alternatives (see Figure 28).

Differentiation

The organization which wishes to pursue a strategy of differentiation will be operating throughout the complete market rather than addressing one or two specific segments of the marketplace. The organization will probably be marketing a fairly wide range of products but to be successful in this strategic context the company and its products will have to be differentiated in some way from the competitive offerings. The product must in some way be 'unique' in terms of the customers' perception. In fact, differentiation is all about creating brand identity and loyalty. The power of a well-known and revered brand helps avoid price competition and it often offers scope for relatively higher margins in the marketplace than would otherwise be the case.

To be a practical strategy the difference between the organization's product or services and the competitors' offers must be sustainable and believable over the longer term. Costs for the differentiating organization will probably be slightly higher because of the costs of developing and maintaining a 'unique' position in the marketplace but costs will still have to be close to the industry average. It is a mistake to believe that differentiation can be used to disguise inefficiency.

Another point worth making is that any given marketplace will only be able to support a relatively small number of clearly differentiated positions. This is because customers only have a finite ability to recognize and, more importantly, to believe different product propositions. Apart from the very specific skills which the differentiating organization will need to gain and keep its position there are problems in terms of the buyer perception of the uniqueness. Buyers, both industrial and consumer, are notoriously fickle and perceptions of what is a credibly differentiated position is likely to change over time. The organization must carefully monitor the situation and adjust its market position over time if it is to endure.

Finally, and this is often a factor which is not readily appreciated by managers, the costs of developing and maintaining a differentiated position in the marketplace can be extremely high. Most of the costs will be associated with promotion and marketing support. The potential rewards from a differentiated strategy are quite significant but it is not a route to be recommended for those organizations driven by short-term considerations or even less for the faint hearted.

Cost leadership

To follow a strategy of overall cost leadership means that the organization will do everything in its power to drive its cost base down to the point at which it is able to produce products or services for the marketplace at a lower cost than any of its competitors. Cost leadership is an absolute term. By driving to be *the* lowest cost provider it means that there can only be *one* in any marketplace. In simple terms this means that given the unfortunate situation of a price war the lowest cost provider will be the last one in the marketplace. At the point where everybody else is making losses the cost leader will, by definition, be the last organization making profits.

A point that should be made is that lowest cost does not have to mean lowest price. There is nothing to stop the lowest cost provider actually marketing at a price which is similar or even above its competitors. As every marketing man knows cost does not influence price. The market influences price while cost influences profits. Marketing at an average or relatively high price level just means that the lowest cost provider will be making larger profit margins than anyone else in the marketplace.

The skills and management attitude required to pursue and achieve a strategy of lowest cost are very, very different from those which we have already looked at for the organization which wishes to achieve a differentiated position. To achieve overall cost leadership the organization must dedicate itself to cost reduction activities. If the lowest cost position is to be achieved (and in this strategy there are no prizes for second place) the organization will have to be ready to invest a considerable amount of money. The cost leadership position tends to be quite capital intensive, especially in information and production technology. It will probably also require a high degree of product standardization. As far as the organization is concerned, the prevailing mental attitude among management and the workforce must be one of unrelenting commitment to cost control. This attitude must permeate the entire organization and everything it does.

Strategy as we know is all about the longer term. Over the longer term the overall cost leadership position does have one or two dangers. For example, cost inflation has been known to erode the advantage over time. Organizations which are involved in international business must also make sure that their production and high cost areas are located in parts of the world where they are able to maintain and drive down the average cost per unit. Also there is a problem in the area of technological change. Technology has an unnerving habit of advancing by quantum jumps. Just imagine the despondency in the organization that had managed to drive its total cost base down to the lowest possible level in the market for mechanical wrist watches when all of a sudden quartz technology arrives and renders years of work obsolete at a stroke.

Probably the biggest single danger for the organization pursuing the cost leadership strategy is that the whole focus of the business can tend to orient towards the internal. Improvements in production and technology needed to drive down the cost base may deflect top management and marketing's attention away from the all important customer need. This may be further aggravated by the very significant cost savings to be made from a standardized product range. If, at the end of the day, we manage to achieve the lowest cost position but are producing products or services which the market does not value, and therefore will not buy, we have gained little more than pyrrhic victory.

Marketer's note

If your organization decides to follow this strategic route your position in the organization will be quite difficult. You will have to find a way of managing two potentially conflicting aspects of the business. Without your ability to keep a very close contact with the developing and evolving needs of the marketplace the organization will soon become production and finance led, it will start to lose contact with customer requirements. This will adversely effect market share and this drop in volume may in turn effect the organization's ability to keep its unit cost base low. A classic downward spiral.

However, to keep the organization relevant to marketplace needs you will probably have to be the one who will insist that some money is spent either in promotional support, non-standardized product ranges or even market research.

Your diplomatic skills will serve you well here.

Focus

The organization which pursues a focused strategy concentrates its effort, not across the entire market as in the case of the differentiation strategy, but on one or more specific segments of the marketplace. As with the differentiated strategy the organization will need to develop a credible position in the marketplace in as much as the customers will have to perceive some uniqueness from the focused organization and will have to understand its specialization in a segment(s). We will deal with the specific aspects of market segmentation in Part Two but for the moment let us concentrate on the overall strategic approach of focus as opposed to the other two generic strategies of differentiation and cost leadership.

A focus strategy, if successful, is a very powerful way of building barriers to competition in a small but, preferably, profitable part of the overall marketplace. The management and marketing skills required of the focusing organization are similar to those required of a differentiating organization in that success will come from the organization's ability to tune its efforts into customer needs. The focus organization will need to be even more precise in this matter than the differentiated organization since the focused organization has, by definition, fewer customers in its target market. It will then need to make its offer that much more attractive to that target segment if it is to achieve a profitable level of penetration.

Societal trends in the 1980s and 1990s of increased disposable income, the need for higher levels of individualism and self-determination have been apparent through most of the western world. Much of the recent growth in new businesses has been the direct result of new firms emerging to meet market demand currently unsatisfied by larger organizations with their more standardized, global approaches. The 1990s has seen both an acceleration and a variation in these trends. The UK and some other markets are edging towards what is variously described as 'post-industrial' or 'post-modern' societies and trends are appearing that offer great challenges and opportunities for marketers. Individualism and the associated search for personal identity have accelerated in the first part of the 1990s creating a wealth of potentially profitable niches for focused organizations to occupy. While in many markets a handful of large, differentiated players still dominate the business, their power is showing signs of absolute decline. Growth in many instances is coming from smaller, focused players who are appearing to meet and satisfy specific demands.

Contrary to common belief, focus is not just another word to describe a small market share. Nor is focus achieved by the organization operating in segments which it defines rather than segments which have been defined by and are recognized by the customer. The truly focused organization is not forced to operate on prices which are determined by the competition. The whole reason for being focused is that the organization can defy comparison with competitors and is relatively free to operate at prices set by itself.

If your organization is to successfully pursue a focus strategy, this will call for a complete and total dedication of the organization to the needs and wants of your specific customer target base. Your product/service range will probably be quite narrow but at the same time deeper so as to offer greater choice to a restricted part of the marketplace. Your whole organization's operations will also have to be seen by your target market as being consistent with the specialized stance which you have taken in the marketplace.

Also, we mentioned that a differentiated strategy is not for the faint hearted. This was with direct reference to the amount of investment needed to achieve and maintain the position. For the focused organization we also call for a certain degree of nerve, and this, in my experience, has always been the single largest problem for organizations who wish to pursue the focused route. To achieve the focused position the organization must be *seen* as being a specialist by its target marketplace. This means that it must actively avoid activities and business which fall outside of the target segment. This could mean that the organization may have to turn business away if it's not of the right kind. As you can imagine this is often less than popular, especially with those who are not customer and marketing oriented.

Finally, the risks. The focused organization, while it should be protecting itself from competition by building barriers around itself and its target segment, is also running certain risks by placing all of its eggs into one or two baskets. There is always the risk of a fundamental shift in the marketplace and the mass emigration of customers to new markets. This is known as the empty segment syndrome. Secondly, there is the big question about how we define the segment into which we are going to focus our attention in the first place. Once we identify the segment we focus our activities to developing products and services exclusively to that segment and we grow with the segment. There is always the risk that as the segment grows we could become prey to even more focused organizations who come in and stake a claim to one particular part of our target segment. In other words we get carved up from underneath.

Marketer's note

The single most important secret to success in a focus strategy is that of the organization's market orientation. If you have only a small part of the market to aim for, the job of getting and keeping extremely close to your customers is made that much easier. You will have to become an expert on market segmentation which, although everybody has heard of the term, is an extremely difficult concept to understand and to implement properly.

Having said all this, probably your most important function in the organization will be that of gatekeeper to the marketplace. Without firm control the various elements of an organization will find it easy to develop new products and/or services which seem like 'a good idea' or even 'terribly easy to make in our spare time and with spare capacity'. It must be your job to ensure that every additional product introduced by your organization actively enhances the image and position of the organization as a specialist, focused producer and that new products don't push the organization back into an 'all things for all men' position. Essentially you will have to take and maintain a long-term marketing view and you will have to resist the short-term demands which are often made either by the finance and/or the sales factions of the business.

Stuck in the middle

This is not a generic competitive strategy as such. It is the result of not following through on any one of the three strategies described above. To explain how this position arises let us take the example of the following quite 'fictitious' organization. The organization in question is in fact a composite made up of a number of firms featured in the business pages of any good business magazine and could easily be in any market providing any product or service. The sequence of events is so familiar that probably all of us can imagine a number of companies which act in just this way.

The organization has been reasonably successful for a number of years and so has not recognized any need to develop a clear and distinct long-term strategy. Competition increased during the late 1980s and early 1990s and at a certain point it became clear that unless something was done then the business was going to be in a perilous state. Top management got together and looked at the situation, wondered what it ought to do, started looking at which parts of its business were being hit hardest by competition and saw that the historical core of the business was still sound.

Someone suggests what we ought to do is to concentrate on what we are good at, 'let's drive for a specialist position and let's hype the prices'. This seems like a reasonably good idea and the organization pursues this for six months, nine months, a year without seeing any concrete return on the bottom line. They have, of course, kept fighting the competition in the allied areas as well as deepening penetration of the core market but competition is still making in-roads. 'OK', somebody says, 'what we ought to do is to spend some money on advertising. Broaden the scope, let's get some more people involved in this marketplace and let's get out and push the name, push the products and widen the appeal.'

This is agreed and the organization then embarks on a reasonable size advertising campaign. It puts the pressure on the sales force to extend the distribution channels, extend the coverage of the product range, maybe brings in one or two product variants to move the organization forward. About a year later sales have increased somewhat but profits look largely unchanged. Worry and concern sets in again and somebody says 'well what we ought to do is to start planning some cuts round here to control the costs and improve the profits'. Naturally, one of the first things to go is the advertising campaign and ancillary areas. So the move now in the organization is to develop cost cutting exercises and improve the margins through a cost reduction approach.

Naturally enough it doesn't take very long before the superficial economies are all used up and cost cutting, to be taken any further, will start to eat into the core of the business. Rather than do this people will start looking for alternative ways to beat off competition. Maybe by this time the effort then starts to return to elements of either focus or differentiation and around the circle we go once again.

This 'fictitious' organization is one which is completely dominated by short-term considerations and obviously lacks a long-term strategic view.

The problem is not that it doesn't try various strategic approaches but rather that it perseveres with none of them. Unless the top management of this organization demands and receives control of the future of the enterprise, the organization will continue its circular route trying one strategy after another. Effectively it is stuck in the middle of the process: never managing to break out of what is a vicious circle leading ultimately only to its own demise.

Worse still there appears to be safety in numbers. It isn't likely to be the only organization in the marketplace which is stuck in this vicious circle. These are the organizations which are doggedly trying to maintain the all-things-to-all-men approach to the marketplace. They find it difficult to compete against clearly and credibly positioned competition. They find it difficult to maintain a customer and market orientation because the nature of the customers that they think they are serving changes on too regular a basis. As the profit situation steadily deteriorates over time they inevitably become prey to shorter and shorter time constraints and end up led by either short-term sales cultures or short-term finance requirements. These are just additional hindrances to their ever breaking out of the circle.

The only solution for organizations which find themselves stuck in this position is to attract particularly strong management capable of forcing the organization through the pain barrier. Undertaking a rational analysis of the marketplace and the opportunities and threats which confront the organization must be followed by a decision on the best strategic route for the future. A relentless drive for that position is the only thing that will break the fatal circle.

Marketer's note

Should you or your organization find yourself stuck in the middle the situation is not completely lost. However, for your organization to break out it needs two key resources.

One, it must have very strong management of which you may be part.

Two, it must somehow negotiate a medium-term period free from short-term financial pressures. If the organization is to break out it will inevitably incur a few years of below-par profit returns. In an increasingly competitive environment it is unreasonable to expect the organization to re-orient itself and to set itself off on a new clear strategic direction without some investment.

If, in your opinion, your organization is unable to provide both of these resources it may be time to look for somewhere where you can do more good.

Growth strategies

Here any sensible commentator must become wary because growth is such an emotive area. To illustrate the point I offer you two excellent quotes, both of which I believe completely:

'Growth for its own sake in the ideology of the cancer cell.'

Ed Abbey

'No company ever shrank to greatness.'

Unknown

It seems that a strategy for growth is good – if it is the right sort of growth. But then, what on earth is the right – or the wrong – sort of growth? Peter Doyle (Warwick university) suggests that strategies should be judged on three interrelated criteria:

- the ability to create growth;
- the ability to create customer value;
- the ability to create sustainable performance.

He suggests there are three sorts of growth strategy that can be identified.

1 **Radical growth strategies**
   Radical growth strategies tend to be acquisition-led, marketing department-led or PR-led. This is very much the 'growth for the sake of growth' school where the organization experiences explosive growth but in the process of acquiring companies or markets adds little customer value and creates little sustainable advantage. Doyle cites examples of this approach: Ratners, Coloroll, WPP, Hanson, Blue Arrow and others.
   Such growth strategies are essentially short term. Senior management needs to appreciate that short-term benefits usually carry a long-term cost. Unfortunately, investing in creating customer value entails a short-term cost for a long-term benefit. Sadly, as long as managers are measured on today's results alone we can expect radical growth strategies to remain popular.

2 **Rational growth strategies**
   Rational growth strategies tend to exploit strategic windows in the environment and concentrate on new technology, new segments or new channels in order to grow. While this approach creates growth and some customer value it is not easy to sustain performance over the longer term. Such strategy is necessary but insufficient to continue the growth

trend since it tends to appeal to price-sensitive customers with whom it is often difficult to create relationships, it is easy to copy or be leap-frogged by further innovation. Examples of this approach are Microsoft, Direct Line, BSkyB, Intel and others.

3   Robust growth strategies

Robust growth strategies are much more durable over the longer term. They are focused on creating customer value, but recognizing that as no strategy is sustainable over the longer term unmodified, through creating an organization that learns and constantly reappraises its direction. This approach starts to recognize that often the organization is more important than the strategy; building a strategic organization with the systems and people necessary to keep strategy up to date is more important than just building a good strategy and standing back.

Robust strategies are built by organizations that focus on customer retention rather than budgets, on effectiveness rather than efficiency, on commitment rather than control and on processes rather than functions. Examples of this approach are: Marks & Spencer, British Airways, Unilever, 3M, Coca-Cola, Toyota and others.

Doyle also explains why robust growth strategies are rare. He places the blame on management attitudes, including: the belief in the 'quick fix' (often driven by short-term bonuses!), never done it in the past so don't know where to start and, of course, the belief that 'we are different' and we can defy the rules that have been the ruin of others.

Customer value is, of course, the key to a practical and successful strategy and we will return to this topic in more detail later.

Sustainable competitive advantage

The concept of sustainable competitive advantage is not a new idea. It can be found in the early origins of economics, basic marketing and in everyday common sense. Simply stated, if an organization is able to do something better than its competitors it will make better profits. If an organization is only as good as everybody else it will only make standard profits. If an organization is worse than its competitors at what it does it will make inferior profits – nothing too difficult there! (See Figure 29.)

Since the avowed aim of competitive strategy is to find ways of avoiding competition and making superior profits then, logically, the search must be for ways of achieving some form of advantage over our competitors which will enable us to make better than average profits. Also since business and commercial activities need to be directed at the longer term,

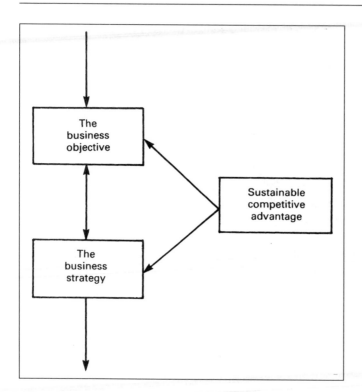

Figure 29
Sustainable
competitive
advantage

the advantage itself must be sustainable over the long term to generate reasonable and consistent profit flows.

Competitive advantage

We have already touched on a number of elements which refer to the concept of competitive advantage, for example, when we were looking at the initial data gathering stage we considered the internal resource/performance audit and were looking for particular strengths that the organization may have in its business domain. We then continued the analysis to look at opportunities in the environment for our organization. We were also looking for structural opportunities in the industry and competitive opportunities within the marketplace. It is in these areas that likely competitive advantage is to be found.

Identifying and selecting the most appropriate competitive advantage is not as easy a process as it would appear to be at first glance. In the marketing texts of the 1960s and 1970s we would read a lot about the same thing but then it was called a USP (unique selling proposition); although at the time the concept was applied mainly to product features rather than organizations. Every organization will probably find a reasonable list of characteristics which it believes it might be able to turn into competitive advantage; but it may also find that its competitors have the same list and uniqueness is difficult to find.

Unfortunately, wanting and succeeding are not the same thing. Firstly, to achieve a true competitive advantage the organization is most likely going to have to make some significant investment in the area – certainly if the advantage is to be made sustainable. This will be discussed later. Investment then requires resources and resources are always in limited supply. This will, de facto, limit the number of competitive advantages which the organization can actually develop.

Second, a competitive advantage has to be an advantage over the competition. Looking more closely at the industry and competitor analysis we carried out, it is important that the organization chooses areas of advantage that have true value in its particular industry and competitive situation. For example, there seems to be little point in working to secure an advantage in the area of domestic sourcing of say, television receiver components when the competition can just as easily source raw materials from overseas suppliers at no significant additional inconvenience. Equally it is difficult to justify capital strength within an industry which is not capital intensive.

The third and possibly most important aspect to competitive advantage, as has already appeared in the strengths and weaknesses analysis, is that it is important that market-based competitive advantage is perceived as an advantage by the customers concerned. It must be seen as adding customer value. For example, the personal computer manufacturer who works hard to develop a competitive advantage in the area of ergonomics and design of its products, will only have achieved a competitive advantage if the target customers perceive that ergonomics and product design are an important element of the product mix. If product design is way down the priority list behind basic elements like speed of processing and compatibility with other systems then the product design advantage is an illusion.

Sustainability

All the way through this book I have emphasized the importance of looking to the longer rather than the shorter term. The area of competitive advantage is no exception. Short-term windfall profits from a lucky guess can be no substitute to long-term, above average profit returns from carefully calculated and properly exploited competitive advantage in the marketplace. An important consideration therefore, when considering the possible areas in which the organization might develop a competitive advantage, is which of the alternative candidates for competitive advantage would be more easily maintained over the longer term. The various attractiveness of the alternative advantages must be a consideration of the ease with which competitors can overcome the advantage. This, if thought through properly, is likely to reduce the potential list quite alarmingly.

Many textbooks attempt to reproduce lists of areas of sustainable advantage that the organization might wish to consider. Over the years, the lengths of the lists have all shortened. With the widespread application of knowledge and technology, there are few areas inside the organization that can now offer any long-term advantage. Having said this, a short-term advantage may still be worth having – but it will have to be replaced eventually. When we look at today's competitive markets it becomes obvious that long-term sustainability is rare. There are only really three areas where this sustainability can be found:

1 **Industry advantage**
   Currently most of the top performing companies in the world (return on assets) happen to be pharmaceuticals. The obvious advantage offered by the nature of the industry and patent protection is obvious. There are similar examples.

2 **Strategic assets**
   The ownership of *brands* can create a powerful and profitable sustainable advantage. Pepsi can reproduce the taste, even improve on it – but it can never be Coke. Another example of strategic asset would include BA's control over the most important landing and takeoff slots at Heathrow airport.

3 **Core competencies**
   The particular knowledge and skills owned by an organization can be a powerful advantage. As long as they are not easily copyable and can be kept secret or safe they are sustainable too.

When we view the competitive advantage concept over the long term, it is quite clear that a number of what might be considered to be competitive advantages are very dubious. For example, financial strength. With the efficiency of modern capital markets it is now relatively easy for organizations of all shapes and sizes to raise extra capital should it be required. The increased mobility of labour makes it difficult to build competitive advantage in personnel and managerial strength. Increasingly rapid change in technology can render even patented technical processes obsolete long before the expiry of patent protection. Distribution advantage is also more prone to attack from competition than in the past. Mostly due to more innovative approaches by competitors and the increased preparedness of customers to accept different distribution methodology. New product development is another area where competitive advantage may not be sustainable over the long term. We can all think of examples of organizations that were extremely innovative with products but soon lost control of the markets which they in fact created. Names such as Sinclair Computer, Laker Airlines, Hoover Vacuum Cleaners, Timex Watches, Philips Compact Discs and Apple Personal Computers number among a much longer list of organizations which found it difficult to maintain their product-based competitive advantage over the longer term.

Marketer's note

This area of sustainable competitive advantage is critical for the overall success of the organization through the medium to long term. It's important because it gives the organization the opportunity of imposing its will on the competitive marketplace, of choosing how it is going to compete and on what grounds. If your organization can get its sustainable competitive advantage right then you will be working in what Hugh Davidson calls 'an offensive marketing organization', in other words you will be taking control of your own destiny. You won't be forced just to react to competition. You won't always be on the defensive reacting to what other organizations are doing. Your own role in the process has two principal elements.

First is to make sure that the competitive advantage which the organization chooses is relevant and actionable given the particular competitive and market circumstances of your organization. If it happens to be what the senior management wants as well then this is an additional bonus.

Second, in your role as the manager responsible for maintaining the interface between the organization and the outside world it is up to you to ensure that sufficient analysis is carried out to be able to identify the most profitable competitive advantage open to the organization. We have spent some time considering the types of data gathering which might possibly be carried out by your organization. The problem of the selection of a sustainable competitive advantage for the organization, I am sure, clearly demonstrates the importance of designing and maintaining a quality management information system.

The business objective

Assuming you have been following the general flow of the book this far and that you haven't jumped straight to this section in the hope of finding

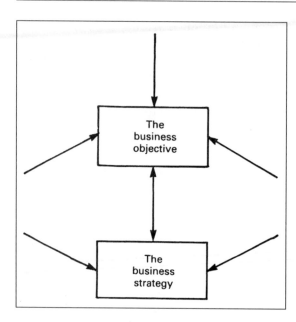

Figure 30   The business objective

some instant miracle cure to the ills that have been dogging your organization for the past twenty-five years, then you might just have enough understanding about your organization to start working on the business objective for the future (see Figure 30).

Just to recap then. What we have found out so far are answers to the following questions:

- Who are our stakeholders and what do they expect in the way of returns from the organization? What are the potential conflicts?
- What therefore is the longer term financial objective which the organization is dedicated to achieve?
- Who are the key implementors in the organization and what are their own personal values?
- What is the vision of the key implementors and how would we best describe their strategic intent?
- Out of these various factors we should have a clear statement as to the corporate mission.
- What are the particular strengths and specific weaknesses of our organization?
- What opportunities and threats exist in the broad macro environment?
- How is our particular industry put together and what is the relative importance of the five competitive forces which make up the industry?
- Where is our competition, who are our competitors, what are our competitors able to do and where are the opportunities for our organization in the competitive environment?

- What business are we currently in at the moment (in all honesty) and what business have we decided that we want or need to be in?
- Drawing on these various elements and combining the improved understanding of the situation has then led us to look at competitive and growth strategies. Of the options available what do we believe offers the best hope for the future (that senior management will accept).
- What do we believe is the sustainable competitive advantage that our organization should be looking at developing and that will help us deal with increased competition over the longer term?

In short we should now have a fairly clear idea of:

- where we are;
- why we are here;
- what we are capable of doing;
- what we face in the outside world; and
- what we are going to do about it.

The next job for the organization is to agree the business/corporate objective. Again, this is not a job for the marketer but for the managing director/general manager in consultation with the strategic team. Nevertheless, marketing needs a clear objective in order to be able to set its own (marketing) objective and, if a clear overall objective for the organization is not specifically stated, a hypothesis will have to be made. Although the development and agreement of an overall business objective for the organization is never an easy exercise it is nevertheless essential.

The business objective is defined as **the goal or the aim to which all activities of the organization are directed**. Naturally, if the organization does not have a single clear, concise business objective then it is more than likely that activities will be directed in a number of different and possibly conflicting directions with the net result that the organization is seriously wasting resource in both terms of money, time and management effort. Assuming the organization's management team has followed the process so far outlined in this book, they will be more or less agreed on the common direction for the organization and they will have in their minds an outline idea of where they feel the organization ought to be in three, five or ten years time (the precise timescale depends on the nature of the organization, its market and the speed of change of its industry base). Following on from this, the business objective ought really be little more than a formalizing of the common agreement which should now have already been reached.

We can use the business objective as a way of defining, in more quantifiable terms, our view of what our organization is going to become. There is no doubt that an organization requires a sense of shared commitment and common vision for the future. The question remains, how will we know when we have got there? This is precisely what the business objective aims to provide. So, now for some basics.

Multiple objectives are easier to agree and everybody can include their 'pet objective' into the grand scheme of strategy. But beware, time saved by not seeking a single, overriding objective will soon be lost in the horse-trading and politicing that takes place as soon as more than one objective fights for the same limited resource.

The business objective should be no longer than one sentence, twelve to fifteen words is ideal (if it's more than this it gets confusing and complicated, and people have more problems understanding exactly what the organization is trying to do). Just to start you off on the objective the first word is 'To . . .'.

The business objective should be achievable. There is no point in simply codifying wishful thinking. An objective, to be effective, has to be seen by everybody as being achievable and being realistic. Over-ambitious objectives simply do not motivate and are seen as unreal hoaxes emanating from senior management who are obviously out of touch with reality.

The objective should be quantifiable in some form. There obviously has to be some time limit on the achievement of the objective and there must also be some form of quantifiable success criteria. This is normally in financial terms but need not be limited to such measures. It is a sad comment on human business life, but what gets measured gets done. If the organization measures short-term profitability that is what it gets – for a time anyway. It is worth repeating that the financial measures of success are *not*, themselves, the objective of the organization. Thinking back to the ideas about competitive and growth strategies, if the secret to longer term success is creating customer relationships and customer value why not use these as the measures of success? What gets measured gets done!

The business objective must be consistent with both the internal capabilities of the organization and with the desires of the key implementors and their personal vision of the future. The objective must also be consistent with the external environment and the opportunities and constraints which we have identified for the organization.

Finally, and very importantly, the business objective must be both understandable and capable of communication throughout the organization. While we are not saying that the business objective must be turned into some form of snappy advertising slogan, it needs to be concise, it needs to be simple, because it needs to be translated down through the entire organization. In terms of communicating the message, lower levels of management will have to understand the objective if they are to be able to convert the objective into sub-objectives in functional areas, such as marketing, operations, finance and so on. They will need to understand the implications of the objective since they are the ones who will have to implement action to achieve the objective. The final test here should be – does everybody in the organization understand what the organization stands for and what the organization is out to achieve?

Only if people truly understand the business objective can they start to relate what they do on a day-by-day basis to the needs of the market-place which the organization serves. Two of the best examples of business objective which I have come across in recent years are that which was used at the end of the 1980s and early 1990s by Barclays Bank plc in the UK where the business objective was defined as 'Number 1 by 91'. This was understood throughout the entire organization and people were able to relate to what their organization was trying to do. A second example comes from the USA and goes back a few years beyond this. That was the objective of NASA. In the early days its objective was very simple – 'to get to the moon'. To reinforce this sense of understanding, a photograph of the moon was distributed to every person in the organization and placed above their desk. When, at any level, someone was asked what their organization was about it was a simple job of pointing to the picture and saying 'to get there'. Unfortunately for both organizations, the problem became a little bit more complicated once they achieved their primary objective and a second, next stage objective was not developed in the same simple unambiguous manner as the first.

Marketer's note

The setting of the business objective is yet another wonderful opportunity for your organization to shoot itself in the foot. It will invariably do so unless you keep a very tight control over the proceedings at this point. We already have a very clear and concise long-term financial target which the organization has to achieve. This should be regarded as safe, sacrosanct and it will be achieved.

The business objective is all about how the organization is going to operate in the market place in order to achieve the financial objective which it has set itself. So, in the case of Barclays they believed that being number one in the UK market was the business objective which they needed to attain in order to achieve their separate financial objectives – which might have been set in terms of return on capital employed, profit figures and so on.

It is imperative that as the marketing person you ensure that the business objective is couched in understandable market-related terms. The whole exercise must not be allowed to degenerate into a series of spreadsheet-generated financial targets and thresholds which will have absolutely no meaning for anybody else in the organization.

Business strategy

Once the business objective has been set and agreed by all the managers who need to have a sense of ownership of the process, we are ready to move on to the question of business strategy (see Figure 31). Once again we will be looking for a short concise statement which crystallizes all of the fairly detailed thinking carried out up to this point and which again is easily understandable and capable of communication throughout the organization.

Our business objective will tell us concisely what we have to do, where we have to be and by when. This must be the 'aim' or 'goal' of the whole organization. If the business objective is the aim, the strategy is all about the means or the how. What we are looking for in the business strategy, and you will note that the term is singular not plural, is **the one route which is both necessary and sufficient to achieve the business objective** that the organization has set for itself. Another fairly basic guide for you at this point: the business strategy should always start with the word 'By . . . . .'.

For any given objective there is normally a series of alternative strategies which may be seen as being viable ways of achieving the objective.

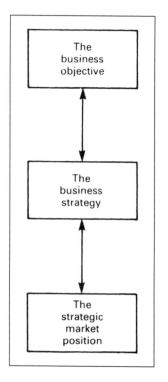

Figure 31   Business strategy

To take a perhaps over-simplistic example let us assume that your objective is to get from your home in London to your corporate headquarters in Brussels. There are obviously a number of alternative strategies for achieving this objective. You could drive from London to Dover, you could then pick up the ferry from Dover to Calais and drive through France to Belgium and Brussels. You could take the Dover to Zeebrugge or Ostend ferries and drive down from there. Alternatively, you might decide to get on a train at London, travel through the Channel Tunnel rail link direct to Brussels. You might decide to fly so you travel from London through to Heathrow; Heathrow to Zaventem and from Zaventem to Brussels which may involve the use of trains or taxis. You might even be one of those élite who has access to a company jet or helicopter. Whichever route you choose your preferred strategy will probably be based on other aspects such as the time available, the relative desire to see other stops en route, the convenience and timing of the schedules and so on.

Bringing the entire question back into the realm of business strategy, the discussion and decision is an essential part of the process since it clarifies top management's views on the environment and the ways in which it wishes its organization to operate. What is clear is that the organization can, and ideally should, only choose one single strategy to achieve its objective. Moving back to our travelling from London to Brussels as an example, if there was to be a meeting and five different people had to get to Brussels, if they all took five different routes it would be most unlikely that anybody would arrive at the same time and therefore the meeting could not take place.

Deliberate or emergent strategy?

Hearking back to the brief commentary on 'the great strategy debate' in an earlier section of this book (you see what happens if you don't read it in sequence!), we saw that the central argument about business/corporate strategy in the 1990s really revolved around the degree to which the market and business environment was capable of prediction. Proponents of deliberate strategy as explained by Porter and others argue for creating detailed plans for the strategic planning period and putting the weight of the organization behind the implementation. The argument is that the market conditions are relatively stable and the organization can exert its influence. The London to Brussels trip is a clear example of this thinking.

Proponents of the emergent schools as explained by Mintzberg and others argue for creating a vision/objective but claim that market conditions are too fluid to make detailed planning worth while. In terms of the

London to Brussels trip, the objective is clear (to arrive in an agreed place at an agreed time for a meeting) but strategy should be left open to allow for changes in market conditions. To push the example probably beyond its reasonable limits, the emergent traveller would set off for Waterloo in good time to allow for last minute changes in travel plans should the rail link be out of action. Finding the tunnel closed the traveller still has the option of a train to Dover or Heathrow or Gatwick to continue the journey by alternative means. Arriving at Heathrow options are still open and the traveller can test flights to Zaventem, flights to Antwerp with connecting trains to Brussels or linking with alternative carriers from Gatwick.

Setting an emergent strategy involves agreeing a general direction that we believe will achieve the objective but then launching testing initiatives and allowing the market environment to show us which way is best.

As we will see later, which strategic route is best much depends on the organization and its marketplace. Although it would appear that most organizations would benefit from encouraging more emergent thinking into their strategic approach.

While there are a number of ways of skinning the proverbial cat, there will be more than one way of achieving the business objective. It may not be possible to reduce the list down beyond two or three similar strategies in the short term. Ideally a single common strategy is preferable since it helps bind the entire organization and helps commit resources to one single chosen route, thereby ensuring that the organization makes best use of its inevitably limited resource. Apart from those markets which are controlled by monopoly or legislation it is extremely difficult to find examples of successful strategies which do not erode over time. Some last for years, some for scant weeks. In any event, it is important that the organization builds flexibility into its approach.

Marketer's note

In the same way as the discussion on business objective, the business strategy argument needs to be firmly grounded in the realities of the marketplace and the capabilities of the organization. When considering business strategy the decision needs to be based firmly on an as unbiased view as possible of your organization's strengths, weaknesses and other capabilities as well as on the present and likely future make-up and structure of the industry and marketplace which the organization serves. You will undoubtedly encounter a number of other arguments such as 'well yes, we tried that five years ago but it didn't work', or even 'I tried that when I worked in such and such an industry and the results were quite different'. Strategy is essentially about the future not the past while management experience is about the past not the future.

It will be your role at this point to make sure that the decision on business strategy is a logical, rational extension firmly based on the decisions made in the process up to this point. It must also be firmly grounded and likely to be practicable within our best estimates of tomorrow's market and industry structure.

Remember that business strategy is all about how and action. It is about what we perceive as being our best chance in the marketplace. Very importantly the marketing objective and the marketing strategy will have to be one hundred per cent consistent with the business strategy and they will inevitably fall out of whatever decisions are made at this time. Since marketing is the primary interface between the organization and the outside world then inevitably you will bear the brunt of making sure that the business strategy is pursued relentlessly. In other words you will have to live with the results of whatever is decided here.

We shall be looking at what constitutes 'emergent marketing strategy' later. At this point though you should be aware that while market conditions are demanding ever faster and greater change from organizations, senior (strategy formulating) managers are not always the first to recognize the need for change. If plans are not to go hopelessly awry it will be marketing's task to build the emergent flexibility into deliberately formulated plans.

The strategic market position

The strategic market position statement is the vital link between the whole area of business strategy development and marketing strategy development proper (see Figure 32). You could almost regard it as the baton change in the middle of a relay race. Unfortunately, since so many books are written either in the area of business strategy or in the area of marketing strategy the links between these two areas simply fail to materialize.

So what then is the strategic market position statement? It is, as its name implies, strategic (it relates to the long term) market (it should relate to the external environment) and position (it should relate to the organization's position relative to its competition in the marketplace). While strategic market position should not be viewed as a simple advertizing slogan, it should attempt to sum up all of the business objective, business strategy, competitive strategy and sustainable competitive advantage arguments into a form which is both easily understood and easily recognizable by the people in the organization who will have to

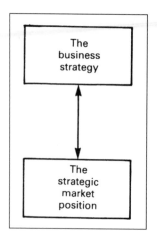

Figure 32   The strategic market position

carry them out. In this regard, the strategic market position statement is very similar to the mission statement only at a lower level in the organization. In the same way as the mission statement, the strategic market position statement should be quite broad and qualitative to allow more precise objectives to follow in its wake.

Strategic positioning

From Porter's work on strategy we have already seen that both focus and differentiation strategies depend on a practical and strategic market position in order to be successful. Both Porter and Levitt assert that in today's highly competitive marketplaces an organization (and its products and services) need to be seen by the marketplace and its customers as offering something different and unique from the competition. This way lies profit. In deciding the strategic market position, the organization will be stating to customers (and staff) what the company stands for and how its products/services differ from current and potentially competing offers.

In fact Porter has gone further. In an important article (*Harvard Business Review*, November/December 1996) he has stated that, while simple 'operational effectiveness' is necessary, it is not sufficient to achieve success in the marketplace. Porter maintains that competitive strategy is about being different – it means deliberately choosing a different set of activities to deliver a unique mix of value. Strategic positioning means either:

- Performing *different activities* from rivals, or
- Performing similar activities in *different ways*.

Porter further argues that the past decade has seen managers caught in a drive for operational effectiveness and growth, imitating each other in a type of herd behaviour, each assuming rivals knew something they did not. He says that the prescription is to concentrate on deepening the strategic position rather than broadening and compromising it. Deepening a position involves making the company's activities more distinctive, strengthening and communicating the strategy better to those customers who should value it.

Positioning is therefore the process of designing an image and value so that customers within the target segment(s) understand what the company and its brands stands for in relation to its competition. It should be readily apparent from this that strategic positioning is a fundamental element of marketing strategy, since any decision on positioning has direct and immediate implications for the whole of the marketing mix. In essence, the marketing mix can almost be seen as the tactical details of an organization's positioning statement.

This being the case, it is important to decide, in detail, the basis of the differentiation that the organization will hold in its competitive arena. The organization needs to identify and build a collection of competitive advantages that will appeal strongly to the target market.

A final word. For those organizations (consumer or industrial) who abdicate or decide not to aspire to a unique strategic position, the alternative is quite clear. Given no reason why they should prefer the organization's products and services over another, customers will compare on the limited information at their disposal – price. The alternative to positioning is commodity marketing and in this business only the lowest cost provider is safe (Figure 33).

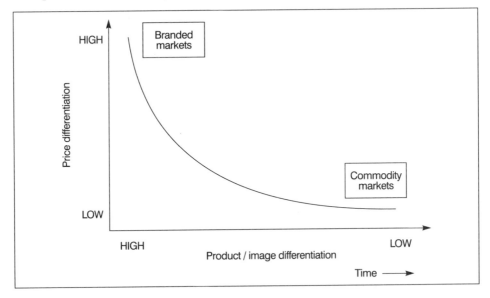

Figure 33   The commodity slide

The positioning process

The process of strategically positioning an organization can be described as follows:

1 Identify the total marketplace and the manner in which the market segments itself.
2 Assess the organization's resources and capabilities and identify the possible alternative competitive advantages which the organization may decide to capitalize in its own marketplaces.
3 Comparing 1 and 2, identify possible matches of competitive advantage to target market needs.
4 Select a particular emphasis (strategic market position) for the organization to pursue over the longer term. The selection must be made from those positions seen as credible by the organization's customers.
5 Implement the strategic position in market terms. This process will require a careful analysis of which market segments to target, which products and services need to be developed and marketed to support the position and the branding policy needed to support the position.
6 Communicate the identified position to the target marketplace in such a way that the customers understand how the organization and its product/service offering is different from the competition and the nature of the additional customer value that will be achieved by purchasing from the organization.

Positioning problems

If the organization or the strategy formulating team fails in any of the steps involved in strategic positioning, this is likely to lead to one of three common problems.

1 **Confused positioning**
   This happens when buyers are unsure of what the organization stands for and do not clearly see how it is different from competitive companies. Customers see no real difference between the products/services presented by the organization and those offered by competitors. It often comes as a shock to some managers that creating a brand name and spending some money on advertising is sometimes not enough – customers have to believe that the name means there will be a real and valuable difference.
2 **Over positioning**
   This occurs when customers perceive the organization's products and services as being simply 'expensive'. The implication here is that the

organization has either misidentified or badly communicated the additional benefits inherent in the offering. Care must be taken to measure response only among the target segment(s), members of non-selected segments should feel that the offering is expensive, the additional benefits were not aimed at them.

3 **Under positioning**

A common problem, this occurs when the message is simply too vague and customers have no real idea of what the organization stands for − no uniqueness is communicated − and how the organization differs from the competition. This can easily happen when managers are unsure of the position they have developed and, consequently, are not confident about making clear claims that might deter past customers who do not fall clearly into tomorrow's target audience.

Positioning traps

When talking about positioning it is important to remember the traps that exist for the unwary:

- Two companies cannot hold the same position − at least not sucessfully. DIfferentiated doesn't just mean different from almost everybody else − it means unique in some way that makes sense to the customer.
- You may have to give up something to get something − having a position in a market means being recognized for doing certain things − and not doing others. If the idea of Morgan cars producing an 'MPV' seems unreasonable to you, you have spotted a unique position.
- Marketing is not a battle of products it's a battle of perceptions − it's not what the independent tests say are the best − it's what customers believe is best for them. Reality always falls a bad second to perceptions.
- Positioning from the company's viewpoint not the prospects − too many companies are obsessed with how their technology or industry describes itself and not from how the customer sees the state of play. Successful positions are relevant to customers − nobody else.

Finally a word on the importance of positioning to the organization's second most important asset − its employees. (For those who had not already guessed, the number one asset is the customers!) A clear and concise position allows the organization to create a sense of purpose and direction among its staff and thereby create the behaviours that its customers will understand and will serve to differentiate it, *in deed*, from the competition. A precise strategic position will enable the organization to create a degree of harmony, understanding and common purpose, certainly among customer-facing staff, that will be essential in delivering on the promise made by the communications.

A position is achieved when the customer feels the difference and believes, for him or herself, that the organization is unique in some important and valuable way. The promise can be made by the communications, the delivery normally depends on the people.

Marketer's note

This is the point at which operational responsibility passes from the business strategy unit to the marketing function in the organization. In the same way as the mission statement was used like a backdrop against which business strategy was developed, so the strategic market position will create a backdrop against which the marketing strategy must be developed for the organization.

It is worth spending some time at this stage making sure that the business strategy development team participates fully in the development of the strategic marketing position statement since this effectively becomes your brief within which more precise marketing objectives and marketing strategies will have to be developed. Consequently you should be concerned with developing a strategic market position which, as far as the business strategy team is concerned, completely sums up their vision, aspirations and thinking in marketplace terms. At the same time it should be broad and qualitative enough for you to be able to develop into precise marketing objectives with a degree of freedom.

Assuming that you are going for the 'positioning' route (if you don't you should start sharpening your cost-cutting knives now) you must be constantly wary of the managers who are really closet-salespeople masquerading as modern marketers. Porter also said that: 'A sustainable strategic position requires trade-offs. Trade-off means that more of one thing necessitates less of another. Trade-offs create the need for choice and protect against competition.' What this means is that we aim to sell more of what we aim to become specialized in – but we must stop selling things that do not fit the targeted position. You can imagine how well this idea goes down with managers targeted or bonused on short-term revenue! But accepted it must be. The alternative will be to spend money on promoting a unique position that is not supported by the company's actions with the result that customers just feel they are being treated like idiots.

Finally, you need to be confident to assert your role as marketer when it comes up to positioning. Positioning, as you know, is about what you do to a product – it's about what you do to the mind of the prospect. The mind of the prospect is, or ought to be, what marketing is all about.

Conclusions – Part One

Now as the baton is about to change and the responsibility for the success of the organization is about to pass to the marketing function, it is probably worth looking back at what we have achieved so far, where the thinking has taken us up to this point. So far we have tried to answer questions such as: What is the organization trying to do? What are the organization's circumstances? What can the organization do? What must it do? And as we approach the end of the exercise, what will the organization do?

Although we have been following the flow chart of the strategic process described in the introduction, we have already said (but it bears repeating) that there is no one way of coming to the all important strategic decisions that the organization will have to develop. The strategic process is, by its very nature, an iterative process – this is why you will note many of the arrows in the flow chart go in more than one direction.

So far we have taken the organization through its broad macro decision-making process, we have looked at the distinctive competencies, what it's good at and what it's bad at, its competitive position, its competitive advantage and so forth. Because we are about to move on to the more micro aspects of strategy, in other words developing the marketing strategy for the organization, this does not mean that the subjects and topics which we have looked at so far can now be safely put away into a box somewhere. We have, in fact, just dealt with a first pass through the specific decision areas. It is more than likely, as we delve deeper into the situation, that a number of the specific areas will have to be re-visited and analyzed in greater detail as our information needs become more precise the closer we get to our target marketplace.

It could almost be argued that up to this point the investigation process has been as, if not more, important than the decision-making outputs. Certainly it is important that the organization realizes that nothing so far decided can be considered as 'set into stone'. At the very best we have become sensitized to the alternatives open to us – the various paths which · it could take in its market operations and which paths are most likely to bear fruits in the short, medium, and long term. Now as we develop the process and get closer and closer to our customers and the market place, we will be able to start getting real feed-back on our plans, our vision and our aspirations for the future. As we develop both the thinking, the understanding and analysis, and generally get closer to the people who pay us our money, we may have to re-visit some of the decisions made in the process as circumstances and external conditions change.

While in no way wishing to denigrate the decision-making process up to this point it is extremely important that the organization understands just how far there is still to go as well as what it has already achieved. Above all the business strategy decisions must contain a degree of flexibility within them if they are not to crack under pressure. The marketplace which the organization serves is by its nature a very dynamic situation and flexibility and adaptability will mark the winning organizations of the next decade. A marketing strategy developed in the absence of a clear guiding business objective and business strategy is likely to be all action and no purpose. A business strategy with no marketing is likely to be all thinking and no action. It will always be achieving a balance between the two that creates marketplace success and a stable and growing organization.

Further reading to Part One

Abell D., *Managing with Dual Strategies*, New York (Free Press, 1993).
Bevan in *The Loyalty Effect* by F. Reichheld and T.A. Teal (*Harvard Business School Press*, 1996).
Davidson H., *Even More Offensive Marketing*, Harmondsworth (Penguin, 1997).
Levitt T., Marketing myopia, *Harvard Business Review* (July–August, 1960).
Levitt T., *The Marketing Imagination*, 2nd edition, New York (Free Press, 1986).
Mintzberg H., *The Rise and Fall of Strategic Planning*, Hemel Hempstead (Prentice Hall, 1994).
Porter M., *Competitive Strategy*, New York (Free Press, 1983).
Porter M., *Competitive Advantage*, New York (Free Press, 1990).
Reis A. and Trout J., *Positioning: the battle for your mind*, New York (Warner Books, 1982).
Whittington R., *What is Strategy and does it Matter?*, London (Routledge, 1993).

Part Two

Where do we want to be?

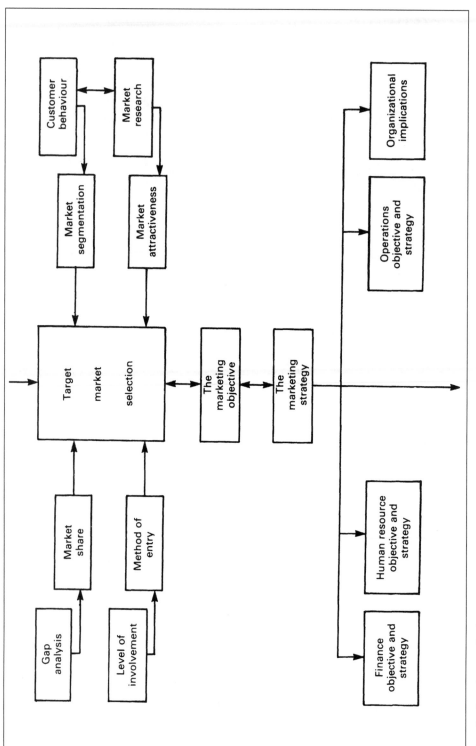

Developing the marketing strategy

Chapter 5

From business to marketing strategy

'In war, the general receives his commands from the sovereign.

'Having collected an army and concentrated his forces, he must blend and harmonise the different elements thereof before pitching his camp.

'After that, comes tactical manoeuvring, than which there is nothing more difficult. The difficulty of tactical manoeuvring consists of turning the devious into the direct, and misfortune into gain.'

Sun Tzu, 500 BC

So we arrive at the question of marketing strategy proper. When I circulated the first draft of this book for comments a number of people asked why they had to get so far into a book on marketing strategy before coming to the topic itself. The answer was (and is) that we started looking at marketing strategy on page one and have never left it.

One of the problems with marketing is that people tend to confuse what it ought to be with what it often is in many organizations. Too many trained marketers and marketing managers seem to content themselves with the mundane marketing issues such as advertising, promotion, direct mail, writing the brochures and producing the sales presenters. This is all valuable activity, don't get me wrong, but while it certainly is marketing it definitely is not strategy. Marketers need to be involved in the broader strategic issues facing their organizations, if only to make it possible for them to develop a proper marketing strategy when the baton passes. In the absence of marketing involvement in business strategy development

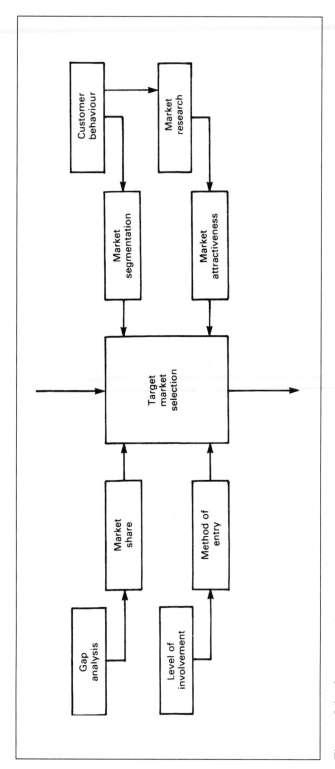

Figure 34 Start with the market

the marketer will be left with the problem of trying to make the best of objectives and a strategy to meet financial or sales driven goals.

Marketing is first of all an attitude of mind, a philosophy, a way of approaching business. Marketing is also, but secondarily, a set of specific techniques. Part One emphasized the first aspect of marketing, Part Two will tend to emphasize the second.

Always start with the market

'We are not fit to lead an army on the march unless we are familiar with the face of the country – its mountains and forests, its pitfalls and precipices, its marshes and swamps.

'We shall be unable to turn natural advantages to account unless we make use of local guides.'

Sun Tzu, 500 BC

Successful marketing, as we all know, starts with the marketplace. In the same way then, detailed marketing strategy must necessarily start with the detailed analysis of the marketplace which we are targeting. In the marketing organization, all activity will stem from the marketplace, from an understanding of its needs and its wants, and success ultimately comes from our ability to satisfy those needs by bringing the necessary resources to bear (see Figure 34).

I know that the temptation is sometimes irresistible, but we must put aside thoughts of existing organizational strengths and particular product or service advantages until a little later on. First comes the customer.

Target market selection

Before we start, however, there are some definitions which probably need to be clarified. Like many other words in normal, everyday use, the term 'market' can be and is used in such a variety of situations as to make marketing activity quite difficult. Historically the word market referred to the physical location where buyers and sellers came together to transact. In a marketing sense, the word market means more than just the physical location. Those of you who have come to marketing from economics will recognize the word market as the situation which encompasses both buyers and sellers. In marketing terms however, the word market refers exclusively to customers (see Figure 35).

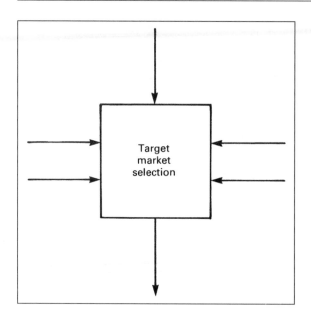

Figure 35   Target market selection

We can take the marketing definition of the term 'market' and see it as a collective noun for customers. Even then we find further complications. You may often hear people talking about certain types of demographic markets such as the 'youth market', the 'grey market', the 'ABC1 market' and so forth. You may even hear terms such as the 'car market' or the 'personal computer market' referred to. These are often called product markets. You will most certainly hear terms such as the 'UK market', the 'US market', the 'German market', the 'North/Scottish market' (even the 'Common market' – whatever that means!). If you have also come across the words market segment in your travels, you can be forgiven for getting slightly confused at this point as to what is a market and what is a market segment. In marketing, as in many of the younger disciplines, terms and terminology are still quite loose. While this allows a lot more flexibility to authors such as myself, it does little to really help the marketing practitioner to put his ideas into action.

Now, I have no objection to everybody choosing their own pet definitions and describing these common terms in the way in which they feel to be most helpful. If you are happy that you understand the difference between a market and a market segment as far as your business is concerned, then you are probably well advised to keep to the definitions which you have evolved.

However, for the rest of this section of marketing strategy, and to avoid any on-going confusion in the area, I will take a fairly broad definition of the word market. I will take my lead from the previous discussion on business strategy. Specifically, the decisions made in the area of what business does our organization want or need to be in will give me the primary guidance as to the general target market in which I am going to be a player. Assuming that there has been the right level of marketing input into the business strategy decision-making process, then the definition of what business the organization is in will have a strong marketing slant. Ideally it will be described in terms of customer needs rather than in technology or customer group terms. Furthermore, it will be quite clear from an understanding of the business strategy process whether the organization is fundamentally a domestic, international or global player, and the question of geographical markets will not be at issue.

A sound, market-based business definition will lead on quite naturally to a description of the organization's target market. Business definitions such as 'fluid transfer', 'home improvements' and 'long term personal financial planning', will give us a clear indication of the types of customers who fall within our scope and those falling outside.

Then we come to the whole question of market segmentation. Using the term 'market' in the broad sense proposed above, each of the organization's primary markets (it may have more than one) will be capable of being subdivided into a number of market segments (and possibly subsegments). The organization, of course, need not be active in all segments of that marketplace. This, as we shall see, does not necessarily present a problem in itself. To the contrary, it shows the organization where it could possibly extend its activities in the future or if it does not wish to extend its activities, shows the organization how it can differentiate itself from its competitors by being other than a full market player.

Given these working definitions of the term market and market segment, it is time to turn back to the flow chart to look for a process which will help us uncover exactly what our customers expect from our marketing strategy.

Customer behaviour

Since the word market is a collective noun used to describe your organization's potential customer base, if we are to understand our market, we need to understand the customers who make it up.

Good marketing strategy will inevitably spring, not from doing what we are necessarily good at, but from doing what our customers want us to do. From supplying the goods and services that our customers actually want from us. Inevitably then this means that an understanding of the customer (their needs, wants and motivations) is the most important ingredient of any marketing strategy (see Figure 36).

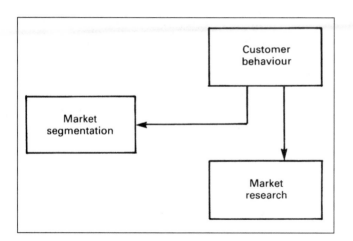

Figure 36
Customer behaviour

In simple terms then, what the organization has to find out is:

- What do our customers need?
- What do our customers actually want from us?
- What will our customers need from us in one, two, five, ten years time?

These are deceptively simple questions. Unfortunately, and here comes the really bad news, no one really understands what makes customers behave the way they do. Yes, I know that the books abound with theories and diagrams and complex flow charts, and as long as these are used to describe past customer behaviour with the value of hindsight, then no problem. Unfortunately, what we are interested in is being able to predict customer behaviour in the future. It is prediction which leads to a proper allocation of marketing and business resource – in other words, where do we pump the money? Into which products and services should we invest our very expensive time and money for maximum payback? While understanding will never give us one hundred per cent predictability among our customers, it will help to reduce the margin of error in our investments and frankly this is the best we can hope for.

Looking at our customers from our inevitable position of organization and product-based interest, it comes as a shock to many marketers that the customer is actually asking apparently irrational questions such as:

- Where can I get it?
- Can I get it now?
- What is available?
- Can I afford it?
- Who am I buying it for?

- What else is affected by this purchase?
- Brand 'A' or Brand 'B'?
- What do I know about Brand 'A'?
- Do I know somebody else who has bought it?
- Who can I ask about it?
- Do I like the people?
- Will I feel comfortable using Brand 'A'?
  . . . and so on and so on.

Very few of the questions, certainly in consumer markets and surprisingly enough in commercial and industrial markets, centre around the detailed technical aspects of any product or service. Japanese-inspired quality control and production has led most buyers to assume that the product or service which they purchase will actually do the job for which it is intended. This level of expectation has meant that people have started to concentrate on the 'softer' aspects of products and services, sometimes described as the intangible elements of a product offering (we will look at this in more detail in Part Three). The important questions, at least as far as our customers are concerned are things like:

- What will the purchase and use of this product or service do for me and my status among my peers?
- Will I enjoy consuming this product or service and the relationship which it brings with the producing organization?

These questions, of themselves, are never easy to answer. The key to understanding the importance of these questions and how this importance is likely to evolve over a time, comes from an understanding of what motivates the customer to buy certain products and services and to shun others. This understanding of customer motivation is certainly critical to the professional marketer and the eventual development of a robust, solid and practical marketing strategy. Let us look then briefly at some of the variables which go into creating an understanding of customer motivation. Looking at the following list, you are almost sure to spot that the whole question of customer behaviour is immensely complicated. The following variables are just some of the elements which come into play when a customer is about to choose between your product or service offering and that offered by your competitor:

- Cultural context
- Social stratification
- Reference groups and sub-cultural influences
- Family influences

- Learning processes
- Evaluative criteria
- Attitudes and attitude change
- Belief systems
- Personal values
- Personality
- Persuasive communication
- Problem recognition processes
- Search and evaluation criteria
- Information processing
- Brand loyalty
- Diffusion of innovations
- Consumerism
- Environmentalism
  . . . and so on and so on.

You can see how all these various aspects of individual personality and individual psychology can play a role in the choice process. Each one of the variables on this list is currently a specific area of detailed academic research and many of them have been the subject of in-depth research for a number of years – even decades. In each one of these areas, theories and hypotheses have been propounded on a regular basis but still there is little of a truly predictive value which has emerged from this world-wide research activity. In other words we may be getting closer to understanding why and how people act and react but we are still short of our ultimate goal of being able to predict customer reaction to any given marketing action.

Take, just for an example, the whole area of attitude and attitude change. Attitude research has been a popular academic pastime for over eighty years, with important work having been produced by people such as Fishbein, Festinger, Ajzen and others. Today, there is still nothing conclusive to show that attitude is linked to behaviour. Nevertheless this doesn't apparently stop many organizations spending millions and millions of pounds, dollars, francs or marks with advertising agencies worldwide in an attempt to change the attitudes of their customers. Even if we assume that advertising and the communication process is able to change attitudes (a separate area of research which is still current – and still inconclusive) what do we know about the effect that a change in attitude has on actual customer behaviour, in other words, will a positive attitude lead to a purchase of our products and services? Certainly the research is able to show equally forcefully that a behaviour change creates an attitude change as well as the other way around. Now, you must understand that I am not out simply to knock advertising (well, not too

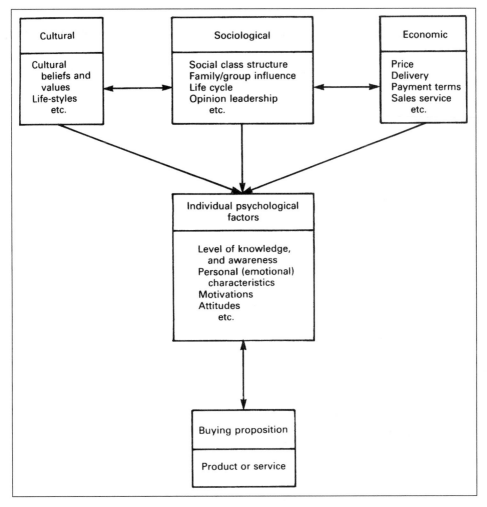

Figure 37   The complex pattern of buying influences. *Source:* Adapted from Chisnall P.M., *Marketing – a Behavioural Analysis* (McGraw-Hill, Maidenhead, 1975).

hard anyway) but it never fails to amaze me how much we can take simply on faith, especially in the more glamorous aspects of marketing such as advertising.

In an area like customer behaviour, the research is quite extensive – this means that the number of elegant models and diagrams is very impressive indeed. I have taken great care to be very selective in my choice of diagrams in this area, trying to choose only those which actually add something to the practising marketer's understanding of the area. I have actively avoided those which unnecessarily complicate the problem or imply that the problem is capable of some sort of scientific solution.

Chisnall (see Figure 37) has attempted to put a number of the more important variables into some sort of overall scheme which illustrates quite well the interrelationships which come into play every time the customer chooses in the marketplace. Chisnall identifies four principal areas of interest to the marketer. These are cultural aspects, sociological aspects, economic aspects and individual psychological factors. Refreshingly, Chisnall does not attempt to put any numbers next to these various factors as do many proponents in the area. This is a wise move on his part since attempting to reduce any of these psychological factors to numbers is necessarily doomed to failure. All it usually means is there is an excuse to feed the whole lot into some sort of computer program and generate a model which everybody believes but is no more use than gut feel anyway.

What is very useful about Chisnall's diagram is that it shows the wildly differing variables which come into play in consumer choice behaviour. These range from the pure economic factors such as price, delivery terms, payment terms, level of after sales services and so on, to cultural beliefs and values and lifestyles which tend to determine, often at a subconscious level, the sorts of products and services which people find intrinsically attractive, or instinctively abhorrent. When talking to practising marketing people about these concepts, as I do on a regular basis, it always is very interesting to go through this process imagining yourself to be a customer rather than a producer. It is not difficult to recognize the various factors which you personally bring into play under these various headings when considering the purchase of, let's say, a motor car, a personal computer, or a package holiday. If you were to think through this process for yourself slowly (and dare I say it, honestly) you could probably easily identify the factors which you bring to bear and how they eventually influence your purchase decision among the various buying propositions on offer to you.

In spite of the fact that most marketing people are also customers and consumers of products and services in their real lives, it is amazing the number of people that, as soon as they get behind a desk, suddenly turn from customers to economists. In the structured situation of the office, there appears to be a change of mind set which says 'Well I know the world is like that but it shouldn't be', so we will concentrate on the top right-hand box and we will deal with our customers as if they are logical, rational, decision-making machines. We will concentrate on the economic aspects such as price, sales, service and so on because these are the things that people ought to be valuing, however, as we all know, they don't, *we don't*.

To get down to the basics of motivation, we have to go back to the very beginings of the theory and strip away some of the more modern embellishments which, in my view, confuse rather than clarify the situation.

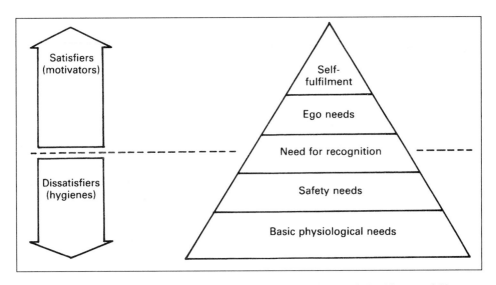

Figure 38 Motivation models. *Source:* Herzberg F., *Work and the Nature of Man* (William Collins, London and New York, 1966); and Maslow A.H., *Motivation and the Personality* (Harper and Row, London and New York, 1954)

There are two basic models in the area of motivation which I find to be the most helpful, certainly when superimposed, one on top of the other. The models themselves come from very early work by Maslow and from Hertzberg (see Figure 38).

In the diagram I have merged these two models, which, when taken together start to paint an interesting picture of customer motivations. Firstly to take Maslow, most people are reasonably conversant with Maslow's work since it has been around for a long time – it certainly forms the underpinning for most motivation models in modern day text books. Maslow looked at what he called the hierarchy of needs; he put this together into a simple pyramid and his argument is roughly – that man has a number of sequential needs and he will seek to satisfy these needs in a sequential, understandable and therefore predictable manner. First of all man has a series of what Maslow calls basic physiological needs – these are basically for food, warmth and sex (not necessarily in that order). Only once these have been satisfied, will man start to be motivated by the next category of need which Maslow calls safety needs, once the needs for personal safety have been satisfied he will then start to be motivated by the need for recognition, and then ego and then self-fulfilment and so on. Interestingly, Maslow argues that as soon as one basic level of needs has been satisfied, for example man feels secure and safe then the need for more safety will no longer be a motivating force.

The need has been satisfied, man moves on and is then motivated by the need for recognition among his peers, need for status and so on.

If alongside this we place the work by Hertzberg, the results of his research do tend to support Maslow quite strongly. Originally, Hertzberg was carrying out his research in relation to the motivation of people in their workplace. What Hertzberg found was that there were a number of factors inherent in the workplace which people found essentially dissatisfying about their job – for example, money. Continuing his research Hertzberg found, interestingly, that once people's perception of, for example, lack of money had been satisfied, additional money on top proved not to be a powerful motivator and people did not become more productive or more satisfied in their work. Hertzberg found, like Maslow, that there are a number of factors in the workplace which, if they are absent, are often quite serious demotivators to people's performance. But once this absence has been rectified, increments failed to motivate people further. Hertzberg labelled these two elements, the 'motivators' and the 'hygienes'. Overlaying the two models the division line between motivators and dissatisfiers tends to fall somewhere in the area of Maslow's need for recognition. However, the actual division line is difficult to draw, people being what they are!

The important step now is try and bring these two theoretical approaches down to the real world. As with all theories, if we can't use them to improve our performance, if they bring no value to bear on the real world and the real marketplace, then they must be considered to be of dubious value. There is no virtue at all in following a theory slavishly and finding out that it does you no good.

The job now for the practical marketer is to find out exactly what these terms mean for his own product or service. Given the marketplace within which your organization operates, you must be asking questions or rather you should be directing your market research to be finding out the answers to the very basic questions like; what does safety, recognition, ego, self-fulfilment mean in the context of your market, your product or service and your target or potential target customer base? Which are the specific aspects of your product or service offering which can be classified as hygiene factors? Which aspects of your product offering are real motivators?

Working through the Hertzberg concept with one of my clients, we were having difficulty seeing how to apply the ideas until one of the management group recognized elements of an analysis they had been carrying out a few years earlier. 'What we tried to do, back then, was to separate the product features into two groups – those features we had to include in our offer just to be on a par with the competition, these we called "ticket to the game features". These were the things we had to offer just to be considered by the customer. Then we tried to identify those features that would insure our purchase over the competition's. These we called the "winners". The trouble we had back then was working out which was which!'

Ticket to the game factors and winning factors are in fact excellent labels for Hertzberg's theoretical concepts. As this company found out, however, the single biggest issue is trying to work out which factor falls into which category. If we follow Hertzberg's ideas then it is extremely important to identify the groupings of factors because the ultimate marketing strategy put together by your organization will need to 'suffice' on the hygiene/ticket to the game factors and 'exceed' the competition only on those factors that are considered motivators/ winners. But before you nod sagely and move on to the next section it is worth while understanding what trouble you can get into if you don't clearly understand the difference between these two types of factor. Just to make the point, let us look at what has become a common problem for most organizations in the 1990s – customer service. Chastised by recent economic recessions, consumers in the late 1990s are no longer content to accept anything less than the levels of service and support that they believe organizations should be delivering. Many organizations, surprised by seeing their customers' bared teeth for the first time, have flung themselves into the problem and are investing serious amounts of money in attempting, variously, to be 'the M&S of our industry' or 'to exceed our customers' service expectations' and so on. More action without thought! But is customer service a motivator or a hygiene factor? If it is a motivator then the more you give the more sales will result. If it is a hygiene factor then surely the task needs to be delivering the right level of service and not exceeding customer expectations. Just because customers are screaming that the service levels are not right does not necessarily mean service is a motivator. Before you protest violently that, of course, it is a motivator – at least in our industry – just think how many waiters you need round a single restaurant table before you get annoyed at too much service. Or how many shop assistants you need to ask whether they can help you before you decide that you would be better off shopping in another department store.

Lack of customer service is causing immense problems with certain customer groups and they are fighting for recognition and to be treated with the level of respect and understanding which they have a right to demand – after all they pay the money. However, it is doubtful (certainly in my mind) whether adding more and more and more customer service is actually going to be a significant motivating force in a number of sectors. Service, as we know, does not come cheap and I have visions of a number of organizations investing more and more into areas which, once put right, do not actually guarantee any form of increased return from this significant marketing investment. Ever-increasing customer service is not guaranteed to attract more and more customers and thereby improve market share. If it turns out to be a hygiene factor but not a motivator this is not a good allocation of limited marketing resource.

'Quality' may also turn out to be a hygiene factor rather than a motivator. The biggest single problem with TQM initiatives is that they are too often based on production rather than marketing concepts. The majority marketplace doesn't actually want a Rolls-Royce, it just wants a standard Ford, GM or Renault that works properly. As with customer service the secret is finding out the *right* quality level and being able to stop at that point. To find out what is 'right' – ask the market.

We should concentrate on looking for the motivating factors in our chosen target marketplace and then aiming to deliver the right level of customer service and quality commensurate with the market needs.

To conclude this section on customer behaviour, I am including my personal favourite from the whole range of theories which are on offer and that is called the black box theory (see Figure 39). What the black box theory says is that we do not understand how the buyer or the customer make their choice among competing offers but something happens inside the buyer's mind (we will call the black box). This activity is a mixture of buying characteristics and something to do with the decision-making process but we are not quite clear what actually happens. Nevertheless, the two boxes to either side of the black box are much more interesting. In the left-hand box we have the marketing and other stimuli, we have control over the marketing mix which (denoted here in terms of the four Ps – product, place, price and promotion) and we mix these as a form of input stimuli to the customer. The customer is also influenced by other external stimuli, such as economics, technological, political, cultural change as we have already seen.

So these stimuli act on the customer who makes some form of decision based on internal processes which we must admit we don't completely understand at the present time. This results in a number of observable responses or outputs. The choice of a given product or product offering, a certain brand if this is relevant in your marketplace, through a certain dealer or intermediary channel, for a certain amount of money, at a certain time and so on. The marketer's job then is to judiciously manage the marketing stimuli which is directly under his control, closely monitor the environmental elements which will affect his marketing activity, to try and understand the basic motivations of his customers, going beyond the basics is unlikely to very successful, and then closely monitor the buyer's response to these inputs. The process then continues. By manipulating those elements under his control he can judge the output in terms of the buyer's response to any changes that he makes or that are made for him by the environment. Over a period of time, the marketer will

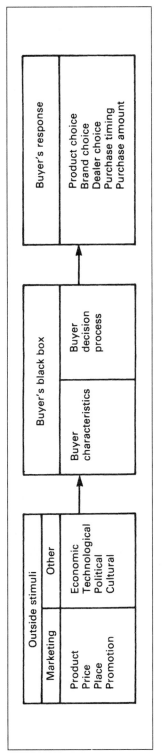

Figure 39 Model of buyer behaviour. *Source:* Kotler P., *Marketing Mangement* (Prentice Hall, Englewood Cliffs, NJ., 1984).

understand what inputs are likely to generate what type of outputs. In this way the marketer gets closer and closer to his targets and understands, or at least gets closer to understanding, what is likely to turn his market on and what will turn his market off. This is not to say that the odd surprise will not happen and on a quite regular basis. Target customers are likely to react in a totally unexpected fashion but then again this is what makes marketing interesting.

Marketer's note

This is it, this is the big one, this is where the marketer starts to earn his or her money. 'The customer is the business', Levitt said this and I have already quoted him and others on this subject. The future of you, your organization and the sales revenue will depend exclusively on how well you know your customers and what drives them to behave in any given way. It is so obvious I wonder why I even bother writing this down. It is so obvious you are wondering why you are reading it yet again! Amazingly enough it is still a brand new idea in many organizations. Here we are, groping into the new millennium, and still we are surrounded by organizations and managers who believe they know what the customer wants – and convinced that the product is more important than anything else. Ah well, we said marketing was going to be fun we didn't say it was going to be easy.

Just to break out of the realms of the 'ideal' for a moment – understanding what the customer wants is one thing, providing it is another.

If, in the process of your analysis, there is an identified mis-match between what your organization currently offers the market and what the customer actually wants, you need to understand what is causing the organization to behave in this way. Does the organization really not know what the market wants? Is this knowledge being ignored or suppressed? What is making the organization produce what it does?

Tricky questions like these need to be answered. If there are significant blocks in the organization to change, more market information, of itself, is unlikely to alter things. The organization will not progress.

Market research

A special section on market research in a book of marketing strategy may, at first glance, appear to be out of place since market research is commonly recognized as being one of the more technical and detailed aspects of the whole marketing function. In fact, the marketing strategist

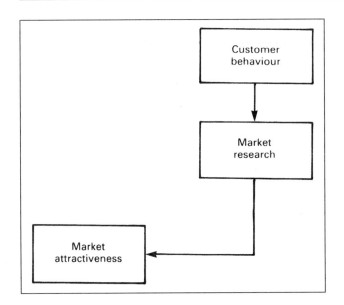

Figure 40 Market research

does not necessarily need to be terribly well versed in the mechanics and techniques of modern day market research. However, it is essential for any practical strategy that the marketer has a very clear idea of what market research can do and what it can't do. (See Figure 40.) Above all how to direct market research projects such that they will produce usable results. Therefore, I see my job in this book as giving the strategic marketer an overall understanding of what market research is all about but not subjecting anybody to a blow-by-blow account of the technical workings of modern research methodology. Such knowledge, if you feel the need is probably even now sitting secure in your marketing reference library.

Before we start, it is probably wise to deal with one or two definitions. At least in this way we can all agree on what we are talking about from the beginning. The first problem of terminology which we might encounter are two terms which tend to be used synonymously – 'market research' and 'marketing research'. Now, using these words interchangeably doesn't seem to cause too many people problems, however, I think it is useful that we understand where these words originally came from. Market research officially applies to research into markets, in other words, their size, compositions, buyer's needs and wants and so forth. Marketing research on the other hand covers research into the organization's marketing activities and how it attempts to address its markets.

Another pair of terms that tend to be used interchangeably by people, but here it causes much greater problems in understanding, are the terms 'data' and 'information'. While data can be defined as things which are known or granted from which inferences may be drawn, they are essentially the raw material of market research. Information, on the other hand, is probably best defined as that which reduces uncertainty in the receiver. If you are struggling to understand a word of what I have just said, then you have just received a whole chunk of data. I will now try to turn this data into information through the use of an example. Imagine that you are at a party (yes I know that a busy marketing strategist has no time to go to parties but just bear with me for the moment) you are being introduced to somebody new by a mutual friend. During the process your name is given, this is of itself data, but since you knew your name already it had reduced no uncertainty on your part at all. The person you are being introduced to is named to you and this can be considered as information because it has now reduced a whole area of uncertainty about this person you have met for the first time.

The distinction between data and information is an important one because the development of a marketing strategy is in absolutely no way aided by the accumulation of random data on markets or on marketing activity. It is only by the careful acquisition of practical and relevant information that areas of doubt and uncertainty can slowly be reduced and efficient and effective plans laid for the future. It goes without saying that information is much more difficult to acquire than data. A library is full of data but it is only the careful selection of the right books with painstaking analysis that produces the information needed. It also goes without saying that while data are the raw material of the market researcher, the commissioner and/or the user of the market research is only interested in acquiring good quality relevant and usable information.

The market research process

In its simplest form any market research project can be broken down into five distinct stages. It matters little the size of the project, the complexity of the project or even the importance of the project to organization's long-term goals, these five stages of a market research project should always be evident. It is worth going through these stages briefly so that we can better understand what is involved in market research and therefore how to control it.

Defining the problem and the research objectives
Any market research project which does not have very clearly defined objectives at the beginning is likely to run out of control in a very short period of time indeed. It is essential that the people commissioning the research, the people using the research and the people carrying out the

research have a very clear understanding of what everybody is trying to do. Research will always be more effective and cost efficient if it is directed at filling in precise and identified gaps in market or marketing information. Simple curiosity is never enough to justify any form of market research project.

In my experience, a useful control mechanism right at the beginning of research project is to make sure that everybody involved, including those who will be doing the research, understands very clearly what the results of the market research projects will be used for and exactly which decisions will be made as a result of the outputs of the project. It is always very easy to be carried away with the mechanics of a market research activity and the setting of clear objectives helps to keep people on the single track needed.

This stage should also set down the time scales and the intended method of reporting.

Developing the research plan

This is the point at which the whole thing starts to get more complicated and technical and quite frankly the marketer needs only understand a minimum of the jargon to be able to contribute to the discussions and to make sure that the researchers will be delivering what is needed at the end of the day. So let's run through the principal points.

First there is the question of data sources. There are two main sources of data open to the researcher; the first is primary data, this is original data collected directly by the organization which could be seen as more relevant to the problem in hand but tends to cost more money to collect. The second form of data is what is called secondary data and this is data which already exists somewhere. It may exist in the form of government statistics, data produced by private organizations or it may already exist inside the organization but just may not be in the right form for analysis at the moment. Secondary data should always be the starting point of a data collection, it is normally cheaper to collect but may of course be less relevant to the question in hand.

The next area in the research plan is how we are going to collect the primary data, should it need collecting. There are two broad types of data to be collected, these come under the headings of qualitative research and quantitative research. Qualitative research will normally precede quantitative research in a project. Qualitative research tends to be concerned with the behaviour organizations, competitors and customers and is mostly interested in asking why people act in a certain way, what people want. A more important aspect is its feeding role to quantitative research. Qualitative research will help to identify the questions that need to be asked. The second stage on a research approach is quantitative research and this is, as the name would imply, a broader scope of research where we just try and find out exactly how many people want a given product offering and how many people act in a certain way. It is putting numbers on to the qualitative outputs.

The next section of the research plan will probably include some indication of the research instruments to be used in the collection of the data (e.g. questionnaires). It may also include some information on sampling techniques and contact methods by which data will be collected from respondents.

Collecting the data
Data collection is the next and probably the most expensive phase in the research project. This is the point at which the field work is carried out.

Analysing the data
Once the data has been collected, depending on the nature of the research, analysis may at this stage involve the use of computers, both PCs and mainframes. Depending on the nature of the analysis to be carried out fairly advanced statistical techniques may be brought into play.

Presenting the findings
This is the stage of the research project when the results of the surveys or field work or whatever the research plan envisaged, are presented back to the commissioner and/or the user of the research.

This is the point at which you find out how good were the research objectives and the briefing. Ideally, any presentation of market research results should avoid any of the deep statistical analysis which was carried out. It is not relevant to the people listening to the presentation – it should refer extensively and continually to the research objectives and it should be aimed at delivering information rather than data.

What can market research do?

Maybe this final section ought to be called 'What can't market research do?' since nowadays market research has become a major tool in the armoury of the marketer. In fact it has got to such a stage in some so-called advanced marketing organizations, that managers will not move a muscle without a market research to back up any activity.

The first thing that has to be said about market research is that it is definitely not an alternative to management decision making. No form of market research, no matter how deep, complicated and detailed, can ever be seen as a substitute to creative decision making by professional managers. At its very best, market research can remove some doubt and clarify some options and alternatives. It may even be seen as a tool which can improve the quality of decisions but it is not of itself a decision-making mechanism.

Market research, in common with a number of scientific and pseudo-scientific approaches in marketing, suffers from the widespread complaint of 'spurious accuracy'. Market research results can never be completely accurate since they are dealing with human nature. They are dealing with a dynamic marketplace and of course sampling methods have been used and then grossed up to give total market results. There will always be a form of inherent bias in market research results and this error should be plainly and clearly understood by everyone reading the results. Therefore there is not only a place but there is an on-going need for creativity and imagination when dealing with market research results, and certainly when making any attempt to apply them in the marketplace.

Last, it should always be remembered that market research is not an end in itself. Market research is purely and simply a means by which some risk can be removed from marketplace activity. It is the marketing activity at the end of the day which counts and not the market research itself. If there is no activity resulting from the market research then the entire exercise has been completely pointless.

More market research please

Marketing strategy (and the marketing strategist) doesn't need market research but desperately needs some answers. Good and practical marketing strategy has to be based upon reasonably well-understood customer needs, wants and motivations if it is to provide longer term solutions that customers will buy. The better we understand our customers and their needs the better the quality of the marketing strategy will be and the better the bottom line will look. Unfortunately all that glitters is not gold and all marketing research documents bearing the name are not what they appear.

Market research implies research into the workings of the marketplace. Who are today's and tomorrow's prospective customers? What are today's and tomorrow's likely needs? What will they buy? What selection will they choose from? How much will they pay etc.? Unfortunately, most organizations' research budgets do not appear to be spent answering these types of questions. The majority of market research spend (at least in my experience) seems to be dedicated to product research. Batteries of questions ask respondents their thoughts and attitudes on existing products, new product concepts and modifications. Hundreds and thousands of pounds and dollars are also spent assessing customers' reactions to likely changes in price, colour or design, and promotional and communication changes. All this is extremely useful data but it doesn't help the development of a marketing strategy. Marketing strategy requires information on customers (not our products!). We need to know how our customers lead their lives, how they run their businesses, how they regard their families, what they do in their leisure time, then we can begin to do the marketing job and blend package design and modify our product or service so that it meets the needs they have – not just the needs we think they ought to have.

Real market research is not easy. Maybe that's why it isn't common. Interestingly enough, the reasons given for not conducting this type of research clearly demonstrate some of the problems facing marketing and marketers today:

- 'We've never done it.'
- 'Qualitative research is all a bit touchy feely.'
- 'How do you find out what the customers themselves don't know they want?'
- 'This organization works on numbers – not loose concepts or ideas.'
- 'The market research agencies we use just don't do that sort of thing.'
- 'Sorry, the finance people just wouldn't buy it.'
- 'The product managers hold the research budget and they have their product targets to meet.'
- 'There's no budget for that sort of thing, every pound/dollar we spend has to be set off against an existing profit centre.'

Marketer's note

This very brief overview of market research, what it can do and how it is done is not intended to be an all-embracing, all-inclusive view of the market research topic. Rather, I have tried to give a broad overview of what can be realistically achieved from market research and how the whole area fits in to the development of a robust marketing strategy.

You should always remember, and try to make clear to everybody else in the organization, that market research will only ever be a cheaper and relatively lower risk substitute to the real thing. The real test of any marketing strategy is moving into the marketplace with the real product and/or service offering and seeing how real customers react – they will either buy or they will avoid your offering. That is the true test of your success.

Lest we forget that everyone, including market researchers, are fallible we should always bear in mind that had Sony listened to the results of its market research, the *Walkman* would not be with us today!

Market segmentation

Once we have started to get a feeling for where the market is and what the market wants, the next stage is invariably how the market breaks up into separate units, groups or segments. We then move into the area of market segmentation – a wonderful field full of mines and traps for the unwary. Market segmentation, niche marketing, are terms that we all hear frequently, often use regularly, but surprisingly few people really understand the concepts behind market segmentation. (See Figure 41.)

Market segmentation as a marketing tool came to the fore in the 1980s and will be increasingly important to marketing strategy in the 1990s and beyond. The reason for this growth of interest in market segmentation is directly related to the evolution of most marketplaces, certainly consumer markets. While the 1960s were typified by mass production and volume sales, the 1990s will be typified by people's search for a greater sense of individualism and a search for identity. People nowadays are much less ready to settle for a mass produced standard item, be it product, service or even industrial. The search today is for something special, something different, something which reinforces my own sense of my identity as a person, as an individual, as someone separate from the herd. The modern

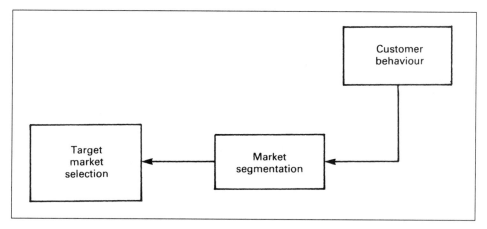

Figure 41 Market segmentation

day array of product choice (for example there isn't just one Sony Walkman, there were 176 on offer at the last count) stands witness to this growth in choice which is being demanded in most advanced market-places in the world. So how shall we go about segmenting the market-place? Can the marketplace be segmented? If it can, who does it and how?

First let's deal with the easy bits – what do we mean by market segmentation? There are very few occasions that I wheel out pat defini-tions but market segmentation is one of the rare instances where a defin-ition can be quite useful. One of the best comes from Kotler, 'market segmentation is the sub-dividing of a market into homogeneous sub-sets of customers, where any sub-set may conceivably be selected as a market target to be reached with a distinct marketing mix'.

From this quite precise definition we can see that market segmentation is all about the identification of 'homogeneous sub-sets of customers', that is, customers who are alike in some way or other. Where any one of these groups 'may conceivably be selected as a market target', in other words we can go for one or all of these groups but we can treat them as a stand alone market target. The final implication, 'a distinct marketing mix', is that the segments, once identified, may actually demand something different from us as a producer, in other words the marketing mix, in terms of either the product, the pricing, distribution and so on, can conceivably be different from segment to segment. Such a breaking up of our marketing into a number of different mixes is obviously much more costly in terms of marketing investment and control but the argument goes that with a more relevant mix you would improve your penetration of a given market segment and the increased volume would pay off the additional costs incurred.

It has been regularly argued, certainly by the more purist marketing academics, that given the evolution of society and its needs, individual-ism and so on, that the ultimate market segment is a segment of one. That every individual is moving to create their own position, their own identity and their own space in the world and everybody has different needs so we have segments of one person. Unfortunately, barring the few odd millionaires scattered around the western world, the segment of one is unlikely to be completely viable, at least for most producers. A compro-mise position must be found.

There are a number of ways in which we can actually test market segments. The first comes from Yoram Wind, who sets out five principal rules for good robust segments:

- measurable;
- accessible;

- substantial;
- mutual exclusivity; and
- homogeneous in response to marketing variables.

The first rule he sets is that the segment must be measurable, in other words, we must know where it is, how big it is, and exactly how it differs from the market at large and other segments in particular. The second rule he sets is that the segment must be accessible. There could be a perfect segment in the marketplace but if we can't actually get to it with our communication, or our delivery channels then that segment remains purely hypothetical. The third rule is that the segment must be substantial, in other words, it has got to be big enough for us to make profit out of. We must bear in mind the extra expense incurred in managing more than one marketing mix through our market segments and of course people's willingness to pay a premium price. The fourth rule that Wind sets is that of mutual exclusivity. This is probably a little purist in its approach but the argument is that a true segment will understand and relate to messages directed at it but will be completely turned off by messages which it inadvertently receives but which were originally aimed at another segment. The fifth rule that Wind set is very important. He maintains that to be a good segment, the response of the people within the segment must be homogeneous. In other words, they must all act in a uniform manner and respond in the same way to the marketing input into that segment. This is a good collection of rules to stand by and although they may appear to be just so much common sense, it is surprising how many people, when looking at market segments, forget some fairly fundamental questions. They form a sound basis on which to look at initial segmentation approaches to the marketplace.

Segmentation bases

The next question is – how can the market possibly be segmented. Well, here the list is practically endless. Frankly, you name a segmentation base and someone somewhere has tried it and probably someone somewhere else will swear that it is the only way they segment their particular marketplace. Markets have been broken up on a geographical basis, for example international, national markets, regions, by county, by town, even by house and by street number. Markets have also been broken up in terms of demographics, by age, by sex, by family life stage, income, by occupation, or education, and so on. More recently psychographics have been in vogue and markets have started to be broken up by social class (although this is becoming less useful as time goes by), lifestyle which is very important for certain product areas, and personality. There are also behaviourial bases for segmentation for example, the use occasion of the product, benefits sought, store usage, usage rate, price sensitivity and so on.

Probably one of the most powerful bases for segmentation is that of benefits sought. Benefit segmentation is not new – as a concept it has been around for almost thirty years, nevertheless it still forms the basis for most segmentation, certainly in consumer markets. To cite an original example, the toothpaste market is segmented in the UK, Europe, USA and Australia, on effectively a benefit segmentation basis. To explain, toothpaste cleans teeth; this is addressing the standard need of people who buy toothpaste. However, there are a number of other benefits associated with toothpaste, and it is these different benefits which forms the basis of segmentation in the marketplace. There are certain people who are very concerned with having fresh breath and how that affects their broader social relationships – certain products are designed to satisfy this need, and are targeted into this particular market segment. Another segment is most concerned with tooth decay and prevention of cavities so another market brand is directed at that market segment. The 1980s saw the arrival of a new range of tooth-pastes which were specifically geared at people who felt that they had sensitive teeth and sensitive gums and additional product enhancements were built in to satisfy the particular needs of this segment, and so the story continues. While benefit segmentation is still a very powerful tool, it does require a good understanding of the underlying benefits demanded from the marketplace; it also needs a very close association with the customer and the ability to forecast future needs as or before they arise, if the new, enhanced products are to be launched in a timely fashion.

Probably the most powerful aspect of benefit segmentation is that it forces the marketer to understand a fundamental truth about market segmentation and that is that it is not the organization or the marketer who actually segments the marketplace; it is the marketplace which segments itself. People fit themselves into market segments. Our job is not to divide the marketplace – our job is to identify how the market divides itself up and then to package and present our marketing mix accordingly.

Following this argument, there needs to be an additional two rules to good segmentation over and above those suggested by Wind. These are:

* Is the segment recognized by the customers themselves?
* Is the segment recognized by the intermediaries in the channel?

In other words do the customers recognize themselves as being a part of and identifiable with a given market grouping? If they don't, not only

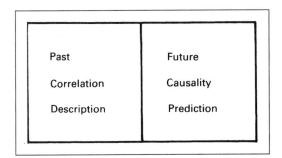

Past	Future
Correlation	Causality
Description	Prediction

Figure 42 Problems with segmentation

will they not understand or identify with the promotion or communication aimed at them, they may actually reject this enforced membership and wreak their vengeance on your product offering.

Second and equally important – if the channel intermediaries and distributors don't recognize the existence of various market segments then they are unlikely to cooperate in the marketing activity. It is then unlikely that you and your organization will be able to satisfy the needs of a given market in a proper fashion.

The problems with segmentation as is currently practised in very many organizations can be summed up as in Figure 42. Most organizations talk about segmentation in terms that relate to the three words in the left-hand column. When asked how they segment and what they are doing in the area, invariably people will start to describe the past experiences that they have had with their customers; how people reacted; what they did and even an analysis of where their sales have come from in the past, some form of ex-post rationalization comes into play at this point. As we all know when we are thinking clearly, the future is unlikely to be a straight-line extrapolation from the past, much as we would like it to be so. Of course, as marketers trying to put together a marketing strategy which will deliver the business what it needs, our concerns must be for the future. Our concerns must centre on where should we invest our marketing spend, where should we invest our energy for both short- and long-term returns from the marketplace. The past has gone. There is some value to be gained from understanding the lessons of the past but only if they can be brought into play and can improve our future activity.

The second problem is that when you press people to explain the rationale behind their segments you are often presented with a whole series of correlations. In other words, our customers in this segment have such and such characteristics. This may be a good correlation but it is not a solid enough base to build our strategy for the future. What we need to uncover is some degree of causality. There may be some relationships which an in-depth study of our existing customers could expose, however, it is dangerous to build a strategy on relationships which are not causal. In other words, is there an underlying motivational reason why people act in a certain way that we can understand from their circumstances. Correlations are interesting but like coincidences they are unreliable and a dangerous basis for building relationships.

Finally, there is a misunderstanding between description and prediction. An in-depth description of our existing customer base and our existing 'segments' in terms of age profiles, sex, income, occupation, education, family lifestage or even socio-economic grouping is only really valid if we have some evidence to support the belief that these characteristics are motivational. That is to say, that the segments with these characteristics will, because of this description, act in some way which is different and unique from the rest of the marketplace. Once again, it is prediction of the future which is important. Now the only thing we know about the future is that our ideas and predictions will be wrong – our job is to reduce this margin of error and in some way shape or form to improve the return on our hard-earned marketing spend.

So what then can we conclude from this very brief discussion of market segmentation. First, we can say that it is an important area and is likely to become more and more important as time goes by. Second, its importance is generating ever more deeply thought out models and ideas about the best ways to segment the marketplace. As with all these 'new' ideas, while the aim is to make life easier and more understandable for the practitioner, I feel that they often tend to confuse rather than clarify.

Segmentation is about the sub-dividing of a total marketplace into homogeneous sub-sets of customers. It is about improving the effectiveness of our marketing. It is about targeting our marketing more accurately into sub-groups of customers in the expectation of improved targeting that will produce a large number of satisfied customers and thereby improve the bottom line result.

As I predicted in the first edition of this book, market segmentation has become more and more important during the 1990s. However, market segmentation, dealing as it does with people as its raw material, cannot and should not be approached in a scientific manner. If you believe, as I do, that the only workable long-term segmentation base comes from the marketplace and not from ourselves, no matter how well versed in the science of marketing, then it is only by getting closer and closer to the target marketplace that we will be able to identify the existence of real market segments and thereby learn to adapt our marketing strategy accordingly. This process is necessarily long, messy, and fraught with danger. Nevertheless, past experience has convinced me that the markets and our customers are only too happy to tell us where they are, what they want now and what they might want in the future. The only thing your organization needs is someone there to hear.

When, and only when, proper behaviourial segments have been identified in the marketplace, the next important job is to attempt to describe these segments in such a way that practical operational marketing can be brought to bear on them. This is the point at which terms such as demographics, lifestyles, usage patterns, and so forth can properly be brought into play as long as we remember that these are descriptive terms and they are subject to change over time. For example, if we look at the market for domestic washing detergents and if we imagine for the moment that there is a segment out there which we might entitle the 'caring mother segment'. It could be argued that the women who buy detergents to reinforce their self-image as a caring mother will be buying products according to the specific promises made within the offering. This is the basic motivation. If we then move to the next stage market segmentation and look at how to describe these segments, we might find that currently these women fall into certain socio-economic groupings, maybe they cluster in certain geographical regions, possibly they have husbands in certain recognizable categories of employment, they may live in certain types of houses in certain areas. These are all descriptive aspects of the segment and will be extremely useful once we move down to day-to-day operational marketing planning. However, it is extremely important to remember that the entire marketing strategy will be directed at these women because of the need they have to be seen as caring mothers, not because they happen to live in a certain type of house or in a certain type of area or suburb.

Future development

Even more important, in strategic terms, the next stage of the segmentation process is to attempt to project the future development of the segments. The questions we need to be asking ourselves in this area are as follows.

Is the segment growing or declining?

Here we are interested in two broad aspects of growth and decline. What is the projected future of the segment in terms of volume sales and profitability? Despite much argument to the contrary (as we shall see later) there is not necessarily a link between volume sales and profit. Declining volumes in certain market segments can still be extremely profitable for the organizations which service them (look at the present price of re-positioned soap flakes in the laundry market). It's much more a question of how the segment is managed rather than what the segment is doing.

Is the segment changing?

There are three aspects to this question of change. First, we need to try and get a feel for how the composition of the segment is likely to be changing over time. Is the segment starting to attract new and slightly different members to its centre? The late 1980s and the early 1990s saw a rapid growth in the green movement in Europe. This not only vastly increased the size of the segment it also quite dramatically changed the nature of the segment and its needs and wants in the marketplace.

The second aspect of change relates more to the nature of the products and services which we would expect this segment to be demanding in the future. In other words, do we see any significant change in the way in which the members of the segment are likely to translate their needs in terms of the products and services which they will buy in the future?

The third area of segment change must be the movements of the segments over time. More precisely, do we see the array of segments changing in its overall structure. There are two ways in which this structural change can occur. Segments may merge and combine to create larger more 'shallow' segments and of course larger segments may tend to fragment over time into smaller more precise market targets for the organization to approach.

While this is an extremely important analysis to undertake, it's also probably the most difficult, but the degree of analysis which the organization will need to undertake here will very largely depend on its business strategy decisions developed earlier. In other words, the organization aiming for a differentiated position in the marketplace will need to retain a certain degree of flexibility which will allow it to operate in a number of related market segments while still retaining its differentiated market position. The focused organization on the other hand will necessarily have to get much, much closer to its fewer market segments, and will have to predict fragmentation and merging long before this phenomenon arises. It must be prepared and able to continue to service changing segment needs as they arise. Failure to do this by the focused organization will leave it very vulnerable to competitive attack from the outside in its core markets.

Market attractiveness

Once we have a clearer idea of our marketplace and the segments which comprise the overall market, the next question we have to face is what to do with them. There must be some degree of selectivity about our approach to market segments for two important reasons. (See Figure 43.)

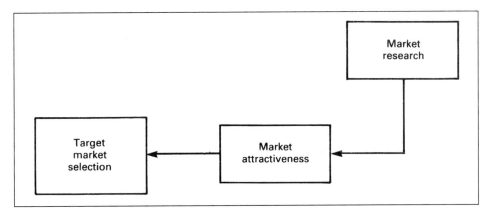

Figure 43 Market attractiveness

First, marketing and business resource is necessarily limited therefore we must choose where to invest our resource for the right level of returns. The second reason why selectivity is important concerns customer perceptions. In the 1960s and 1970s the large conglomerates could lay claim to being in a variety of different businesses. Their size was a major factor in this argument and customers accepted the claim that an adequate product and service could come from a large, non-specialist organization. The 1980s and the 1990s are seeing this claim being less readily acceptable in the marketplace. Quality, it is perceived, is more likely to come from specialization. The organization should then select market segments which will reinforce this image in the marketplace.

The first step in bringing about a strategic evaluation of various market segment attractiveness is to go back to the analysis conducted in the early stages of the business strategy and to list the resources at our disposal; our strengths and weaknesses; the opportunities and threats faced with new environments and our competitive position. All these aspects have been covered in Part One.

Selection criteria

Once we have identified and listed our basic key competencies we must then look at the total potential market and its segments. We need to organize our attack on the market according to some priority. We do this by looking at the segments according to a number of fairly clearly defined criteria (see Figure 44).

The order that I have used here need not necessarily be the one that you and your organization follow – that will largely depend on your own

Criteria	Weight	Segments				
		1	2	3	4	5
1 Long-term volume growth						
2 Long-term profit growth						
3 Short-term volume growth						
4 Short-term profit growth						
5 Organizational image						
6 Offensive strategic reasons						
7 Defensive strategic reasons						
8 Internal resource/capability						
9 Relative competitive strength						
10						
11						
12						
Total						
Priority						

(Ratings 1–10, 10 = Highly attractive)

Figure 44 Target market attractiveness

individual circumstances. There will also be additional criteria to be included that are specific to your own market situation.

A simple and convenient (although not mathematically accurate) analysis of market/segment attractiveness can be carried out with the diagram shown. After listing all the relevant criteria and the market segments in question, you (or a team) can attempt to rate – I use marks out of ten – each segment against each criteria. Simply adding up the columns for each segment at the bottom will give you an idea of which segments to look at first (highest totals) and which ones to leave to last (lowest totals) – or to the competition. A more advanced exercise, but just as subjective, is to add weightings against the evaluative criteria according to their relative importance to your organization now and in the future.

Long-term volume growth
These are typically the growing market segments which will generate large amounts of tomorrow's volume. Don't forget of course that if you

spotted them as a growing segment, it's not unlikely that your competition has spotted them too.

Long-term profit growth
Profit growth and volume growth need not necessarily be contained in the same segment. Long-term profit growth could come from a declining segment where competition is vacating the segment and leaving more profit opportunities for our organization. The key words here of course are long term.

Short-term volume growth
As we have already seen, long-term vision and strategy is essential for the survival of the organization. Nevertheless, it is important that the organization lives long enough to realize the potential coming from its future markets. In other words, we have to generate volume sales today if for no other reason than to make sure we are around tomorrow. The same applies to the next paragraph.

Short-term profit growth
Short-term profits are as important as long-term profits. It is the short-term profits which allow us to invest in the future. These segments should be identified and should be carefully nurtured.

Organizational image
There are things in life other than profit (heresy, I hear you cry) at least more important than directly attributable profit. In the same way that the mens' wet shaver market has used the concept of selling razors at an extremely low price and making all the margin on the blades, so we can extend this idea into strategic terms. There may be segments within which the organization must be a major or at least an active player if its strategic market position is to be credible in the marketplace. It may be that these segments produce no profit of their own but by being in this segment we are allowed to be in another segment where profit is generated. Combined segment profitability must be positive over the long term but individual segment losses need to watched very carefully indeed.

Offensive strategic reasons
The organization's business strategy may involve the development of new segments or the creation of bridgehead segments which in themselves hold no intrinsic value for the organization, but which will allow the achievement of the organization's business objective over the longer term. Again, beware short-term losses/investment turning into a long-term disaster.

Defensive strategic reasons

These are segments which may appear to be much less attractive to the organization in terms of volumes or in terms of profits or maybe even in terms of image and company positioning. However, falling out of the initial research in competitor analysis and competitive opportunities, it may become apparent that our competitors' strategies might take them into certain market areas which could in the long term prove quite dangerous for our organization's position.

The sad case in point here was the UK motorcycle industry. At one time, UK motorcycle manufacturers practically dominated the market for the large engine sizes. When the Japanese first entered the UK motorcycle market with mopeds and machines in the fifty to eighty cc range, the domestic industry did not consider this to be a major threat. They rather despised the 'toy' end of the marketplace and did not see the Japanese entry as major competition. Now of course there is no real domestic motorcycle industry in the UK. The pattern is being repeated by the Japanese in the telecommunications and office equipment marketplaces with similar results.

History shows us then that bearing the cost of operating in certain strategic market segments to control the activities of our competitors may pay dividends over the long term.

Internal resource/capability

There will always be segments which we could tap purely because we happen to be good at producing the products and services that the segment demands, however, just because we have the internal ability and maybe the short-term profit looks attractive, this does not necessarily mean that we should be attacking these segments. If you still feel the need to understand the reasons why attacking such segments could be dangerous then refer back to the introductory section of this book about production versus market orientation.

Relative competitive strength

As in the previous paragraph, there will also be segments where your organization has definite competitive strength and advantage over the competition. Again, it may or may not be a wise decision to attack these segments. Always look to the long term and the strategic rather than the tactical issues involved.

I realize from what has been said so far, that you could probably argue to take your organization into almost every segment available based on one of these arguments or another. As with all things in marketing, we must deal with the question of balance. The successful organization is one which properly allocates its limited resource and does so by judiciously balancing up the needs of the short term versus the needs of the long term. By balancing up the needs of profits today versus profit (or even super-profits) tomorrow. By balancing of the need for a consistent credible position and image in the marketplace against the current strengths and capabilities of the organization. By balancing the offensive strategic activities against the defensive strategic activities and understanding likely competitive responses towards these activities.

Gap analysis

Gap analysis is another one of those wonderful marketing terms which can mean everything and nothing. The unfortunate thing with the term gap analysis is that if you hear it on three occasions it will no doubt be applied to three different analyses, and the concept of the gap will likely mean three different things. While on the one hand this can be quite confusing for the novice, it can also be quite powerful. The whole concept of gap analysis itself is very simple, it can and is applied to a number of different problems in the marketing arena. The reason for including this section on gap analysis in this discussion on marketing strategy is that gap analysis can be a useful way of training the mind to look for market and marketing opportunities. (See Figure 45.)

In its simplest form, gap analysis is all about identifying gaps, analysing gaps and then seeing how these gaps might be filled to the profitable long-term benefit of the organization. The problem arises when the term gap analysis is applied only to one form of gap. That's OK but unfortunately three different commentators will use the terms in respect to their own personal favourite form of gap and will ignore the others.

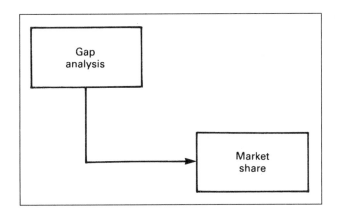

Figure 45   Gap analysis

Here we are going to look at the various forms of gaps which might be analysed by the marketing organization and various ways in which, strategically, these gaps might be filled.

The gaps which we will look at are:

- the performance gap;
- the market segment(s) gap;
- the product (needs) gap;
- the image gap;
- the activity gap; and
- the competitive gap.

The performance gap

The performance gap (see Figure 46) is the most common example of gap analysis to be found in the marketing literature. It applies quite simply to the question of how, in market and marketing terms, the organization should plan to achieve the financial and other performance expectations which are laid down in the guiding business strategy. The procedure for carrying out gap analysis on the performance requirements is reasonably straightforward.

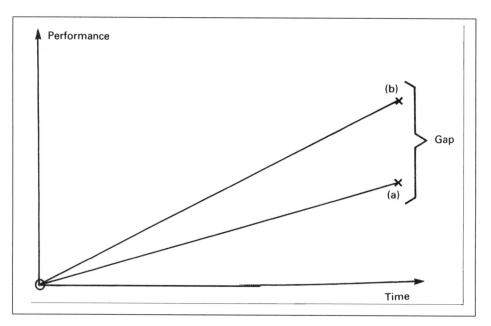

Figure 46   The performance gap

To illustrate the case, let us imagine that your organization has well-developed strategic plans and, so, has a reasonably clear idea of the position that the organization should be in in say ten years. This position may be quantified in profit terms, in turnover terms or in market and market share. To be robust, a business objective should be ambitious and should stretch the organization. This objective is represented by point (b) in Figure 46.

If we were to draw a straight line (extrapolating from past experience) we could plot the likely performance result at the same time, if there were no change to the way in which we were doing things at the moment. This position is represented by point (a) on the diagram.

As we would expect, ten years out there would be a gap between the targeted performance (b) and the expected performance (a). If we subtract (a) from (b), we are left with a shortfall, or in other words a gap. Simplicity itself!

Whether this gap is expressed in financial turnover, in profits, in market share or in volume sales terms is largely irrelevant. The marketing problem now is how can we fill this gap with new activity.

One word, however, before we continue, we have assumed so far that the gap to be filled is a question of expanding the organization's business. This need not necessarily be the case. We can also envisage the organization which either, overall or in a particular division, is facing certain market decline over the planning period. In this case, the business objective will involve controlling the market decline. The problem of the gap then will be one of controlled market shrinkage and maintenance of financial results. This is certainly the situation being faced by many large organizations which have moved from a previously government-controlled or regulated industry into a freer and more competitive marketplace. The UK's British Telecom (BT) after deregulation would be a good example. The marketing problem facing BT was not one of market expansion – it knew that new competition was about to arrive – indeed competition was being encouraged by government legislation. It was evident that BT's market share could move in only one direction, downwards. In this case the problem facing the organization was to control the market decline and in some way to manage actively which business/segments should be passed on to competition, which business/segments the organization should fight to retain for its future years.

When we consider the alternative ways of filling a gap (the more usual expansionist gap), we are still helped by the early work of Ansoff (see Figure 47). According to Ansoff there are really just four ways (others have added to the matrix but not really to the concept) in which the organization can expand its operation to fill the performance gap. In ascending order or 'risk', these are:

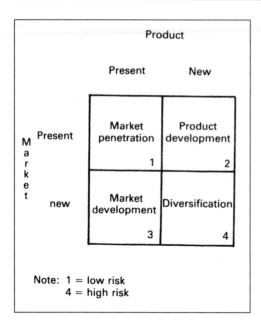

Figure 47 Ansoff matrix. *Source:* Ansoff H.I., 'Strategies for diversification', *Harvard Business Review*, Sept–Oct, 1957.

- market penetration;
- product development;
- market development; and
- diversification.

Market penetration

The first option open to your organization is simply to sell more of your existing products or services to your existing marketplace. In other words to increase the level of penetration which you already have into your existing market segments. Market penetration as a strategic approach to filling the identified gap will of course depend on the level of penetration which you have already achieved in your existing market segments. It will also depend on competitor activity and the likely development of your key market segments over the next ten years. Are these increasing in size, declining, fragmenting and so on. Market penetration is the least risky of the four alternatives to fill in the gap since your organization will be dealing with products and services it knows and understands, and more importantly with market segments which it knows and understands.

Product development

This approach involves a continuing concentration on existing markets and market segments but developing additional or replacement new products. This is aimed at increasing the level of sales through an expanded product range to the same marketplace. The product development approach is slightly more risky than market penetration in that it entails developing new products and there is never any certainty about how well these will be received by your market segments. There is also likely to be some degree of cannibalization – in other words adding a fourth product range to an existing range of three will not automatically increase your sales by the same percentage. A number of sales can be expected to be cannibalized from the existing range into the new product and it is of course the net growth in the market for profit potential that will need to fill the gap.

Market development

Market development as an approach means that the organization concentrates on the existing range of products but looks at ways of marketing these same products or services into new markets or market segments (this may include overseas markets). At first glance, this would appear to be a very attractive option but on closer inspection we can see that the risk involved is higher than both market penetration and product development alternatives. First, it is unlikely that a product will move satisfactorily from one segment to another segment without some form of modification to enable it to meet the different needs of a different user group. As soon as we modify products in any way, be it just packaging or presentation, we have can expect additional marketing costs of stocking, management control, promotion activity and so forth.

The biggest single problem, however, comes not from changing the products or services, but from moving into new segments which, by definition, are not as well understood. Since, as we have already seen profits flow from markets not from products, it is the understanding of the markets and market needs that generates success. There will be a lot of learning to do for the organization that embarks on a market development activity.

Diversification

Diversification is the riskiest of the four options suggested by Ansoff, involving as it does the marketing of new products into new market segments. While the potential returns can be high from a completely new venture such as this, the organization must realize that it is moving off into completely new territory. It may have to learn whole new product areas. New technology resources may be required. At the same time the organization must learn about the needs of completely new markets.

Diversification was certainly flavour of the decade in the 1970s but the 1980s have shown all but the most hardened expansionists that 'sticking to your knitting' is more likely to generate secure long-term profits. For those that are interested, a number of surveys were carried out in the late 1980s looking at the results of the 1970s diversification and the growth of conglomerates. Almost without exception the large conglomerates of the 1970s have now been broken up, willingly or unwillingly, and we have seen the appearance of a new business expert – the disinvestment specialist. While fifteen years ago, the business literature was full of words such as economies of scale, diversification, conglomerates, width of operation expertise and so on, now we are faced with words such as specialization, concentration, focus and niche business. The 1990s have taken this focused approach even further with 'outsourcing' being used as a management process to rid organizations of everything accept the skills and competencies considered critical for the future growth of the business. The outsourcing route began with the easy targets such as the in-house printing department and the staff canteen as managers realized that these services could be more efficiently and effectively bought in from outside specialists. The outsourcing movement has proceeded into more interesting areas recently with organizations now outsourcing their entire IT function to outside specialists and one national airline now considering outsourcing its finance and accounting department! Diversify by all means, but understand exactly what you are doing and why you are doing it.

The next step in the process is to look at the gap between extrapolated (a) and targeted (b) future performance and work out the most appropriate way of filling that gap with a mixture of the four very broad macro alternatives offered by Ansoff. If for example we think that ten years out it would be most sensible to have filled fifty per cent of the gap through improved market penetration, say twenty-five per cent market development and twenty-five per cent product development, then that will give us fairly good indications about how we should direct our marketing strategy and our marketing resource to achieving those results.

The most attractive option for the majority of organizations will likely lie in the area of market penetration. Not quite so exciting I know but often the most effective and profitable.

The market (segments) gap

You have probably heard the expression, 'there is a gap in the market' voiced on a number of occasions. It is another application of gap analysis but this time applied to the identification of the market and its constituent segments. The process for identifying market gaps is quite different from that used for identifying performance gaps and is essentially based on some technique which involves the concept of perceptual mapping.

It is evident that no organization ever completely understands its marketplace. If you followed the previous discussion on market segmentation, you will understand that we are faced with so many unknowns when we deal with customer/human behaviour that we can never be quite sure whether we have highlighted and identified all the market segments which exist in the market. Even if we did it successfully two or three years ago, how far has the situation changed today? Even worse, it is every marketer's nightmare that he has overlooked some magical segment in the marketplace that is not only capable of producing enormous profits but is also wide open for competitive entry. While a regular update of the market gap analysis can help to show the evolution and growth of new segments, it can never be sufficient to put our minds completely at rest.

In its simplest terms, any marketplace can be described in one or much more usually a series of maps – unfortunately, nowadays, high-powered computers are able to somehow conceptualize more than one dimension of a map at the same time thus confusing all us lesser mortals completely. (See Figure 48.)

Essentially a perceptual map of a market consists of two criteria which are important to the customers who make up the marketplace. Remembering our discussion on segmentation, true segments are motivational in nature and therefore the criteria we should be using are motivational criteria. In Figure 48, we could imagine two (in a series of) maps used to describe, say, the motor car market. Just to explain the workings of the mapping process, let us assume that the criteria shown on the maps are as follows:

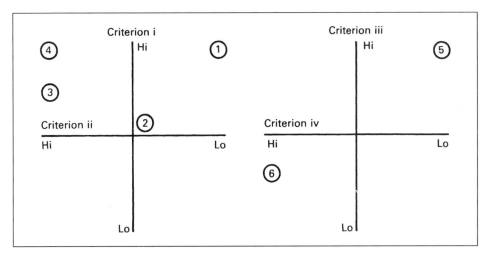

Figure 48   Market mapping

- economy;
- performance;
- safety; and
- styling.

Very simplistic, I know, but we can imagine that market research has shown the existence of the following market segments motivated by a motor car offering:

- high economy/low performance;
- average economy/average performance;
- above average economy/high performance;
- high performance/high economy (the holy grail!);
- high safety/low styling; and
- below average safety/high styling.

If we were then to overlay the existing product offerings on the same maps (based of course on customer perceptions of the benefits which each brand offered) we would be able to see the match between what the market wants and what the market thinks it is being offered. Gaps may be evident between need and offering, although all may not be capable of satisfaction (high performance/high economy or high performance/low price).

To look at a real example, a major European retail banking organization conducted in-depth motivational research of its prime marketplace and drew out a number of key criteria which motivated people to use banks and other financial institutions. After a long period of fairly detailed market research, they discovered that the two most important criteria that were being used were whether people felt confident in dealing with financial institutions, and secondly whether money, in itself, was important in their lives. Without going into detail of the analysis, to continue the example we will consider the extremes of these two continua, we have four separate and identifiable market segments:

- Those who are confident in dealing with institutions and to whom money is important.
- Those who are confident in dealing with institutions but to whom money of itself is not important.
- Those who lack confidence but to whom money is important.
- Those to whom money is not important but also lack confidence in dealing with the institutions.

It takes little imagination to see the very different marketing strategies which will be required to successfully penetrate these four segments.

Once potential market segments have been identified in this qualitative way, the next step is to find out how many people actually identify with these various broad macro segments. If, for example, the bank above were to discover that the 'low confidence/low interest in money' segment included less than five per cent of the population, maybe it should think twice before attacking this segment at all.

As with all pseudo-scientific methodologies in marketing, we run the risk of the technique becoming more important than the output. If you feel the need to know more about mapping techniques generally there are a number of good publications which describe the process in more detail. There may even be someone in your organization who understands the process and who can carry out the analysis for you – this leaves you free to concentrate on the implications of the analysis. The most important thing to remember about gap analysis is that the value of the outputs are only as good as the thinking and the input which goes into the analysis in the first place.

As we discussed in review of market segmentation, there is a great temptation to use descriptions of behaviour such as demographics too early in the analysis. It is the underlying motivators which are most important to long-term marketing strategy and these must be used for any map criteria function at a strategic level. Above all, anybody using these mapping techniques must realize that they are only a first stage in the identification process of possible and potential market segments. Maps are a conceptual approach to laying out the marketplace in visual form and showing what market segments may exist. After this, any detailed marketing strategy must be preceded by much more detailed research and analysis to uncover the precise needs of the market segment, the size of the segment, the distribution of the segment and ways in which the segment might be accessed profitably. Market gap analysis will not generate these results on its own.

One, very last, comment. Maps are sometimes used by managers who want to express their subjective views as objective facts. Don't fall into this trap.

The product (needs) gap

Gap analysis here is taken one level down and can now be used to look beyond the market at a specified market segment. The objective of product gap analysis is to plot, again visually and conceptually, the specific needs of a market segment and the corresponding products which are perceived as satisfying those needs – the analysis should include both your organization's products and competitive offerings.

There are two common methods of visually depicting the product gap. The first is to use the mapping procedure described above, but here remember we are concentrating on one particular segment rather than the overall marketplace. We are concerned with uncovering the most important needs/wants of the members of the market segment – these should also be the key criteria by which they differentiate and therefore choose between the competing product offerings made to them. There are a number of well known and tried techniques for listing this information but this is getting to a level of detailed market research which is really not the subject of this book.

As an example, let us take the case of a sports-related health drink. The most important needs may be taste, price, energy content, artificial additives and so on. Out of this analysis a series of maps contrasting each time to key criteria would produce visual representations of the various composite needs of the marketplace. By then merging these various maps (probably computer-aided if you are able to understand the output) we could envisage an optimum product offering of medium price, good taste, no additives, high energy content.

The next stage is, again, to move from qualitative to quantitative work and to attempt to discover the relative importance of the product attribute combinations within the overall market segments (S1, S2). A touch of reality is always useful when using these techniques, for example, the extreme positions of all the maps should be considered cautiously. If there is no demand for a high additive, high price, high taste product it is not worth pursuing; the high energy, high taste, very low price position may be very popular but if it can't be produced there is little point in the organization pursuing it too far.

Once the product gap analysis has been quantified in this way, the third step is to return to the members of the market segment and to find out from them how they position the various existing products/services/ brands (B1, B2) against the composite positions which have been identified from the previous research. This final addition to the map will now produce an overall visual representation of the market needs in terms of the benefits or solutions which it is seeking from products, as well as the relative positioning of your organization's products and the competition's products within the marketplace. Gaps may suggest themselves in terms of unoccupied space on the map (see Figure 49).

Gap analysis is never more than an initial, conceptual approach to finding out what is going on in the marketplace. The very best gap analysis can point towards specific research which may need to be carried out in greater depth. The most important contribution that gap analysis can make to marketing strategy is to provoke questions. The sort of questions that this form of product gap analysis should be provoking are:

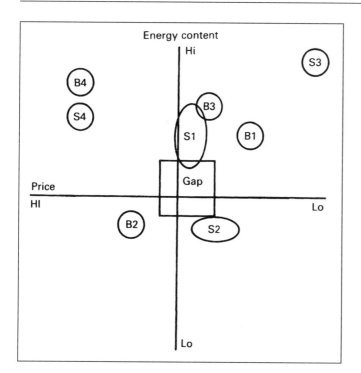

Figure 49 Product (needs) gap

- Is there a difference in how we are positioning our product and how the market appears to be perceiving this position?
- Is there a sufficient and understood difference between the various products within our range?
- Are we positioning close to competitive offerings and if so are we clearly differentiated from them in the marketplace?
- Are there any empty areas of the map which would appear to show unsatisfied demands that we may be able to develop profitably?
- If so, can these areas be developed with whole new products or are we facing a repositioning?

The skill of marketing is in, not how we ask, but how we respond to these questions.

The second and very popular approach to product gap analysis is by using what is called a cluster diagram. Once again we have the modern computer to thank (blame?) for the rapid rise in popularity of this procedure since it does require some fairly powerful number processing to produce results (see Figure 50).

In its simplest terms, cluster analysis involves taking all of the information we discussed previously from the members of the market segment (needs/wants, the relative importance of the needs, perceptions etc.) and

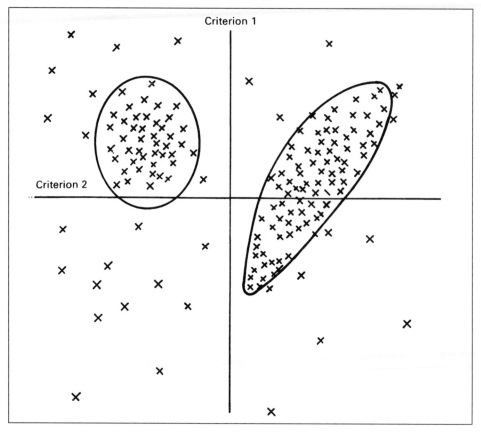

Figure 50   Cluster diagram

feeding these into the computer database. The computer analysis will then generate its own series of maps internally and will finally produce one or a series of diagrams which plot the various responses according to the most relevant criteria. The analysis of the output then consists of identifying the denser plots (clusters) of these responses. The clustering will be attempting to sort responses to produce major clusters with as much similarity within groups and as much difference between groups as possible. While the computer is able to generate the clusters from the input data it is the analyst's job to identify and label these clusters in market terms.

The image gap

Image gap analysis can be considered to be something of an offshoot of the previous forms of gap analysis. Using the techniques described above, the main objective of an image gap analysis is for the organization to plot the perceived image of its corporate identity of its product range and individual product lines in the eyes of these target market segments. It is also useful to plot these image perceptions comparatively against competitive offerings. The sort of questions which image gap analysis should be able to provoke might be:

- How does our target market perceive us as an organization?
- How do they perceive our products in terms of quality, pricing, reliability, etc.?
- How does our image relate to that of the competition?
- What is the difference between our existing image and how we would like it to be?
- Is our target image position vacant or occupied by a competitor?

The activity gap

Activity gap analysis can, if you prefer, be considered part of the image gap analysis. It really extends the process from image gap analysis and asks one more very important question. Given, first, our existing image in the marketplace and, second, the marketplace image that we need to have in order to achieve our business objective, two questions follow:

- Are there any precise activities that we are not doing that the market would either require from us or expect us to be doing?
- Are there any activities which we are currently doing which the market would consider to be incompatible with our market image?

By activities here, we may mean segments approached, products marketed and also the method of marketing in terms of distribution channels, pricing policy, promotion policy and so on. Again a comparative analysis would be useful – comparing the responses for the competitors as well as ourselves helps to give an additional fix and point the way for future marketing strategy.

The competitive gap

The competitive gap is another derivative of the previous gaps that we have already discussed. Nevertheless, it warrants a separate mention since it is directly related to the areas of business strategy, competitive advantage, competitive opportunities and competitive analysis.

In the area of business strategy we will be concerned primarily with the organization's strengths and weaknesses and the competitor's ability to compete at a business level. In terms of marketing strategy, we will be much more concerned with our activities in the marketplace and our competitors' ability to market in an effective and efficient manner. So the emphasis must shift from detailed business analysis, economic and financial comparisons to one of comparing the all important customer perceptions of ourselves and our competitors.

Straightforward maps, based on marketplace descriptions, showing the different positions which are held by ourselves and our major competitors can be a powerful competitive tool. Competitive gap analysis can be an invaluable aid when attempting to position your organization and your product/services. Gap analysis can highlight the areas of marketing activity where the competition is strongest and also where the competition is perceived to be weaker. Since head-to-head competition is always expensive in terms of retained profits it should be avoided wherever possible.

The analogy of a map through a minefield does have I feel, some validity when we start looking at the area of competitive gap analysis.

Marketer's note

Gap analysis, in all its various forms, can be quite a powerful tool for analysing and describing situations in the marketplace. However, as with any analytical technique, while there are benefits which flow from its use, there are also dangers for the unwary.

The first point to make is that with any form of analogy the output is only as good as the input. Low quality input can produce nothing but low quality output, even when reduced to three decimal points!

Second, the aim of gap analysis and mapping is to give a pictorial representation of a situation which we believe subjectively exists in the marketplace. It should be seen as a precursor to more detailed market research. It is unlikely to be sufficient analysis on its own.

The third main danger is likely to come from your colleagues, while you may understand the nature of cluster analysis, mapping, gap analysis in general, managers who have graduated from a more scientific and disciplined function such as engineering or accountancy may find it difficult to appreciate the essentially illustrative nature of the process. Worse, the harder you have to 'sell' the ideas, the more they are likely to see them as objective representation of 'facts'. They may want to read too much into the results and may push for marketing strategy decisions to be made too early.

Just to end the section on gap analysis, I leave you with one thought – there may be a gap in the market but the art is discovering whether there is a market in the gap.

Market share

I have decided to include a short section on the important subject of market share at this point in our discussion of marketing strategy. This is done, not with the intention of going into the subject in any great depth and looking at the many theories and concepts which abound in the area, but rather with the intention of trying to dispel one or two myths. There is, in my opinion, a need to help the marketing executive of the 1990s deal with the topic of market share in a more reasonable fashion than has been done hitherto (see Figure 51).

The idea of market share is certainly a key concept in the development of marketing strategy but it is just that – a concept. It is not, and cannot be, a definitive scientific measurement of our relative position in any given marketplace. Its primary importance comes from the fact that we use it as a shorthand method of relating our position in any given market-place to that of our competitors. As we have already seen, it is not the only method for comparing ourselves with our competitors – it is probably not even the most efficient. It does, though, have one great virtue – it is very easy to understand.

As well as the term market share, often expressed in punchy percentages, we also come across terms such as market leader, market follower, dominant market position and so on. The question is, just what do these terms mean? More importantly, can they actually add anything to the general discussion on marketing strategy?

The first problem which faces us is how to actually define the market-place. If we take the example of the car market, we hear regularly about the relative market positions of Ford and General Motors in various markets across the world. If we look beyond the simple numbers, we

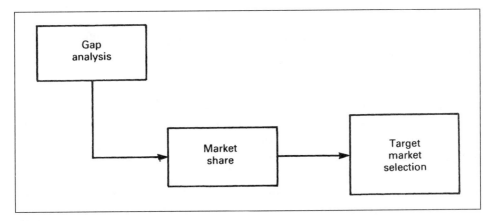

Figure 51　Market share

suddenly find other definitions such as 'the volume car market', 'the commercial market', 'the luxury car market', 'the sports car market', 'the economy car market', and so the definitions proliferate. We should remember that any time a measure is used for comparative purposes, then it is essential that the base used for the measure is a standard base otherwise comparisons have no meaning. Also, modern trends would seem to indicate that people are moving away from the concept of a mass market, markets are fragmenting and the appearance of quite different and quite novel segments can only conspire to provide even more complicated measurements (and so of less comparative value) in expressions like market share.

So we get the quantification of market share – down to single percentage points, even decimals of percentage points! There are two questions which the rational investigator will raise at this point:

- Just how were these measurements taken?
- Knowing that the marketplace, any marketplace, is a dynamic system, what validity have these measurements over any reasonable period of time?

The big trouble with quantification is that as soon as numbers are placed on any concept, everybody starts to believe them. Few, if any, people will look behind the numbers.

Last, there are all the absolute terms to consider such as 'market leader', 'market follower', 'dominant market position' and so on. We must ask ourselves whether these terms still have any real value in the 1990s. Depending on how we define the marketplace, a ninety-eight per cent market share can quite reasonably be described as a dominant market position. On the other hand our five per cent market share, if all of our competitors have one per cent or two per cent each, is also a dominant market position. But does this mean that the pressures on the dominant organization will be the same in these two markets, that their strategy should be the same and that in fact they will have to act in the same way? I strongly doubt it.

You are probably thinking that all this is a somewhat pessimistic view of what you believed was a fairly simple and easily understood measure of your organization's success and performance in its marketplace. You should understand that much of the thinking on market share originated in the 1970s and the original work carried out by organizations such as the Boston Consulting Group. Twenty years ago the world was different and the mass market was a reality – growth in economies and markets and organizations was a prerequisite and size was quite reasonably correlated with profit. The logical route then was to grow, to increase market share and thereby increase profits – a simple equation.

The 1990s is looking less and less like the 1970s and serious questions are now starting to be asked about this preoccupation with growth and market share. Why should this be? Most of the cause, not surprisingly, resides with the marketplace or the customer. Generally, disposable incomes have improved over the past twenty years and expectations have risen to match – no longer are people satisfied with standard mass-produced products, they are now much more concerned, certainly in the advanced western markets of the world, with products and services which enhance their perception of themselves as individuals and not as simple mass consumers. Everywhere, east and west, we are seeing the rejection of the values of a mass-production society. All this simply makes the economies of scale for a mass production that much more difficult to achieve. Unfortunately, it also makes markets more difficult to control.

In the 1970s, the large, dominant organizations could look forward to significant economies of scale through large standardized production lines as well as a degree of control over the marketplace and the ability to dictate, at least to some extent, what people would buy. Now, more sophisticated buyers are actively searching out products and services which are different. This 'new' demand is tending to be serviced by smaller, flexible, more innovative organizations – organizations not hidebound by a long history and strong beliefs in the 'right way to do things'.

In short, for the new millennium, size looks less and less likely to be correlated with profitability, and of course profitability must be the ultimate goal of any organization. Absolute size, per se, is looking less and less attractive as an objective. Add this to the diminishing role of dominant organizations in controlling the marketplace, it is not surprising that many, more enlightened organizations are starting to re-think the role of market share in their overall marketing objectives.

Marketer's note

For those of you that would like to understand the techniques and mechanics involved in identifying relative market share, a reasonably easy to follow explanation of the two BCG models as well as the McKinsey/GEC model and the product life cycle analysis is to be found in *Marketing Plans* by Malcolm McDonald (published by Butterworth-Heinemann).

If you do decide to make use of these models do remember that they can be treated as purely conceptual models, in which case trying to put numbers to them is a fairly dangerous exercise. Alternatively, if you wish to pursue them in a more technical and scientific way, you should know that the mathematics underlying the models is extremely complicated indeed, and in fact based on models of markets that have, in many cases, disappeared.

One final word of warning for the unwary, any model, whether in marketing or in any other discipline is only as good as the data on which it was initially based. Many of these models, dealing as they do with human nature and consumer behaviour, require inputs that are essentially subjective in nature. Where the inputs for a model are subjective, no amount of complicated mathematical processing is going to transform opinions into facts. If you start off by feeding in opinions then you will get opinions out – albeit to mathematical precision.

One last observation. Preoccupation with market share can tend to reduce all strategic decisions to the tactical level. This comes as a great relief to many of the 'hands-on' marketers but does the organization no long-term good at all. Tactics will be important – at the right time.

A rallying call, as if you need one, when dealing with the market share zellots could be 'revenue is vanity, profits are sanity'.

Level of involvement

We have already seen, in the discussion of market attractiveness, that the organization's target market can be made up of a number of discreet and different segments. We have also seen that these different segments vary or can vary quite markedly in terms of their significance and potential for the organization whether it be in profit, volume or long-term strategic terms. It logically follows from this argument then that when the organization is considering its various market segments, its degree of commitment to different segments can and almost certainly will vary widely (see Figure 52).

There are a number of ways in which the organization can engage in marketing to its various market segments. The organization is able to choose strategically the level of involvement which would most suit it on a segment by segment basis and can choose how it markets to various segments. The range of choice, in ascending order of involvement in the market segments are:

- casual or accidental marketing;
- third-party marketing;
- proxy marketing;
- active selling; and
- active marketing.

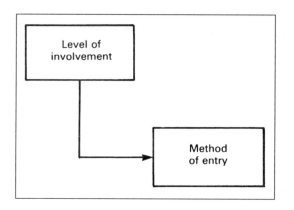

Figure 52 Level of involvement

Casual or accidental marketing

This is essentially a passive form of involvement. The organization may be selling into a particular market segment without even knowing it. There are typically three reasons for this type of marketing (it might be argued that this is not a marketing choice if the organization sells into a segment without realizing it – but it is marketing).

First, casual or accidental marketing can be caused by an uncontrolled distribution channel, for example, intermediaries buying from other intermediaries and selling the product or service on through channels to consumers other than those originally planned for and targeted for by the organization itself.

Second, it could be due to the end user or consumer who has discovered a secondary or additional use for the product or service and who is purchasing in order to achieve solutions or acquire benefits completely different from those originally foreseen by the organization. Examples of these type of secondary usage would be the use of Coca-Cola as a soaking agent to remove rust from metal.

The third and probably most common reason for this type of marketing is quite simply the lack of precise organizational and product positioning by the organization itself. An imprecise or fuzzy market positioning not only makes clear differentiation and market penetration more difficult it also encourages end users and potential end users to experiment with the product or service in question.

It is, in fact, quite disappointing to discover just how frequently organizations are surprised by the usage to which their products or services are put. It must also be said that while these alternative usages may come as a surprise to many marketing departments they are often much less of a surprise to the sales force who knew about it all along – there is a message here I believe.

While this sort of casual or accidental marketing may occur in a large number of organizations, it does not really represent any true commitment or involvement in the marketing process. Nevertheless, its occurrence needs to be identified and understood. If there is a significant amount of casual or accidental marketing happening in your organization, then you should be asking yourself some questions. First, is your existing targeting to your primary market segments tight enough? In other words, are you making the most of your segment opportunities and making a product offer that your target audience can identify with?

Second, you might ask yourself whether there is evidence, or sufficient evidence, to believe that a whole new target segment exists in the marketplace that you had not previously identified. More opportunistic organizations may even see such accidental segments as a way of unloading unexpected surpluses or even obsolete stocks as long as there is no direct link between the 'accidental' segments and your primary target segments and that there will be no knock-on effect of such 'dumping'.

Third-party marketing

Third-party marketing means selling and marketing into a segment but not through the overt use of the organization's name and image. Own-label marketing falls into this category. There may be a number of strategic reasons why the organization does not wish to be seen to be marketing into a given segment at a particular time.

It may be justifiable for the organization to generate revenue flow and also maintain the general buoyancy of the market segment although it does not wish to be actively associated with that segment either because it would not fit with the overall image of the organization or because the time is not yet right for its inclusion in the organization's sphere of business. In these instances it can be quite useful to become actively involved in these market segments but through the offices of a third party. The packaged food industry is rife with examples of organizations which maintain premier branded products with large sophisticated marketing support but at the same time are very active in the supply of bulk products for own-label brands ostensibly produced by the supermarket chains.

In a number of instances, third-party marketing by large organizations is carried out simply for revenue purposes. In the past, some organizations have risen from supplying own-label products and, having a certain size of operation, have graduated to compete in the branded sector becoming a threat to existing players. A number of organizations now see involvement in the own-label market as a way of blocking out potential competition from the far more important and lucrative branded markets.

Proxy marketing

Proxy marketing is quite closely linked to third-party marketing but is an increase in the level of involvement of the organization in certain market segments. Proxy marketing can be seen as similar in style to licensing and may indeed even involve some form of joint venture between two organizations for marketing activity into a given segment. Often based on some form of longer term partnership agreement between two or possibly more organizations, proxy marketing can give real benefits to all parties of the agreement.

This method of marketing is most often used where an organization has quite significant product and marketing expertise in certain market segments but lacks the specific expert knowledge of additional market segments to enable it to market in these new areas successfully. The search and acquisition of a partner who understands in more detail the intricacies of the 'new' target market segments can bring benefits to both parties. Marketing by proxy in this way, while does not necessarily encourage long-term expansion of the organization into the new segments (legal arrangements may prevent), can be extremely useful for organizations who wish to expand their area of operations but are aware that they have limited and possibly specialized expertise that would not allow them to annex new segments without major investment.

Active selling

Another approach employed by some organizations, although not necessarily always to be recommended, is active selling. By active selling we mean that the organization has decided to participate actively and openly in a segment. It is typically a high level of involvement in the marketing process, although the use of the word selling rather than marketing implies that the organization is led more by short-term sales requirements than by any need or desire to develop long-term customer relationships. Nevertheless, the active selling approach to market segments is a very high level of involvement and does signify a quite high level of commitment, certainly in terms of management time and resource to developing a market segment for serious revenue purposes.

Active marketing

This is the highest level of involvement that an organization can decide to take with regard to its market segments. By active marketing we mean that the organization has decided that the segment in question is important to its long-term future. It has decided to invest the executive time and finance required to properly understand the present and likely future needs of the customers who make up the target market segments and will develop long-term plans to satisfy these needs. Typically the organization's activities in these segments are highly visible and marketing activity is concerned with market segment defence against incursive competition as well as with the development of the market segment and the organization's penetration of that segment over the longer term. In the case of active marketing we would expect most of the organization's business activities to be carried out in these segments, in other words the organization is into the market segment with both feet.

The discussion on the level of involvement in market segments shows that as the organization considers the universe of its market segments it finds a wide range of possibilities for marketing involvement as well as a wide range of profit possibilities. The larger the organization, the wider the range of choices open to its management. Even the smaller organization can successfully operate in a range of market segments through a mixture of types of involvement appropriate to its own position and resources.

Marketer's note

The list of different levels of involvement which I have given above is meant to be neither absolute in their definition nor so clearly separated as I have made them appear in their description. My intention was rather to illustrate the range of choices open to the organization in the way in which it may deal with its target market segments. The decision to approach a given market segment is not necessarily an all-or-nothing decision, you do have a choice over the degree of involvement which you are willing or able to take on.

Also, there is no implied progression through the five stages for example, an organization does not have to progress from casual or accidental marketing through to active marketing going through all the stages. There are some examples of this happening but it should not be seen as a blueprint for future activity.

After having read through this section, and having direct responsibility for your organization's marketing, you may want to look a little closer at your organization's marketing activity throughout your various segments. There are a few questions that you may want to ask yourself about your activity. For example, can you see evidence of your marketing being exclusively in one of the areas described above or are you more flexible in your approach and do you tend to tailor your level of involvements to the needs of the market segments and your overall understanding of your organization's goals? Naturally the size of your organization will also be a major factor in this question – the larger the scale of the organization, the more one would expect to find a variety of levels of involvement as different segments are brought into play over the long term of the strategic plan.

A second question which can be quite telling is, in your opinion, has the present situation and levels of involvement come about as a result of accidents and lack of marketing control or can you identify evidence of a more planned and structured approach to the market segments in which you operate?

The last question you might want to ask yourself (this of course rather depends on the answers which you have been able to digest from the past two questions) is about the history of your levels of involvement in market segments. The level of involvement is strategic in nature. It is a strategic decision – which segments to approach in which order and with what allocation of resource. In a number of organizations, these decisions tend not to be made at strategic level, rather, the organization's different levels of involvement are often the results of piecemeal tactical decisions having been made lower down the organization. A piecemeal, essentially tactical approach to the organization's level of involvement is unlikely to be the most efficient method of allocating scarce resource over the longer term. If you find that these decisions have historically been made at a tactical level, this may be the opportunity to grab back the reins on an important strategic area.

Method of market entry

Distribution, for both manufactured products and for services, has long been recognized as a critical area of marketing and marketing success. However, the extremely important distinction between the problem of market entry and distribution policy per se has, up to now, not been properly recognized in the domestic marketing literature. (See Figure 53.) I have broken this important area into two separate sections – the method of market entry which is all about how the organization should get the product or service into the target market; and the distribution policy which we will consider in Part Three within the larger question of distribution or 'place' policy. The second reason for making this split is that we should consider method of market entry as a strategic decision whereas distribution policy is effectively of a more tactical nature. The

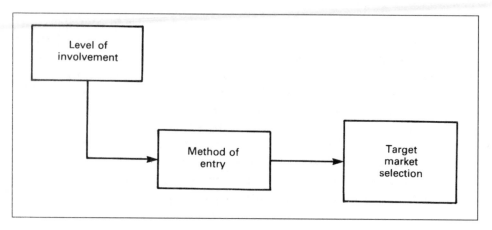

Figure 53   Method of market entry

distinction between these two areas will become apparent as we look more in detail at the whole problem which faces the organization at this point.

   The distinction between the method of market entry and internal distribution policy has long been understood and very well explained in the marketing literature related to international marketing. It has long been seen as one of the most critical decisions to be made in international marketing since the chosen method of entry many not only require large amounts of organizational resource but also because the chosen method of entry will largely dictate the freedom that the international marketing organization has to operate and market within the foreign country at a later date. The distinction between market entry and distribution policy has not traditionally been drawn in domestic market situations because, while overseas markets are visibly very different from each other, it was always felt that the various market segments within one domestic market were much more homogeneous in nature. Today, with the growth of individualism and the fragmentation of society, it is proving to be much less the case. Different market segments within one country can often vary greatly, both in terms of their needs and their general description. Consequently, as the various market segments diverge there is less and less justification for a standardized distribution or method of entry policy for all the segments.

   Method of market entry, is also important because it is this which, by and large, will dictate the freedom and potential for the organization to market within that segment over the short to medium term. As we shall see, method of market entry like the whole area of marketing strategy is essentially a question of balance (see Figure 54).

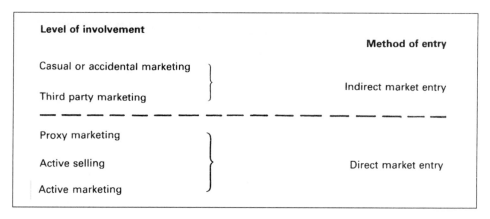

Figure 54 Level of involvement and method of market entry. *Source:* Adapted from Terpstra V., *International Marketing* (Dryden Press, 1983).

In general terms, there are two very broad methods of market entry. The organization can choose to enter a market indirectly or directly.

Indirect market entry

There are a range of indirect market entry methods, but the one character-istic which links all these methods together is that the organization does not intend to build a direct franchise with the end user of the product or service which they produce. Typically, indirect market entry methods involve the use of some form of intermediary or middleman in the process between the producing organization and the ultimate end consumer. The role of the intermediary will depend on the nature of the industry, the convention of the business and, importantly, the perceived needs of the target marketplace. The organization may consider using wholesalers, retailers, franchises, tailor-made specific marketing organizations, and so on.

The essence of an indirect market entry method is that the organiza-tion will limit itself to marketing to the intermediary or the channel and will not attempt to create a direct franchise with the end user. The middle-men, intermediaries or channel managers will themselves be responsible for building any form of franchise with the end user in the marketplace.

Direct market entry

Methods of direct market entry may also use intermediaries in some form but may also involve the organization in dealing direct with the end user.

The essence of a direct entry method is that the organization takes responsibility for building its franchise or a direct link between itself and its end users. When the organization embarking on a direct market entry method uses intermediaries then its demands on the intermediaries and the channels of distribution will be slightly different from those organizations using an indirect market entry method. It will typically rely on the intermediaries and the channel to provide distribution and logistics services. While the organization may involve itself in some partnership with a distribution network to create the franchise and link with the end user, final responsibility for this long-term organization–consumer link lies with the organization itself.

Where the organization decides to use direct methods of market entry they have the choice of distributing and dealing on a direct basis with the end user, this applies for both outward-bound financial services and also for much after-sales and maintenance. In this case, the distribution channels may be the organization's own or under their direct control, there may be a joint venture arrangement or partnership agreements of some sort to ensure this direct producer/consumer interface.

The organization can also enter markets directly with the use of independent intermediary or distribution channels. If the distribution policy aspects of the market are handled by an independent channel manager then the organization takes much more responsibility on itself for the promotional and branding aspects of the marketing function. The end consumer must be able to identify directly with the producing organization via the distribution channel and is not left identifying itself with the distribution channel itself.

Decision criteria for method of entry

There are two levels of criteria by which the organization is or should be able to decide on the most appropriate entry for any given market segment. The first set of decision criteria emerge from the previous discussion on business strategy and the four broad areas which can be expected to influence the organization's decision are the following.

First, company goals regarding the volume of business required from the various segments. The expected breadth and coverage of different segments in the marketplace and the organization's general market based aspirations over the longer term.

The second major factor which will impinge on this decision is the size of the company both in terms of sales and in terms of resources. The larger the organization, the more it is able to embark on direct methods of entry in more segments since it has the resources to invest in this way.

The third factor which should be taken into mind is the nature of the organization's products and/or services. High-price or low-price products, technologically complicated, technologically quite simple products, will have quite different needs in terms of market support and this will affect the decision on method of market entry.

The fourth area to be considered is the nature of competition both industry-wide and on a segment-by-market basis. If competition is entrenched in the target market segment and a 'conventional' method of market entry has been established by the resident competitor then it may be difficult to choose a quite different entry method, simply because the consumers expectations have already been fixed by competitive activity.

There is a second and more detailed level of decision criteria which the organization should be applying when considering market entry and these fall more under the category of marketing strategy decisions. The following are not meant to be exclusive or definitive but rather should act as a first cut list to demonstrate the variety of choice which is involved.

Number of markets

Different methods of entry will offer different advantages depending on the nature of the different market segments under consideration. It is quite likely that any given method of entry which works well in one market segment will simply not be plausible or feasible in another segment, in these cases the organization will need to be flexible in its approach. Also, if the organization has a large number of different market segments which it wishes to approach then indirect market entry methods may, because of the reduced need for direct organizational resource, allow the organization to approach and attack relatively more market segments than it would be able to with direct market entry methods.

Penetration within markets

The required level of penetration in any given market segment will be a function both of the organization's needs and goals and of the specific market segment and its characteristics. Direct market entry methods offer a potentially higher level of market penetration than do indirect market entry methods. The organization has a greater level of control over the marketing activity and is much better able to focus its attention on the marketplace and the customers within it.

Market feedback

A higher level both in quality and quantity terms of market feedback is possible if the organization has a direct communication link with the target market segment. If, because of the nature of the product and/or the organization and/or the target market segment, the level of market feedback required for successful marketing operation is relatively high (for example the fashion industry) then direct market entry methods will be favoured in this situation. Indirect market entry methods often mean that while the intermediary or distributor of the products and/or service may obtain high quality market feedback, there is no guarantee of this market feedback being passed onto the organization.

Marketing learning

Experience is still the best way of improving our marketing performance over time. A long-term relationship with a market segment depends on the organization's ability to understand the market segments and to predict and move with those needs. The organization that wants to grow with the segment should choose a market entry method which gives it direct experience and involvement in the market and thereby allows it to learn from its successes as well as its mistakes. The organization cannot 'learn by doing' if others are doing the marketing on its behalf.

Control

Management control over the marketing function will vary greatly from almost no control at all (the product is sold into a central wholesaler or distributor who then looks after the entire marketing to the end user) to complete control over all elements of marketing mix (where the organization has embarked on a direct method of market entry to create an enduring franchise with the end user). The extent to which this management control is seen as important to the organization will strongly determine the organization's choice of market entry methods.

Incremental marketing costs

Whatever else marketing does, we all know that marketing costs money. Expanding the organization's activities into further, new market segments will always require an increase in investment and capital in the marketplace. The organization will have to make a decision as to the extent of the investment and how far it wishes to proceed along this route. Generally, indirect entry methods require less additional expenditure while more direct methods may be extremely capital hungry in the short to medium term.

Profit potential

Profit, and especially longer term profit is, as we all know, the ultimate goal of marketing strategy. As we have already seen, the associated costs differ widely among the various methods of market entry, so also (and not surprisingly) profit potential also can be expected to differ depending on the method of market entry chosen. Depending on the organization's ability to market successfully within the target market segment, potential profits, especially longer term profits, should be greater from direct methods of market entry rather than indirect (fewer margins to pay out).

Personnel requirements

While it is obvious that the method of market entry will have a direct impact on the level of financial commitment and investment and long-term potential return that comes from any given market segment, what is often less evident is the additional personnel requirements which can be driven by the organization's choice of method of market entry. Generally, the more direct the method of market entry, then the greater will be the strain of the existing personnel in the organization (in terms of the numbers of people and specific expertise required). The deeper the organization expects to become involved in the target market segment, the more it is important that the personnel within the organization have a degree of affinity and empathy with the target market segments. As the organization then expands into the market segments under its control, the diversity and nature of the people in the organization who have day-to-day contact with the segments will need to expand and vary accordingly.

Flexibility

There are two aspects to the question of flexibility and the organization will have to decide where it feels most comfortable on these continua. The first aspect concerns the organization's strategic view of its future. If we expect to be active in the new market segments for the long term then the organization will need a degree of flexibility in its methods of entry. Any entry method which is right at one point is quite likely to be less than ideal in five years' time. Not only do market conditions change but also the organization's situation and business objective is also likely to modify itself over time. The organization will need some degree of flexibility, in other words, the ability to change to meet the evolving needs of a dynamic business environment. The organization's ability to be flexible and to change as market situations change over time, will be much greater if the organization has already planned for this degree of flexibility when it was originally choosing its method of market entry.

The second important aspect of flexibility concerns the organization's willingness to test its abilities and its offer in the marketplace. Not every foray into a new market segment will be successful, failure is a reality of business life. Indirect market entry methods allow the organization a greater degree of flexibility to test market response in relative safety. Withdrawal from unsuccessful market experiments which have been approached indirectly is less painful for the organization, its markets and its core segments than withdrawal from a market which it has entered directly with all the visibility and exposure which this brings.

Risk

As the organization expands, it tends to do so by annexing segments which are progressively further and further away from its original core business segments. As the organization spreads its interest in this way then of course the new segments carry a relatively higher degree of risk since management starts to move into less and less well-charted waters. Naturally, by using indirect market methods the degree of financial and marketing risk can, to some extent, be reduced but obviously this carries penalties in terms of short-term profits, marketing control and so on. The organization must determine the level of risk it is happiest to take on. The risk associated with its activities should be carefully analysed before deciding the most appropriate method of market entry.

Marketer's note

Method of market entry is another area where strategic decisions are often made at a tactical level. It is important therefore to understand, and make sure everybody else in your organization understands, that method of market entry is in fact a strategic decision and should be taken with care and after sufficient analysis of the alternatives.

The main reason why the importance of carefully selecting the correct method of market entry cannot be over emphasized is because the entry method will dictate the degree of flexibility, control and manoeuvre which your organization has when it comes to marketing in the target market segment. It is one thing to limit exposure and risk by handing a new product or service over to an intermediary, and sit back and count whatever profits arise from the marketplace. It is quite another thing to see the market segment expand rapidly while being managed and marketed in a way which you find uncomfortable and over which you have no control. Even worse, if you have made no plans to eventually take control of the marketplace down the line, you are denying your organization the long-term profit and growth it needs.

Distribution/'place' policy (as we shall see later) is all about how we should physically distribute our product or service within the target market – a tactical marketing decision. How we enter the market in the first place is not

---

part of place policy decisions, it is far too important for that. Ignorance of this distinction between the strategic and the tactical has produced a number of organizations (especially in packaged groceries and UK financial services) that find their entire marketing strategy has become 'distribution-led'. Without sufficient analysis these organizations have simply entered the market through traditional routes and have found themselves torn between satisfying intermediary needs and satisfying customer needs. This is not a situation any self-respecting marketer should fall into. If this situation sounds familiar, look at your market entry strategy, how was it determined? Was it discussed at all? If you were to start from scratch, what would you do now?

Uncomfortable questions can often be the most enlightening!

Target market selection – conclusions

As we have come now to the end of the detailed market analysis stage of the strategic process, I am wondering just how many of my readers are starting to feel more than a little frustrated because we still haven't really started to talk about what we should actually be doing about any of this. While this sense of frustration is quite understandable it should be regarded as something of a hangover from the 'action-manager' syndrome of the 1970s and the 1980s when organizations believed that they had some degree of control over the marketplace itself. As we move through the 1990s to the new millennium, more and more organizations are starting to realize they do not, in fact, control the marketplace and that as time goes by they have less and less power to do so. Success in the future will almost certainly come to those organizations who are best able to read the marketplace, read the needs of customers and react to these needs. These will be the organizations that recognize that the market controls the profit which controls the organization. (See Figure 55.)

What we have covered in this section really falls into two separate categories. First, there is the question of our customers. We have spent some time looking at who our customers are, what they want, how they are motivated and how our customers group themselves into self-standing segments. Finally, we looked at how these segments might be organized and the alternatives open to us in terms of selecting the most attractive market segments to satisfy our broad business strategy requirements. We also looked, albeit briefly, at how information on our customers and their needs might be obtained through the market research procedure.

Broadening the discussion slightly, we then started to look at how we might analyse gaps in the marketplace, gaps of various sorts, including

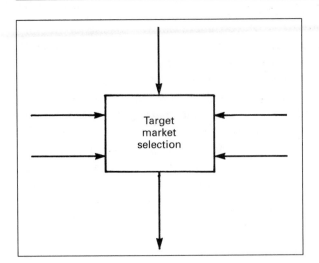

Figure 55 Target market selection

competitive gaps, product gaps and activity/image gaps. Last, we looked at the possible methods of market entry which might be open to the organization given the particular circumstances and situations of individual market segments.

It is very important, when considering target market selection, not to pre-judge the likely marketing activity which the organization could use to annex these markets. It is very important but also very difficult to concentrate on the alternatives with a completely open mind. It is only by having all the alternatives on the table that we can possibly move to the next stage. What is the organization going to do about all this? It is only by uncovering all the alternatives that the organization will be able to decide what it has to do for marketing success and will not be hidebound by considering only what it is able to do at this point in time.

Chapter 6

Developing marketing strategy

'Thus we may know that there are five essentials for victory:

(1)   He will win who knows when to fight and when not to fight;
(2)   He will win who knows how to handle both superior and inferior forces;
(3)   He will win whose army is animated by the same spirit throughout all its ranks;
(4)   He will win who, prepared himself, waits to take the enemy unprepared;
(5)   He will win who has military capacity and is not interfered with by the sovereign.

'Victory lies in the knowledge of these five points.'

Sun Tzu, 500 BC

So now we reach the kernel of the discussion on strategy, how the organization can proceed to develop its marketing objective and marketing strategy (see Figure 56). However, for those of you that have decided to start reading the book at this point, with the expectation of discovering the answers to all your problems crisply explained on just a few pages, I fear you are about to be mightily disappointed.

A good, robust marketing strategy is just not one of those things that we can pluck out of thin air. Developing a marketing strategy is a critical landmark in the organization's progress. If it is going to be done properly, then significant time, effort and resource will have to be invested. This is, in fact, put up or shut up time.

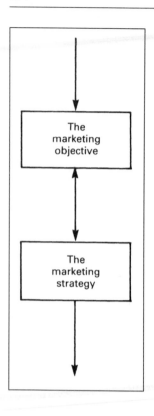

Figure 56   Developing marketing strategy

Those more dogged readers who have at least skimmed through the pages of the book up to this point will have realized, I am sure, that the quality of the marketing strategy decision will only be as good as the quality of the preparation work which leads up to it. If we are to put up, rather than shut up, it is essential that we understand, as far as possible, all the alternatives open to us and the likely outcomes of the various routes that we could take. Mixing my metaphors very badly, we are now at the point of launching a ship – it will be exceedingly difficult to stop half way down the slipway so we must know with a fair degree of confidence just exactly what we are trying to achieve.

Although, in order to explain the implications of marketing objective and marketing strategy, I will deal with these two issues separately. In fact the two areas are quite inextricably linked and should really be dealt with as a combination. The process is very similar to the weighing out of cooking ingredients in old-fashioned kitchen scales. We start with objectives – what the organization wants and needs to achieve in the market-place if it is to satisfy the broader business objective. We then look at marketing strategy – how the marketing objectives may be achieved. Marketing strategy has, necessarily, a cost as well as a revenue element and we may find ourselves having to go back to modify the objectives,

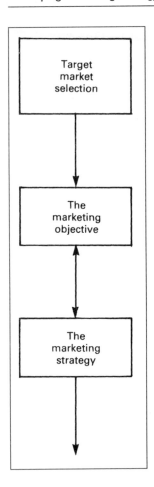

Figure 57   The marketing objective

back to the strategies and back to objectives again so that finally we reach a balance or point of equilibrium where our objectives and our strategies combine to produce the right mix between what we have to do, what we are able to do and the profit that we need to generate.

The marketing objective

While it is difficult to find a modern day text on marketing which does not emphasize the importance of setting objectives, it is equally difficult to find an author who is prepared to commit himself as to the precise nature of marketing objectives – what they are and what they do. To be fair to authors, setting definitions is a quite thankless task given the relative newness of the marketing discipline as well as the number of quite entrenched positions which are to be found in the marketing literature. Any attempt at precise definition of modern marketing terms must inevitably re-label some areas of existing marketing practice as 'wrong'. This, naturally enough, leads to a level of frustration and indignation among the devotees of these previously acceptable behaviours and techniques and, as a result, the words and articles start to fly. (See Figure 57.)

However, not being one to shy from controversy, I intend to lay out what I believe to be the ideal definition of the terms marketing objective and marketing strategy within the context of the overall business and strategic marketing process. Nevertheless, we should all agree that the only true test of marketing is assessed by observable results in the marketplace. If, because of specific market conditions or specific internal organizational conditions, you feel the need to modify and adapt this definition of marketing objectives to suit your own needs and you expect it to produce better results, then you should not feel constrained in any way.

What does the marketing objective do?

The best way of defining any abstract concept is by defining as close as we are able what this concept does and how it is made up. The first question is, what does the marketing objective do for the organization?

Being an objective, it must follow exactly the same rules as previous objectives we have discussed. It must be realistic, measurable, challenging, ambitious, it must be achievable within a set and agreed timespan, and above all, you must know when you have reached it. In the same way that the business objective was the aim or the goal to which all activities within the organization were to be directed, the marketing objective must be seen as the aim or the goal to which all marketing activities in the organization must be directed over the planning period. In short, every activity, both major and minor, carried on in the marketing function must be linked (and be seen to be linked) to the overall marketing objectives of the organization. There is therefore, a very important communications element inherent within the idea of the marketing objective.

In terms of its position within the hierarchy of the organization, the marketing objective must form the solid link between the business objective and strategy and the organization's activity in the marketplace. In skeletal format, the process we have looked at so far has required the organization to determine its mission statement – from this mission statement an understanding of the business environment within which the organization must operate. Senior management's job has been to develop a clear, measurable, understandable business objective and from this business objective a primary business strategy through which the objective will be achieved. After the decisions on the business strategy, we looked at the question of the strategic market position statement, the backdrop against which the organization's market-based activity will be undertaken.

Moving the focus of attention from the corporate to marketing, we have spent some time looking and trying to understand the complexities of the organization's target markets. Our next primary decision point is how to turn the business strategy into a set of clear precise and definable objectives which are capable of being implemented in the organization's marketplaces. This is the role of the marketing objective.

How is the marketing objective expressed?

The only way in which the marketing objective can be expressed is in terms of markets and products. If we stop to think about the fundamental nature of our organizations, the only way in which an organization's business objective and business strategy can be achieved is by interfacing in some way with the external marketplace. The only way the organization can do this is by marketing products and/or services to its customers. It therefore follows that this market/product relationship must be the fundamental plank on which the marketing function operates. The marketing objective then (it seems to me) can only be expressed in market and product terms.

It then also follows logically that unlike the business objective which was singular (one objective for the entire organization), once we move from the internal to the external, in other words the organization's marketplaces, we must come to grips with the need for marketing objectives which are not singular but composite in nature. In other words, we will have to devise an individual marketing objective for each separate market or market segment within which we are currently operating or expect to be operating within the planning period. Naturally, each individual marketing objective must fulfil the same criteria which stands for any objective such as timespan, measurability, and so on.

When you move from being directed by a single objective, to a composite or multiple objectives, it is vitally important that the various component (segment) market objectives be arranged in strict hierarchial order from the most to the least important. This priority ordering must be carried out at the very beginning of the exercise since conflicts are almost sure to arise as we develop the various marketing strategies. There must be an independent and pre-agreed importance of order against which strategic alternatives can be measured.

The work that your organization has already carried out in the identification of target markets, particularly that of market segmentation, customer behaviour and marketing attractiveness, will be used at this point to determine which markets need to be consolidated, which markets annexed and the strategic order in which these activities must be placed. To refresh our memory, the list of criteria which we used to assess market and market segment attractiveness were:

- long-term and volume growth potential;
- long-term profit growth;
- short-term volume growth;
- short-term profit growth;
- organizational image;
- offensive strategic reasons;
- defensive strategic reasons;
- internal resource/capability reasons;
- relative competitive strength; and
- others specific to your organization.

As we stated previously, it will be the primary job of the marketing strategist to strike the critical balance between the long and the short term, between profits today and profits tomorrow and between the needs of the various marketplaces and the strengths and capabilities of the organization.

When you first move into the area of marketing objectives, you should take time to relish the freedom which comes with an essentially theoretical or conceptual approach. For the first pass at marketing objectives we should be concerned primarily with the business objective, the strategic needs of the organization and matching these to the needs of the target marketplaces or market segments. At this stage in the process it is unwise to worry too much about competition and competitive response, it is more important to fix the ideal situation and to lay out clearly what the organization needs (or aspires) to achieve in market terms. The cold light of day will, soon enough, start to cast a shadow on this 'ideal' marketing objective. When we start to consider ways in which these objectives may be achieved, i.e. by developing appropriate marketing strategies, we are almost certain to come up against various things which we simply cannot do because of environmental or competitive positions. This is the point at which we re-visit the marketing objective, we modify and adapt according to the needs of the real world. This should not be a serious problem but it is important to take the opportunity right at the very beginning to position the organization ideally so that when we move away, driven by the practicalities of life, at least we know where we have moved from.

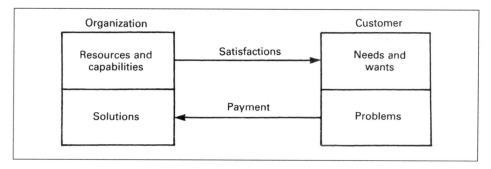

Figure 58 The marketing process. *Source:* Adapted from Wilmshurst J., *The Fundamentals and Practice of Marketing* (Butterworth-Heinemann, Oxford, 1978).

The 'market–product' match

We have said already that the key to the marketing objective must be the market–product match since this is also the key to the business relation-ship between the organization and its customers. It may seem strange to some of you that although we have spent some time considering the nature of markets, we have not yet embarked on a discussion of the product, indeed, those of you following the strategic flow chart closely will see that discussion of product policy comes even further down the list than marketing strategy itself. There is a very good reason for this. As will be explained later, most organizations tend to place much far too much importance on the products which they market – products tend to acquire a life of their own within the organization. This is not only dangerous, it is also very bad marketing. (See Figure 58.)

Products have no intrinsic value of themselves. Products are no more than the most appropriate vehicle, at any point in time, to enable the organization to pass on the benefits or the solutions to its customers which they need. In return for these benefits and/or solutions, the customers send the money in the opposite direction – in fact a perfect relationship.

In our discussions of marketing objectives, we should be concerned, not with the physical products themselves or with the composite service packages for those in the service sector, but with the specific needs of our target marketplace. We should be concentrating either on the specific benefits which our customers require from us or the specific solution to the problems which our customers feel they have.

At this point of the process, it is far more important that we get as close as we can to our target marketplace and that we determine the needs of our marketplace with minds uncluttered by technical knowledge of the products we currently sell. The success of any market–product match depends on the ability to match the market (its needs, wants and problems) to the internal resources and skills of the organization. Whether customer needs are currently being met by existing products is less important in terms of developing long-range marketing strategy.

The measurement of marketing objectives

The discussion around the measurement of marketing objectives is extremely varied. Various marketing texts argue for measurements to be carried out in market terms – this is difficult to disagree with. They suggest measurements such as customer satisfaction, market penetration, market shares, volume sales figures and even the plotting of attitude change. Some texts even go so far as to suggest that marketing objectives should be measured using one or more of these measures in some form of composite measurement scale – the idea is quite appealing but I fear not terribly practical. All these measurements are in themselves valid indicators of marketing performance but they can each, individually, only be applied properly to one specific small area of the marketing function. These measures are really more appropriate if applied to marketing tactics rather than marketing strategy.

Since, in marketing strategy, we are considering the overall performance of the marketing function, we need to look beyond these specific tactical measures. We must look for that measure which is used by top management to judge the efficiency and effectiveness of the marketing function as a whole. This leaves us with one inescapable measure – *profit*.

If we cast our minds back to the very beginning of this book, I emphasized that the marketing function in any organization is the primary function charged with the responsibility for generating profit from the organization's activities. In this case the marketing objective (the aim, the goal to which all marketing activities in the organization are directed) must be measured in profit terms. People have argued with me in the past that profit is not necessarily accumulated in the marketing area, that profit is not a sufficiently marketing oriented measure to use for objectives – I have no doubt that people will continue to argue this with me as the years go by. My response to these arguments has always been that this probably highlights a flaw in the organizational structure rather than a basic flaw in the thinking behind the purpose of the organization and of the marketing function.

There is, in fact, no problem in using measures such as attitude change, market penetration, market shares and so on, but we should think long and hard why we are pursuing these objectives at all. If we are pursuing these objectives for reasons other than profit, the organization may not be long for this world.

By all means you should feel free to use surrogate measures for use lower down the organization if this makes it easier for operational management to identify with their tasks. We shall look later at some examples of lower level objectives which are related more precisely to, for example, distribution, promotional and product needs. Nevertheless, it is essential that the person or persons responsible for developing and achieving marketing objectives are very clear as to the nature and purpose as their organization as a whole. Over the long term, success, and indeed survival can only be guaranteed through a strong profit flow from our markets.

Marketer's note

Just in case you were starting to worry, remember the definition of marketing that is used by the UK's Chartered Institute of Marketing: 'Marketing is the management process responsible for identifying, anticipating and satisfying customer requirements PROFITABLY.' It's sometimes too easy to forget the last word in the melée.

Marketing strategy

When we start discussing marketing strategy, the same terms apply to the words 'objective' and 'strategy' as were used in Part One of this book. The marketing objectives as we have already seen are the aims, the goals to which the entire marketing effort of the organization is directed. Marketing strategy, therefore, to remain consistent with previous definitions refers to the means by which the marketing objective will be achieved. (See Figure 59.) The same shorthand will also apply, the marketing objectives must begin with the word 'To ...' and the marketing strategies with the word 'By ...'.

It then follows that the marketing strategy of an organization must be all about the development and the execution of the marketing mix. If we stop to think about it, there is no other way that the marketing objective of an organization can possibly be achieved other than through the traditional McCarthy classification of the marketing mix, known as the four Ps (product, price, place and promotion). Alternatively, for the service

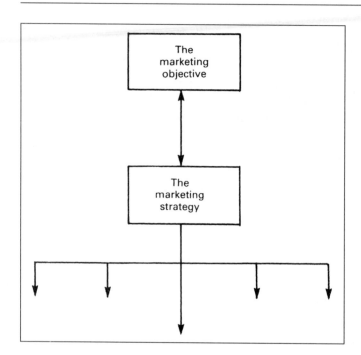

Figure 59
Marketing strategy

sector, the Booms and Bitner definition of the marketing mix (the seven Ps: product, price, place, people, physical evidence, process and promotion) – but more of these two alternative marketing mixes later.

While the majority of marketing texts, at least those that even attempt to define what the marketing strategy is, will agree that the core of the marketing strategy must be centred around the marketing mix. Still, there appears to be a great deal of confusion about the difference between marketing strategy and marketing tactics. Confusion between strategic and tactical activities. Confusion between long-term objectives and short-term manoeuvring.

While the individual elements of the marketing mix are, both individually and collectively, extremely important to the organization's marketing success, it is even more important that the marketing strategist be able to stand back from the everyday detail of product policy and pricing decisions to take a truly strategic view of the marketing activity of his or her organization. The art of any form of strategy, including marketing strategy, is in not being sucked into the detailed discussion. In any business, there are more than enough people who are only too happy to get involved in detailed questions of product design or lengthy discussions with the advertising and PR agencies. These decisions, like mailshot copy decisions, on-pack offers, short-term pricing campaigns and regional sales activity, are definitely tactical marketing decisions. These tactical decisions are exciting, interesting, challenging – I agree completely – but unless someone in the organization is able to stand back from this day-to-day 'street fighting', retain a vision of the wider picture of the marketplace and their organization's broader purpose, then tactical decisions will take over as the major driver of the business. An organization that ends up chasing its tail in this way will never create a secure, long-term position in its marketplace and will always be at the mercy of more committed competition. The tactics-driven organization is its own worst enemy.

Marketing strategy must be about the wider vision and the broader picture. Marketing strategy is:

- managing what is probably the most critical series of interfaces in the entire organization;
- managing the interface between what the organization wants to do and the means by which these aims or ambitions can be realized;
- managing the interface between the internal organization and the external marketplace;
- managing the interface between the organization's capabilities together with the opportunities open to the organization in its industry, and its marketplaces;
- managing the interface between your organization's resources and the needs of its marketplace; and
- about balance and the constant search for a point of equilibrium between these varied and often conflicting forces.

Talking to the advertising agency and briefing the sales force is important but it all comes later. Like a general, who would love nothing more than to get involved in every separate skirmish, the first and most important job is to ensure that the whole army is deployed in the most efficient manner. The general must ensure that he has protected his weaknesses, that he has made as much as he can of the opportunities offered by the terrain and the disposition of the enemy troops. He must remember at all times that his objective is to win the war and that the individual battles and skirmishes collectively take his army in the desired direction. If the general's (or the marketing strategist's) attention is in any way swayed from his long-term purpose by short-term losses or gains then the army will cease to act as one entity and momentum will be lost.

It is true to say that thinking strategically in this manner is not an easy process. The biggest single problem facing the marketing strategist is his or her ability to cut themselves off from the day-to-day marketing detail. If you are in control of a sizeable marketing department then you have to learn to delegate the tactical decisions to others. If you are a one-man marketing department (I remember it well) then it is a question of managing your time so that perhaps once a year you take a fixed period of time to deal with the strategic issues – during this period you make no tactical decisions at all.

Re-drawing the business strategy flow chart in a slightly different manner, I have tried to re-organize the main aspects of the strategy process and to highlight the key areas which the marketing strategy decisions must take into account (see Figure 60). We have already spent some considerable time dealing with the majority of the issues on this reformatted diagram but it is imortant to re-cap, this time from the marketer's point of view. I shall concentrate especially on the broader co-ordination or balancing issues that marketing strategy must resolve between these various, and sometimes conflicting, forces.

Organization goals

The primary areas of concern to marketing strategy under this heading are:

- the mission statement;
- the business objective;
- the business strategy; and
- the strategic market position.

These outputs of the business strategy process give a very clear and one would hope, an unambiguous direction in the development of the marketing strategy. The organizational goals will tell us not only what we have to achieve but will also tell us how we should go about achieving these goals.

The mission statement

The mission statement, always difficult to define accurately, is a qualitative statement about the organization, what it believes and its ethics. It should inform marketing strategy very clearly as to the nature of its market-based activities, specifically what is acceptable and what is not acceptable to all the important groups that have a stake in the organization and its future. Never forget that the organization's marketing activity is at the same time the most powerful and the most visible of all the activities carried out by the organization. It is your marketing activity which will be directly compared against the mission statement and the

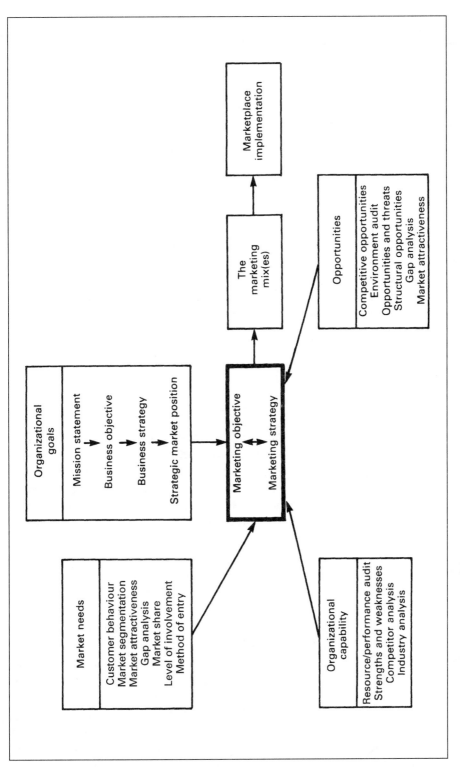

Figure 60 Developing marketing strategies

promises which the mission statement makes. You cannot afford inconsistencies.

The business objective

Assuming there has been some degree of marketing input to the business strategy process, the business objective should be firmly based in market rather than in internal or, even worse, financial terms. In this case, we have a very clear idea of what the organization expects to achieve over the planning period and this should guide us quite easily into translating the broader corporate or business objectives into more detailed objectives which relate to the marketplace or marketplaces within which the organization operates.

A good business objective should be used to keep the marketing strategy's attention carefully fixed on the longer term. We all know how difficult it is to ignore apparently lucrative short-term market opportunities. But we also know (if not always freely admitted) that short-term opportunism is not always the best route for long-term success. The everyday cut and thrust of competitive marketplaces, while exhilarating, can make long-term vision quite difficult to maintain. The business objective should be clearly stated and should be returned to on a regular basis to make sure that our marketing activity is not being driven by the short term at the expense of long-term profitability.

The business strategy

A clear line should flow from business strategy to marketing strategy. The business strategy team will have considered the major environmental factors as well as the organization's strengths and weaknesses and will have decided on the most appropriate route for achieving the business objective. In simple terms, the organization will have decided whether it intends to be a focused organization, whether it will strive for the cost leadership position or whether it intends to operate industry-wide but on a differentiated basis. It is now the task of the marketing strategy to put the business strategy into operation.

The clearest indication here for the marketing team is what they should *not* be doing. For example, the organization that has decided to embark on a focused business strategy has clearly stated that there are a number of marketing activities that it will not engage in. For example, the focused organization will not attempt to market a product range across the whole industry sector, it will not be attempting to compete on a number of diversified fronts and it will not be expecting to spend large percentages of its turnover on above or below the line promotional support for its products. The essential thrust of a focused organization is aimed at picking off a single or a small number of closely related market segments and developing product ranges which extend in depth rather than in width. Consequently, the marketing strategy should concentrate on aspects such as depth of market penetration of key market segment or segments with mixes tightly focused. We can expect pricing policy to reflect premium-priced brands, promotion to be fairly limited compared to more diversified organizations and distribution policy to be specialist rather than aimed at volume sales.

Similarly, for the organization which has decided to embark on a differentiated or cost leadership business strategy. The business strategy will give very clear indications to the marketing function as well as clear boundaries within which marketing strategy and marketing activity must be developed. While business strategy is generic in nature and oriented towards concepts, marketing strategy is active in nature and oriented towards implementation. Consistency between the business strategy and the marketing strategy is all important.

The strategic market position

Another qualitative concept passed down from the business strategy development team. This should act, alongside the mission statement, as a vision or a backdrop against which marketing strategy is developed.

As with all aspects of strategy and organizational goals, if, following more detailed and in-depth analysis of the marketplace, the marketer was to find that the business objective and business strategy were 'unreasonable' it is not the job of marketing strategy simply to ignore the business strategy decisions and to take what appears to be the best route in market terms. Rather, the additional information should be fed into the business strategy process and the business objective and strategy adjusted in the light of the new information which has been acquired.

Market needs

Under this heading we have already considered the following:

- customer behaviour;
- market segmentation;
- market attractiveness;
- gap analysis;
- market share;
- level of involvement; and
- method of entry.

It is worthwhile briefly reviewing the direct impact of these various analyses on the development of the organization's marketing strategy.

Customer behaviour

An understanding of our customer's behaviour, of their needs wants and motivations does not, of course, just happen overnight. Getting close to our customers may take years or even a lifetime but, as we have seen, the closer you can get to your customers, the fewer risks you are likely to run. As far as the future is concerned, and it is essentially the future which must drive marketing strategy, an understanding of how our customers act, how our customers respond and why they respond in a given way is the essential raw material for developing marketplace activity. It is only once we have started to understand what our customers expect from us, what our customers believe we are able to provide them and the preferred terms on which products and/or services should be offered that we can start to develop market-led as opposed to production-led thinking in the organization. We can then start to assess properly the resources available to our organization and consider ways in which these resources might be most profitably co-ordinated.

Market segmentation

Closely linked to customer behaviour, market segmentation is becoming more and more important in the understanding and servicing of our marketplaces. Marketing strategy must, of course, follow the guidelines in the business strategy. The organization following a differentiated strategy will need to understand its marketplace and the sub-segments within it while the focused organization will need to concentrate its effort on one or more market segments which it will pursue to the exclusion of all others. Once the individual market segments have been identified, the extent to which the organization's marketing strategy should adapt various approaches to various segments will depend largely on its image in the marketplace, the resources under its control and the organizational goals.

Market attractiveness

The various markets/segments which the organization has identified as being attractive should have been clearly arranged in priority order.

This order of markets/segments to be attacked, with clear time scales and priorities, will form the cornerstone of the long-term marketing plan and the timed approach to marketing strategy. The priority order need not be considered a stepping stone for the duration but should be reviewed on a regular, but not too frequent, basis as market and environmental conditions change.

Gap analysis

Gap analysis, we have seen, can be used in a number of ways. However, all the various methodologies and objectives of gap analysis tend towards the identification and isolation of various market-based opportunities. Of course, it is important to identify the opportunities open to the organization within its major marketplaces. but just because an opportunity presents itself, it doesn't necessarily mean that the organization has to follow it blindly. There has to be some form of logical, rational, strategic thinking as to which opportunities should to be approached and in which order. The business objective will provide the long-term view needed to assess each opportunity and its potential to take the organization toward its long-term goals.

Market share

Market share, as we know, is used fairly extensively as both a business and a marketing objective. We have also seen that there are some quite interesting problems in the measurement and monitoring of market share that tend to cast some doubts over the validity of market share as a competitive measure. Nevertheless, it can in certain circumstances (for focused organizations) be quite a useful measure. If market share is the measure which your organization is going to use to determine its performance, then enough effort and time must be set aside to ensure that measurements of market share are as solid and reliable over time. Market share is an evolutionary measure important for the organization's long-term future.

Level of involvement

Level of involvement is a strategic concept and will be determined by two broad factors. First, the organization's business strategy, cost leadership, differentiation and focus all have fairly obvious implications for the optimal level of involvement in markets. Second, the marketplace itself will dictate the optimum level of involvement that the organization is able to play, certainly in the short to medium term.

As well as these two important criteria, the marketing strategy should also take into account the resources available to the organization since involvement costs resource. The relative attractiveness of the market/segment will also influence the choice of level of involvement.

Method of market entry

Method of market entry is closely linked to level of involvement and the same forces will act on the organization's choice. An additional dimension when considering method of market entry is that it will have long-terms effects on the marketing strategy. For example, if for reasons of resource, market situation and organizational goal, the organization decides to enter a given market segment through an indirect route, then this is likely to restrict the organization's freedom to deploy fully the marketing mix. It is vitally important for marketing strategy that the long-term scenario be brought into play before decisions are made. Decisions on methods of market entry should be based on future ambitions as well as current resource and capabilities.

Organizational capability

The marketing strategy must also be cognizant of the abilities of the organization to deliver in the marketplace. It is one thing to be ambitious, it is another thing altogether to be unrealistic. The types of areas we have already looked at under this heading are:

- the resource/performance audit;
- strengths and weaknesses;
- competitor analysis; and
- industry analysis.

The resource/performance audit

There is nothing quite so dangerous in marketing strategy as over-estimating our organization's ability to produce real benefits in the marketplace. A true, unbiased and realistic assessment of the organization's resources and how well it is able to deploy those resources is essential to any practical marketing strategy.

It is also quite useful here to draw a distinction between the resource audit and the performance audit. Organizations differ quite markedly in both the resources they can bring to bear on any given marketplace as well as their ability to marshall and deploy those resources at the right point and at the right time. Your track record in resource utilization should be a good guide to your ability to employ resource efficiently in any future marketing strategy.

While we are discussing resources, we should remind ourselves that as well as physical and financial resource, the resource that could tip the scales in your favour will be your organization's managerial expertise. Difficult to measure and quantify on a comparative basis it will include creativity, vision, entrepreneurial spirit and motivation. These manager-ial resources like the 'hard' resources of finance and capital, also need nurturing, refining and developing over time.

Strengths and weaknesses

Once again, two quite different aspects to the question of strengths and weaknesses. First we need a realistic assessment of our organization's strengths and weaknesses in the marketplace, the sort of things that we are both good and bad at – a degree of historical perspective can be used here. This will influence the types of markets we are prepared to take on and the types of new ventures, either product or market led, which we can handle easily. It will also show where additional resource may need to be found.

A second and extremely important facet of organizational capabilities is the marketplace's perception of what our organization's strengths and weaknesses are. Remember that often the marketplace's opinion that we have a particular strength in a particular product and/or market area means that we will be able to achieve significant marketing success in this area even though we may have little or no (production-based) strength in this area relative to our competition. The same naturally applies to weaknesses.

Competitor analysis

The first reason why competitive analysis is important is that it helps to identify likely competitive gaps in the marketplace where our limited resource could be applied for good return. Don't forget that head-to-head competition is extremely wasteful in terms of both profit and resource and it should be avoided at every opportunity.

The second important area of competitor analysis needs some careful thought when developing marketing strategy. All too often eloquent marketers armed with polished plans and strategies will run aground in the marketplace for one simple reason – they have forgotten or just overlooked the likely competitive response to their marketing strategy. Except in pure monopolistic situations, no organization can expect to operate in a market vacuum. Every activity carried out by the organization will have an effect on the marketplace and on other organizations operating in that marketplace – in other words, the competition. Every activity will generate a response of some sort from the competition.

Therefore the net results of any marketing strategy can be calculated as the results of the organization's actions plus or minus the results of the competitors' response to those actions. It is vital that the marketing strategy team takes into account the most likely responses from the competition and builds some allowance for this activity into the strategic plan. No organization is ever measured on the eloquence of the words in the marketing strategy – only results count.

Industry analysis

Similarly to competitive analysis, the industry in which your organization operates has a series of dynamics, factors and trends which will affect all players within that industry. The marketing strategy, if it is to be effective over the long term, must bear in mind these underlying trends and factors and must either work with or against the flow depending on the organization's business objective. In either event, there will be an effect on the bottom-line results and this must be accounted for before any action is initiated.

Opportunities

Opportunities can be found and can be made. Opportunities effectively form the basis of the business as a whole. Most organizations do not necessarily have a problem in finding or making opportunities for themselves. The biggest single problem comes from choosing among the opportunities, the right ones to follow. There are a number of different opportunities and methods for identifying them. We have looked at the following:

- competitive opportunities;
- the environment audit;
- opportunities and threats;
- structural opportunities;
- gap analysis; and
- market attractiveness.

Competitive opportunities

Competitive opportunities will or should fall out of a detailed competitor information system which your organization should try and put into place. By carefully and regularly assessing and plotting the progress of your major competitors (their business objectives, business strategies, marketing activity etc.) you should be able to identify where they think they are headed. Everything the competition does in the marketplace is likely to create an opportunity for your organization as well. One point of warning here, just because you spot the competitors moving into a certain market area, this does not necessarily mean that they have properly gauged and judged the demand. They could have got it wrong. One risk of maintaining an up-to-date and detailed competitor information system is that the herd instinct can assert itself. Always be prepared to make your own decisions grounded on good market-based opportunities. Because the competition moves, does not necessarily mean that a profitable market gap exists for every player.

Environment audit

The marketing strategy is, as we have already said, a long-term activity. While we know that any long-term activity is difficult to plan with significant confidence, we have to make some effort to reduce the risk of the unknown. As the marketing strategy extends its vision beyond the one-, the two-, the five- into the ten-year period, we have to start looking at the environment within which the strategy will be operating. We have to be as perceptive as possible about the likely changes which we can expect to see in the future marketing environment. The four broad headings which are traditionally used in the environmental analysis also serve us reasonably well when plotting scenarios for marketing strategy.

The political environment will undoubtedly change over the planning period. We should be asking ourselves who is likely to be in power and when? What political persuasions are likely to change, and what are the likely major influences on marketing? The economic situation is important in that it will affect our customers' ability to buy our products and services. This, in turn, affects our profit returns and bottom-line results. The future economic environment will also affect the cost and availability of the resources which we need. Technological factors are becoming more and more important in most areas of business and such trends can be expected to continue. In certain disciplines, such as information technology, a ten-year planning scenario is impractical due to the speed of the growth of technological change, nevertheless, some time should be put aside to visualize most likely futures and building into the marketing strategy likely responses to change in environmental situations.

The sociological changes in the environment are even more important for marketing strategy than the previous three factors. There are two very distinct aspects to a sociological audit. The first is the importance of trying to plot major trends in society, a recent example of a major trend which has arisen is concerned for the environment or 'green issues'. While ten years ago, certain industries such as the chemical and petrochemical industries had noted and were starting to respond to the rise in the environmentalism in their markets, other industries such as financial services did not see the rise in the green movement as having a major effect on their business. In the 1990s the major financial institutions in the UK, in Europe and the USA, are all now building into their forecasts and their strategies, the additional costs required to be environmentally responsible organizations.

The second and most commonly overlooked element of the sociological audit is the information that such analysis can give us on the evolution and the development of market segments. It is often quite difficult to separate ourselves mentally from the day-to-day issues of marketing and look forward strategically. Contrarily, it can often be made more difficult, the better the organization is at getting closer to its market segments. This may appear to be a contradiction in terms, but the closer an organization is to its market segments, the more difficult it may find it to look beyond existing segments to the more vague and fuzzy segments of the future. It is often advisable to put existing segments and characteristics out of the mind and look exclusively at the longer term future of society from which very broad macro motivational segments can be drawn. Such broad macro strategic segments can only be produced by a relatively uncluttered mind. One would hope to find a relationship between existing market segments and their expected or planned evolution over the coming years and the broader macro segments which can be identified form a purely futurist analysis of likely sociological change. If, in the analysis, you were to find no relationship between these two pole points then this might imply that the environmental analysis is well off skew, in which case you could be looking and re-analysing all of the environmental factors. Alternatively, it may mean that the extrapolation from the existing market segments into the future is erroneous, in which case your existing market research and current marketing activity needs to be reviewed carefully.

Opportunities and threats

As well as market-based opportunities and competitive opportunities there will be environmental opportunities as well as threats posed to the organization from environmental change. The marketing strategy must take these opportunities and threats into account so that it is best placed to both protect its existing market position as well as develop new areas of business.

Structural opportunities

The Porter analysis of industry competition and industry structure is likely to expose certain opportunities for your organization within the industry. These opportunities, if they exist, are likely to be fairly straightforward. The main questions here for marketing strategists are, first, should these opportunities actually be taken on? Second, will the opportunities actually lead your organization towards its declared business objective? Third, do these structural opportunities match with other opportunities such as competitive opportunities and marked-based opportunities. If they do, then there will be some degree of synergy to be obtained by the organization at this point – if they do not then they may even work against each other. Don't forget that resources are always limited and choices have to be made.

Gap analysis

We have already covered the concept of gap analysis previously under market-based needs but it has been included here because of the other, non-market-based opportunities which gap analysis can be used to uncover. Yet again, it is a question of carefully selecting from among the various opportunities which the organization faces – those which will produce the largest payoff in terms of business objective or marketplace success.

Market attractiveness

For the sake of completeness, the concept of market attractiveness can be added under the opportunities section (this will allow it to be properly compared to other non-market-based opportunities for selection and allocation of resource).

The marketing mix(es)

The marketing mix or mixes are the primary output of the marketing strategy. While the basic concept of the marketing mix is a relatively simple one for most people to grasp, the strategic and the tactical aspects of the marketing mix become confused very easily.

While the various, detailed aspects of the marketing mix and marketing management such as product policy, pricing policy, distribution, channel management and so forth are clearly marketing tactics, it is the role of the marketing strategist to ensure that the various elements of the mix come together into a consistent and coherent whole before they are applied to the marketplace.

If we take the easiest possible example, that of an organization which operates in just one single marketplace, then the marketing strategy for the planning period becomes relatively straightforward. Taking into account all the elements we have identified above, it is then the job of the marketing strategy to create a marketing mix which combines the right product range, which is marketed at the right price, through the right distribution channels, supported by the right level of promotional activity. The operative word here, of course, is the word 'right'. The important strategic element of the mix is making sure that all of the individual mix elements come together and appear to be consistent and reasonable from the target customers' point of view. The optimal product distribution and promotional element of the mix all marketed at the wrong price effectively will destroy the entire marketing effort.

As the process proceeds down to a more detailed practical level different people are likely to be working on different aspects of the mix. It is imperative at this stage that someone is able to remain above the mêlée and orchestrate the various inputs in the right order, the right sequence. No amount of creative and dedicated tactical work can ever make up for the lack of a strategic focus. It is very difficult to emphasize sufficiently the importance of this strategic co-ordinating role in the marketing effort. Like the symphony orchestra without a conductor, each individual section may be playing superbly but the overall effect is one of chaos and cacophony.

The strategic influence on the marketing mix is even more important if we imagine the more realistic situation of an organization which operates in more than just one single market or market segment. We have already seen that the organization will have as many marketing objectives as there are markets or market segments to be addressed by the organization. Naturally enough, for each marketing objective a marketing strategy is required, or in other words, a marketing mix which is both consistent, logical and cohesive. An additional complication now appears, unless the organization is working in completely discreet market segments, then there is likely to be some overlap between the various activities. It is therefore essential that the marketing mixes are not only consistent and logical within themselves but also that the various marketing mixes are logical and sensible when placed side by side. In other words, the job of the marketing strategy is to ensure that the totality of the organization's marketing activity in its various marketplaces adds up to a sensible and understandable corporate image among the customer base. As new activities are embarked on or new segments are opened up so the marketplace as a whole should see the activity as a logical extension of the organization's previous expertise and track record. Consistency and co-ordination will be seen as the hallmark of a successful marketing strategy.

Marketing strategy – conclusions

While we might just simply look at the results of a well-constructed and effective marketing strategy and see one or a series of good quality marketing mixes, the work which actually goes into developing and building a good practical and effective marketing strategy is much, much deeper. Marketing strategy is about striking the right balance between many various and conflicting forces which act on the organization – then turning these into long-term profits.

We must talk about one final balance required of marketing strategy. All of the various influences which play on the development of an effective marketing strategy are themselves dynamic in nature. That is to say that nothing can be expected to stand still for very long. The net result of this ever-changing environment within which the organization finds itself is that the marketing strategy must remain a quite flexible plan for the future. So we meet the final and possibly most difficult balance to be struck – the need for the marketing strategy team to find an ideal mix between a marketing strategy which is firm enough to facilitate longer range planning (and often significant marketing investments), while remaining flexible enough to incorporate amendments and changes caused by the environmental variables without having to completely rewrite the marketing strategy every six months.

There is very little concrete guidance that one can give at this point since the degree of dynamism in the environment, the degree of firmness and solidity required for investment, and the organizational culture's need for certainty will vary from one organization to the next. Marketing strategy is not an easy process, but then things of value rarely are.

Chapter 7

Making the links

'When you engage in actual fighting, if victory is long in coming, the men's weapons will grow dull and their ardour will be damped. If you lay seige to a town, you will exhaust your strength.

'Again, if the campaign is protracted, the resources of the State will not be equal to the strain.

'Now, when your weapons are dulled, your ardour damped, your strength exhausted and your treasure spent, other chieftains will spring up to take advantage of your extremity. Then no man, however wise, will be able to avert the consequences that must ensue.'

Sun Tzu, 500 BC

Up to this point I have emphasized the importance of the marketing concept as a state of mind which should percolate the entire organization. I have emphasized the importance of the marketing objective and the marketing strategy as the essential link-pin between the business strategy and the all-important marketplaces of the organization. It is now time for a little reality. Marketing, important as it is, cannot work in a vacuum (see Figure 61).

The only true test of marketing (as has been said time and time again) is bottom-line profit result in the marketplace. Marketing, both as a function and as a concept, cannot deliver these profits all alone. Marketing and marketing strategy may be responsible for identifying the needs in the marketplace and for showing the organization the way to achieve success, but it cannot generate results without the willing cooperation of the other major functions in the organization. Worse, the best-laid marketing strategies can be effectively destroyed by opposition from other quarters. So important are the effects of these other functional areas

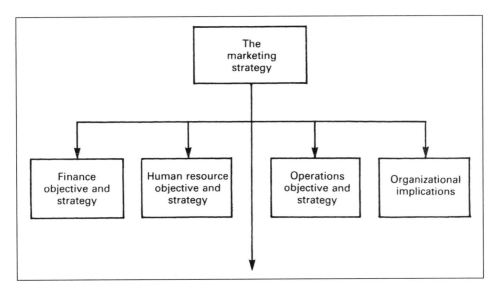

Figure 61 Making the links

in the organization that we need to spend time looking, albeit briefly, at the specific interfaces between marketing strategy and the other important strategies in the organization. This section will not deal with the myriad of technical/tactical differences or points of conflict between marketing and other functions – we are concerned only with the interrelationship of strategic thinking across functional boundary.

Organizational implications

If we view the organization's business objective and business strategy as what the organization wants to do, then the marketing objective and marketing strategy is the translation of this organizational ambition into market terms. The organizational structure and design should be regarded as the internal delivery mechanism which will actually make this activity possible (see Figure 62). While the 'right' organizational structure can actively support the marketing effort and will allow the organization to deliver benefits to the marketplace, the 'wrong' organizational structure can make it extremely difficult and sometimes even impossible for the organization to deliver the benefits the marketplace requires.

The question then is what is the 'right' organizational structure? The answer, naturally enough, is the one which enables the organization to

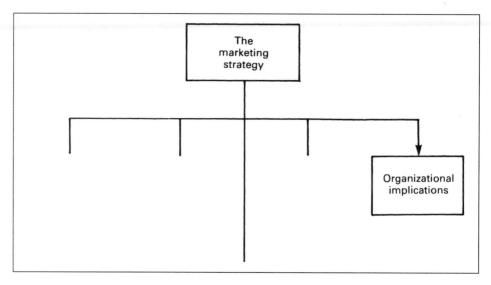

Figure 62 Organizational implications

deliver the benefits which the market requires from it. Unfortunately, I have the impression that this may not help you too much in your deliberations. Organizational structure and design is itself a vast area with its own supporting literature. Our concern here, will be limited to the effects of the organizational structure on the marketing strategy and the marketing effort so we shall not be delving too deeply into the theories and concepts behind organizational design. The interested reader is refered to the many excellent texts on the subject, especially those by Charles Handy.

Good marketing and a practical marketing strategy must (it bears repeating lest we forget) be driven by the marketplace – not by internal organizational concerns. Similarly, from a marketing point of view, the 'right' organization structure is the one that gives me, the customer, the benefits that I want. Unfortunately, too many organizations seem to be under the misapprehension that the organization is designed primarily for the benefit of the people that work within it – a very strange idea when we think who it is paying the money.

As a customer, how many times have you tried to get answers to questions, or solutions to problems, from organizations as diverse as hospitals, restaurants, banks, car manufacturers, and computer suppliers? How many times have you tried to make contact with such an organization only to discover that you have to learn the way their system works before there is any chance of you coming away with even the barest level of service? How many times have you phoned an organization with a query only to be passed from department to department like a hot potato? Don't you sometimes start wondering why, if you are paying the money, you have to jump through the hoops that they put up?

So, keeping firm hold of the indignation which you so rightly feel, try looking at your own organization from the outside – from your customer's point of view. Is it any different? For whose benefit has your own organization been designed? For your customers or for you and the staff? I think now you are probably starting to get the picture.

Life itself is a question of balance and this is no less true in the area of marketing strategy and organizational structure. Before you are tempted to dismiss these ideas as incompatible with the needs of the 'caring 1990s', yes, I realize that the people who work in the organization come in every day and yes, I also realize that it is not easy to get good people nowadays and you have to work hard to get them and harder to keep them. On the other hand, I also realize that it is the customer who pays everybody's bills at the end of the day. Also, just because customers don't come in to the office every day, there is no reason for their voice not to be heard. I also understand that running an organization of any size costs money. I also realize that structuring and designing the organization so that it does exactly what the customer wants may not be the most efficient or the cheapest way of running the business, but maybe the customer is not too worried about our problems. All our customer wants is the right level of service. Maybe, if we can't deliver the right level of service our customer will go somewhere else. If that happens in sufficient numbers, maybe we don't have a business.

The key to developing the right organizational structure is striking the balance between internal efficiency and external service. While the members of the organization who turn up every day are a powerful lobby (sometimes supporting internal efficiency but almost always supporting the status quo), the customer has no voice. This is a role that must be taken on by the marketing function. Marketing should see themselves as the representatives of the market within the organization. It is the marketing function's job to assess the needs and concerns of the customer base and to ensure that the organizational structure is sufficient to deliver the products and service levels which the marketplace requires.

Organizational structure is determined by a number of factors. As can be seen from Figure 63, these factors can be separated into 'inputs' and 'outputs' to facilitate understanding. The inputs include people, or what the industrial psychologists might call the total systems behaviour of the people within the organization. This relates to individual, inter-personal, group and inter-group behaviour, all of which will have an effect on the structure and design of the organization. The control systems and objectives will both influence the organization which will adapt to accomodate the constraints placed on it. Technology will have a significant effect on

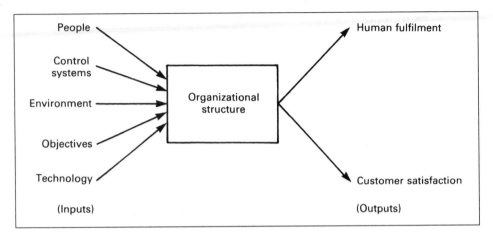

Figure 63   Organizational structure

the organization which must mould itself to its production processes. The rate of change of technology will especially effect the flexibility required within the design. The environment includes the business, industry and the marketplace factors which will determine how the organization must respond to external demands.

The outputs in the diagram are both important and potentially conflicting. For long term success, the organization needs to satisfy its customers (enough said so far about this) as well as satisfying the personal needs of its own people. The argument runs that customers cannot be satisfied by an organization full of unfulfilled people – Sun Tzu put it differently talking about the morale of the troops, but still agreed. Problems can arise when the customer wants the organization to do something that the troops would rather not do. That is when we have to start remembering who is paying the money!

There are two basic types of structure, traditionally termed 'functional' and 'product'. The functional-based organization is structured into sections and divisions according to the nature of the work carried out, e.g. finance, marketing and sales, production, administration, and personnel. The product-based organization ('product' is rather a misnomer) is structured into sections and divisions around the task to be achieved. Bases for division may include product groups, industry sectors, buyer types or markets/market segments. Again there is scope for conflict whichever approach is used for the organizational design. Functional structure tends to give better internal efficiency while product-based structure should give better customer satisfaction. Typically, most organizations tend to spend much of their time looking for the ideal compromise between these two extreme positions.

An additional point on organizational structure is the question of comparative measures. Often, once an organization has understood the importance of external image and desired service levels, it will often use competitors' service levels as a measure for its own performance. This then will generate necessary changes to structure and design. Comparative measures such as this may not necessarily be the right ones. The trend today is for organizations to move away from direct, competitive head-to-head confrontations into more differentiated market positions. Of course, your position and marketplace image will largely be dependent on the products or services which you market and the specific nature of your target market/market segments. Much work and careful analysis will normally go into product design, distribution, management, promotional activities to differentiate your organization from its competitors in some clearly defined way. An organization can also differentiate itself in the marketplace through judicious control of its organizational structure and hence service levels.

One final thought on organizational structure. There is a phrase often used by industrial psychologists that I have always found very useful when considering organizational structure and design. That is 'structure gives behaviour'. It is only by looking beyond the structure to the behaviours which these various structures will give that we can start to see the ultimate effects of any organizational change on the marketplace.

One example I can give here comes from work which I have carried out with two major UK financial institutions. The two organizations were of a roughly equal size, both employing something in excess of 100,000 people in their UK operations, but both were organized in a quite different manner. One was organized along the traditional functional lines that we would expect to find in most large established organizations. The results of this organizational structure were that the organization was often perceived as quite slow moving, quite slow to react, sometimes more concerned with internal systems than external market results and not always as efficient as it might have been in terms of missed profit opportunities. Nevertheless, marketing activity, once it was eventually produced, tended to be quite solid, robust and well integrated.

The second organization was organized on similar broad functional lines but within the function, the business unit system was used. The business units were variable in size but were relatively autonomous and, above all, profit responsible. This organization was seen as more innovative, more dynamic and more pro-active rather than re-active to marketplace demand. Certainly profit, as a concept, was a very important factor in all decision-making processes. On the other hand, the business unit structure did give rise to a number of undesirable behaviours. The foremost among these was a difficulty in co-ordinating various activities that were required to satisfy market demands. While individual business units' attention was constantly focused on bottom-line results, it was the business unit bottom line rather than the organization bottom line. Large organizations require a degree of integration and co-ordination if they are to provide the modern day sophisticated packaged benefits which more sophisticated consumers are demanding. Internal efficiency can also suffer under the business unit system when arguments over 'turf' and feuds between power barons can distract management attention from the ultimate need to satisfy customer demands. These are just two examples of how different organizational structures can generate quite different behaviours. Structural questions are interesting but behavioural questions are imperative. It is the behaviour that must be planned to create successful marketing strategy.

Financial strategy

According to most of the major texts on finance, the financial management of any organization can be seen as having four separate tasks:

- the acquisition of funds;
- the investing of funds in economically productive assets;
- the managing of these assets; and
- the eventual reconversion of some (or all) of the productive assets into future returns to the original investors, creditors, suppliers, employees and other interested groups.

To these tasks we could probably add:

- keeping a record of revenues and expenses; and
- achievement of the long-term financial objective.

Although all these aspects of financial strategy and management impinge on marketing strategy, the biggest area of interest centres on the discussion of the word 'assets'. As stated above, and this is a quite normal (if narrow) statement of the role of financial management, the essential job of the finance function is investing in assets, managing assets and the eventual conversion of assets. The question is what do we mean by assets. A very clear and succinct description of what constitutes an asset, as seen from the marketing viewpoint, can be taken from Levitt, who said (in his article, 'Marketing intangible products and product intangibles' in the *Harvard Business Review*, May/June 1981):

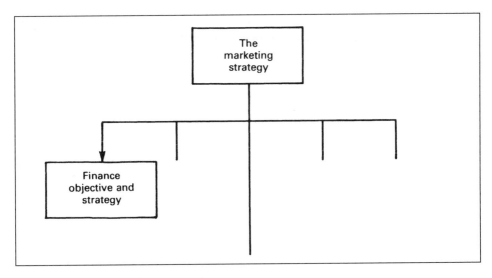

Figure 64   Finance objective and strategy

A customer is an asset that is usually more precious than the tangible assets on the balance sheet. You can usually buy balance sheet assets. There are lots of willing sellers. You cannot so easily buy customers. They are far less willing than are sellers and have lots of eager sellers offering them many choices. Moreover, a customer is a double asset; first, he is the direct source of cash from sale, and second, his existence can be used to raise cash from bankers and investors, cash that can be converted into tangible assets.

If we look at the marketing strategy from this point of view, then the marketing and finance functions have a lot in common. Marketing strategy can be described as the process of investing funds into economically productive assets (the customer), the management of these assets, and finally the eventual re-conversion of some or all of these productive assets into future returns (for returns read profits) to the original investors. To be fair to both parties, I must admit that I have met very few marketing professionals who see their role in quite this way. Nevertheless, the investment in, and management of, assets for a return is the very essence of marketing strategy. Spending money in the hope of a quick buck is the sign of a mind driven by short-term marketing tactics.

So what then about the marketing–finance interface? The two disciplines have more in common than either thinks and there are lessons that each party can learn from the other. There is much for the marketing strategist to learn from the finance function (yes, more heresy but you should be getting used to it by now). Marketing strategy (not marketing tactics) is all about investing in the organization's marketplaces for longer term profit flows. In my experience, the marketing strategies of very many organizations would benefit greatly from the application of a financial discipline. Some simple financial management techniques used on a regular basis by managers, for example, management accounting, capital budgeting, and rates of return forecasting would help focus the marketing mind on profit results. If marketing strategy is about the investment of the organization's limited resource into the organization's most productive asset, I personally see no reason why such large amounts of money should be expended on little more than a wing and a prayer. If marketing strategists wish to be seen as responsible and professional managers, rather than reckless spendthrifts then maybe we have something to learn in the area of financial and managerial control systems.

The finance function also has things to learn from marketing. The first, and most important, is that marketing expenditure is not a cost but an investment and should be treated as such. Cutting marketing and advertising expenditure in the bad times is not managing costs, it is witholding investment on which the future of the organization depends. The nature of marketing investments is often seen as risky and cavalier – this is often a justified criticism. Marketing investment is often more uncertain due to the unpredictable nature of the asset, the customer. While some marketers revel in the mystique of this unpredictability, many more are working hard to create a closer understanding of the target market's needs and so reduce the uncertainty to more manageable levels.

Looking, finally, at the relationship between marketing and finance strategy, we should see that ideally the finance function should take its lead from the marketing strategy. An 'independent' finance function can, while making appropriate decisions in isolation, work against the long-term interests of the organization. The acquisition of funds involves decisions about the sources of those funds and the balance between debt and equity in the organization. The sources of funds can have effects on the customer's perception of the business and the products/services which are supplied – concerns about apartheid and the environment have both led to customer alienation in the 1980s. The balance between debt and equity finance can affect the organization's ability to deal with adverse market conditions – again the 1980s showed the danger of carrying heavy debt into markets with rising interest rates and falling customer demand. The investment of funds in tangible, physical production assets also needs to be directed by the marketplace. Future customer demand will be the most important factor in determining how profitable our investment in productive assets will be. Like the discussion on organizational structure, it may be that short term decisions based on internal efficiency may not necessarily be the most constructive in terms of the organization's long-term success.

In too many organizations the relationship between marketing and finance is one of conflict. We should have the same goals (marketplace profits) and the same enemy (the competition). Teamwork, not conflict, is required – this is provided by a clear and practical business objective and strategy that all parties understand and follow.

Human resource strategy

Distilled to its very essence (and greatly simplified) the strategic human resource function is responsible for two broad areas within the organization:

- recruitment and selection; and
- motivation and reward systems.

The marketing strategy–human resources strategy interface (see Figure 65) will centre on similar areas to those already seen in the previous sections. In other words, is it the job of human resource strategy to recruit, select, motivate and reward in order to improve internal efficiency, or to maximize the organization's external effectiveness within its marketplace? As before, the organization should be seeking the elusive balance between the two. Such a balance can only come through a mutual understanding of the needs and objectives of the two functions.

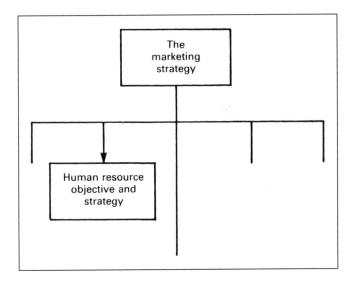

Figure 65 Human resource objective and strategy

Potentially, the most serious area of strategic conflict is in how different roles in the organization are seen. The best way of explaining this is through a practical example. Let us consider two roles in an organization, maybe best imagined by two vacant positions which the human resource function is currently trying to fill. In our example, the two vacant positions are for a telephonist/receptionist and for a manager in the payroll department. The human resource function, in common with all other functions in the organization, has limited resource at its disposal and is concerned with how best to use this limited resource to achieve its objectives. From a purely internal point of view, the position of payroll manager is the more senior position and will require somebody with both technical and managerial expertise. The telephonist/receptionist position on the other hand will be seen as a relatively minor position. Based on purely internal considerations then, the human resource function can be expected to allocate relatively more resource to the recruitment and selection of the payroll manager than the telephonist/receptionist.

On the other hand, for the marketing function and the marketing strategy, the relative importance of the two positions is reversed. When customers attempt to make contact with the organization directly, the telephonist/receptionist is not only the first point of contact with the organization, but is quite capable of typifying and representing your organization and everything it stands for in your customer's eyes. The marketing strategy will determine both how the organization is to be perceived in its target markets and the level of service which the organization will deliver to its customers. The right telephonist/receptionist has the power to either actively and positively reinforce these messages or to almost instantly destroy the often quite sizeable marketing investment which the organization has made, by acting and behaving in a manner inconsistent to projected image. The recruitment, selection and motivation of the receptionist/telephonist might be much more important to the marketing function and to the organization's marketing strategy than that of the payroll manager. The telephonist/receptionist function is a high (customer) contact position whereas internal functions such as payroll manager are low contact positions.

In the service sector the paradox is very visible. Whether we think of hotels, banks, building societies, insurance intermediaries, supermarkets, leisure centres or garages the career path is always the same. We start new employees in the 'lowliest' position in the organization – facing the customer. We then reward those who do well by increasing their pay, calling them managers – and reducing the amount of customer contact. The most successful probably never have to see a customer again! It is not really surprising that customer service levels fall if this is the type of message that the organization is passing down. It is surprising that this traditional way of thinking is so rarely questioned.

It obviously doesn't take a genius to work out that there are vast areas of potential conflict between marketing and human resource managers. Neither function is able to achieve its objectives independently. Both functions need the active support of the other and such active support can only come through improved communications and an understanding of mutual needs to achieve the organization's business objective.

Operations strategy

According to most of the major texts on operations management, the function can be seen as having eight principal tasks:

* process planning and control;
* operations planning;
* facilities design, location, layout, materials handling, equipment maintenance;
* scheduling;
* inventory planning and control;
* quality control;
* operations control; and
* forecasting and longer term planning.

I am using the word operations to cover both the manufacturing and the processing that will be required in any organization, manufacturing or services, to deliver satisfaction to the customer. The service industry also has a very important operations function, although it is often not regarded as such. For example, banking, financial services, hotel management, and health care would cease to function were it not for careful planning, the processing of documents and documentation, scheduling of activities and, where applicable, the traffic flow of people involved in the process.

While no organization can prosper in its business activity without careful regard to efficient and effective operations management, it is not, and cannot be regarded as, the sole aim and objective of industry. Adam Smith noted this in the eighteenth century and, despite the apparent unwillingness of too many organizations to accept consumption as the ultimate end and object of all industry and commerce, Adam Smith's words are as true today as they were 200 years ago.

Leaving aside the tactical conflict points, the areas of potential strategic conflict between operations and marketing centre on (yet again) the relative importance between internal and external influences. Again, the organization is seeking a balance between the internal efficiency of production and the external effectiveness of the products and/or services

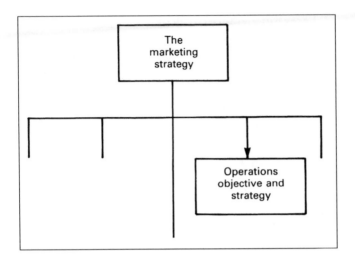

Figure 66
Operations objective
and strategy

produced by the organization. The lead must clearly come from marketing strategy.

There is no doubt at all that what the organization produces must be
driven solely by what the marketplace requires and not by what the
organization is simply able to produce. This is the classic distinction
between production and marketing orientations. While with other areas
of the organization, a certain degree of collaboration is required (albeit
led by the marketing strategy), operations strategy must be driven exclusively by the organization's marketing objectives (see Figure 66). Once the
marketing objective and marketing strategy (themselves driven by clearly
identified and understood market needs) have laid down what the
organization has to produce, it is then the role of the operations function
to mobilize its resource in order to produce what the market wants in the
most efficient and effective manner possible.

Potential conflict arises, once more, from different perceptions. From
different views on what is important. What is important when considering facilities design, scheduling, inventory, quality and forecasting could
differ markedly between the operations strategist concerned with cost
and efficiency and the marketing strategist concerned with satisfying
customer demands.

There is a specific, strategic area that often serves to confuse the relative
roles of marketing and operational strategy – the control of the research
and development function. Whether or not the function or department
operates under the R&D name, it is to be found in almost all organizations, where, due to its essentially technical nature, it is often placed
under the direct control of the operations function. If line responsibility
also involves control this can provide problems over the long term.

It is very important that the R&D function is led by marketing rather than operational strategy. It is essential that the organization's R&D effort is concentrated on finding practical, technical solutions to problems which the marketplace already has or is expected to have in the future. There is nothing more depressing than seeing the marketing effort of an organization being placed behind a wonderful, technical innovation that the marketplace doesn't really want – but we feel duty bound to sell because X million pounds, dollars or francs have been invested in a research programme and we have to show a profit somewhere. The world is littered with heroic failures such as the Sinclair C5, the Ford Edsell, the Egg & Bacon Soup (marketed as a convenience English breakfast), and the IBM PC Junior – I see no reason why our organizations need to be blindly following this trend. It is difficult enough for an organization to become and remain market oriented. One of the ways that we can resist the pressures to put internal considerations above external is to properly control the research and development function so that its flow of new products or services are firmly rooted in market needs rather than technical/production possibilities.

Conclusions

Every organization nowadays needs specialists if they are to achieve the level of efficiency necessary to guarantee profits in ever more competitive marketplaces. The marketing function is equally a specialist function within the organization. The primary difference between marketing strategy and finance, human resource and operations strategy as well as organizational structure and design is that marketing's responsibility and primary focus of attention lie outside the organization. The other functions' responsibility and attention are focused primarily within the organization. It is this internal versus external focus which is normally the root cause of all the usual but senseless and unproductive conflicts which exist within too many organizations.

It is one thing to state boldly that it is the marketing strategy which must give direction to the other areas of the business and the organizational structure, it is quite something else to achieve this happy position. If the organization is market oriented in its outlook, then the position will be much easier to achieve. If, however, as is more often the case, the organization is production oriented and only the marketing function looks outside, then consistency of the organizational effort will be elusive.

At the end of the day, however, we are left with one inescapable fact – if it is only the marketing function in your organization which is concerning itself with the external marketplace, the source of all the organization's profits, then you will be entering a competitive race for customers with a severe handicap. As markets become more sophisticated and more demanding, so competition becomes more intense and margins can be expected to come under greater pressure. In these circumstances, internal squabbling becomes a very expensive pastime.

Unless a common sense of external, market-based purpose can be instilled within the organization, then we will risk the possibility of internal squabbles over procedure, turf or priorities becoming lengthy discussions about how best to arrange the deck chairs on the Titanic as the ship slowly sinks into the sea.

Conclusions – Part Two

Now that we have reached the end of the most important part of this book, the question of marketing strategy, I wonder whether you feel you have answers to all your questions. I suspect not. Well you hardly expected me to do your job for you did you? Marketing strategy is, after all, a very personal activity. Driven as it must be by the individual and unique circumstances of your organization's business and your organization's existing and targeted future marketplaces, there can be no such thing as a blueprint answer to everybody's problem.

What, then, can we say we have learned about marketing strategy? If you have picked up the following points then you have done extremely well. The main lessons are:

- Marketing strategy is all about the conversion and translation of your organization's business objective and business strategy into practical market-related terms.
- Your marketing strategy must be driven primarily from an understanding of the needs and wants of your existing and future marketplaces. This then must be allied to an ambitious but realistic assessment of your organization's ability to deliver the benefits and/or solutions which your marketplace requires.
- The marketing objective and marketing strategy should be seen as a combination of decisions which need to be adjusted and fine-tuned until a balance is achieved and the organization can clearly see the way forward.
- The marketing strategy should lead the way for other important strategic efforts within the organization. It should be used to guide major decisions on organizational structure and design, finance strategy, human resource strategy and operations strategy. The marketing function cannot

realistically be expected to achieve the necessary marketplace results (for results read profits) without the active support and participation of the other key functions in the organization. While marketing strategy should lead from the front, success comes from creating an enthusiastic band of followers rather than press-ganged time servers.

- There is a world of difference between what constitutes marketing strategy and what should properly be termed marketing tactics. Strategy comes first, tactics follow. The two cannot be mixed.

To support the final point, the next part looks, briefly, at marketing tactics.

Further reading to Part Two

Baker M., *The Marketing Book*, 2nd edition (Butterworth-Heinemann, Oxford, 1991).

Cowell D., *The Marketing of Services*, 2nd revised edition (Butterworth-Heinemann, Oxford, 1991).

Cravens D., Strategic Forces Affecting Marketing Strategy, *Business Horizons (US)*, Sept/Oct 1986, Indiana University, School of Business, Bloomington, Indiana.

Engel, Kollat and Blackwell, *Consumer Behaviour* (Dryden Press, Chicago)

Kotler P., *Marketing Management*, 9th edition (Prentice Hall, Englewood Cliffs, NJ, 1997).

McDonald M., *Marketing Plans*, 3rd edition (Butterworth-Heinemann, Oxford, 1994).

Terpstra V., *International Marketing*, 7th edition (Dryden Press, Chicago, 1997).

Part Three

How do we get there?

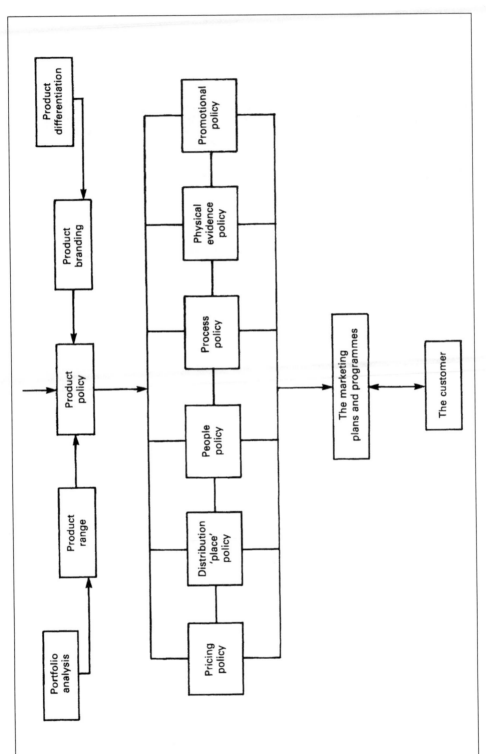

Moving from strategy to tactics

Chapter 8

Connecting with the market

'The control of a large force is the same in principle as the control of a few men: it is merely a question of dividing up their numbers.'

Sun Tzu, 500 BC

As we move from marketing strategy to marketing tactics, it is important to understand the role of this section in a book on marketing strategy. Strategy, of any kind, must be implemented if it is to have any value. Implementation must be monitored and controlled if the strategy is not to be corrupted. For these two reasons, the marketing strategist must be involved in tactical issues. We cannot draw a clear line of demarcation between the two. The problem is not whether the strategic marketer should be involved in tactics (most will find it irresistible anyway), but how deeply to become involved – what to concentrate on and where to stop.

This part on marketing tactics will concentrate on the marketing mix. We will not be trying to cover all the mix elements in great depth, there are many excellent texts that have already done this and I certainly do not consider it my role to try and replicate their work here in a few pages. My main intention is to try and show the fundamental inter-connectedness of the marketing mix elements. While most marketers have a detailed understanding of the various, separate, elements of the marketing mix, what is too often overlooked is the strategic nature of the word 'mix'. As I hope I emphasized sufficiently in Part Two, the key to successful marketing strategy is not that the individual elements of the marketing mix are 'right' or appropriate to market needs on a one-by-one basis, but that they are blended together to create a cohesive and logical approach. Part Three then, will look at the marketing mix but, specifically, at how the individual elements can be blended strategically to achieve the marketing objectives.

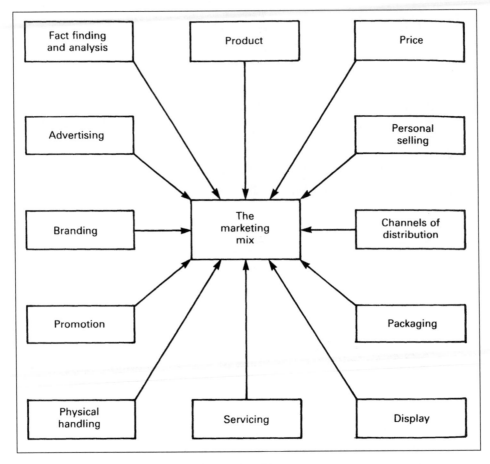

Figure 67 The marketing mix. *Source:* Bordon N.H., 'The concept of the marketing mix', in Schwartz G., *Science in Marketing* (Wiley, Chichester, 1965), pp. 386–97.

The term 'marketing mix' has been used as a shorthand way of describing the combined tactical activities of the marketing function for more than twenty-five years. The first true marketing mix was outlined by Bordon in 1965 when he attempted to sum up the complete range of marketing activities under the headings seen in Figure 67.

This list was developed further in 1975 by McCarthy who reduced Bordon's previous list down to four major sub-headings known as the 'Four Ps' (see Figure 68). While McCarthy's marketing mix had the very important benefit of all the words beginning with the letter p (an invaluable aide-memoire for the harassed marketing man, I feel), we must always remember that marketing remains a complicated and interconnected activity. Reducing the mix from twelve to four key elements just

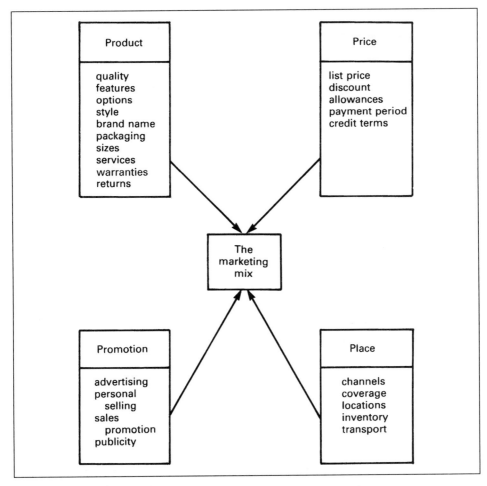

Figure 68 McCarthy's developed marketing mix. *Source:* McCarthy E.J., *Basic Marketing* (Irwin, 1975).

means that the elements themselves become more complicated and will overlap.

In 1981, Booms and Bitner looked again at the marketing mix, this time from a services marketing view, and suggested an expanded marketing mix of the elements shown in Figure 69. The seven Ps mix was developed specifically to deal with the marketing of services which differ from manufactured products in a number of ways. Services are characterized by:

- intangibility – service products often cannot be touched, seen, tasted, smelt or heard (e.g. banking, consulting);
- inseparability – services may not be easily separated from the seller (e.g. doctors, lecturers);

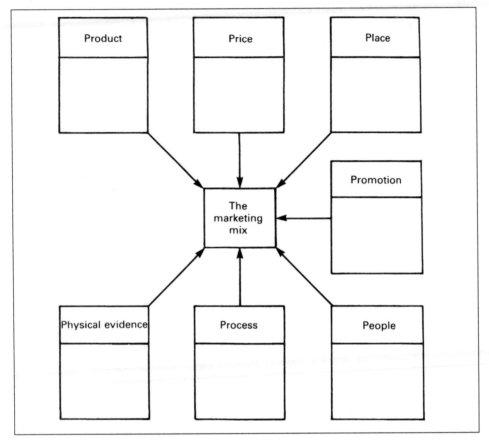

Figure 69 Booms and Bitner's version of the marketing mix. *Source:* Booms B.H. and Bitner M.J., 'Marketing strategy and organization structures for service firms', in Donnelly J. and George W.R., *Marketing of Services* (American Marketing Association, 1981).

- heterogeneity – there are often too many variables to allow the organization to achieve standardization (e.g. hotels, car servicing);
- perishability – services often cannot be stocked or stored (e.g. a hotel room, radio news bulletin); and
- ownership – services often involve access to, but not ownership of, a product (e.g. lawyers, public swimming pools).

The additional three elements included in the Booms and Bitner mix are brought in to broaden the marketer's attention beyond the mechanical product–price–place–promotion myopia. 'People' reflects the importance of staff, sales and service personnel in the customers' choice of which service to purchase. 'Process' reflects the involvement of the customer in the operations/production process. 'Physical evidence' reflects the special importance of increasing the tangibility of services with physical representations that may, in themselves, have little or no value.

In the following, brief, review of marketing tactics, I have decided to use the Boom and Bitner seven Ps approach to the marketing mix for two reasons. First, if we look at the overall size and scope of the service sector (and include government services in our definition), then, in all western economies, services far outweigh manufacturing, both in terms of people employed, investment and share of GNP. The second reason for concentrating on the Booms and Bitner approach to the marketing mix is the important role of intangibles in marketing. The seven Ps mix was developed to deal with the intangible nature of service products, and this provides a special challenge to the marketing function. However, if we look at manufactured products, especially those in consumer markets, more and more emphasis is now being placed on the intangible aspects of the products rather than the tangible – the modern differentiation of cars, clothes and toiletries is more likely to be based on what ownership or use of the products say about you as a person than on what the products actually do. Marketers of tangible, manufactured products have much to learn from service marketers who have had to come to grips with the special problems inherent in marketing intangibles.

One final word on terminology. Many texts talk of product strategy, pricing strategy, branding strategy and even discount strategy. I have decided to keep the word strategy true to its original meaning – and if the general is busying himself with detailed questions like trade discounts, he shouldn't be! I have preferred to use the term 'policy' for these sub-strategic issues.

Chapter 9

Product policy

While product policy is undoubtedly the most important element of the marketing mix, there is still an immense amount of misunderstanding about exactly what a product is and what a product does. (See Figure 70.) All too often, products take on a life of their own and manage to create a dedicated and devoted following within the organization long after their useful life, as far as the marketplace is concerned, has passed. Products, while important, do not deserve to have the right to an existence for their own sake. A product is no more than the most appropriate vehicle, at any point in time, which will carry satisfactions produced by the organization in one direction, and carry profits from the marketplace to the organization in the opposite direction.

A product is no more than a package of benefits. This expression has been in existence for a long time but is still badly understood my many marketers. To explain through an example, in the early part of this century the main mode of transport between Europe and the USA was by passenger liner. The benefit which customers purchased was transportation from East to West, and from West to East. With the advent of load-bearing airliners, the shipping lines lost a large amount of their business, the benefits being demanded by customers had not changed but the product required to deliver those benefits had changed in nature from the ship to the aeroplane, at least for the bulk of travellers.

It is also interesting to note that the organizations dominating the transportation business in the early part of this century were not the same organizations dominating the business in the latter part of the century. In true production orientation style, the early organizations saw themselves as in the shipping business and owed (and still owe) an allegiance to sea transportation rather than their customers. I secretly suspect that despite this

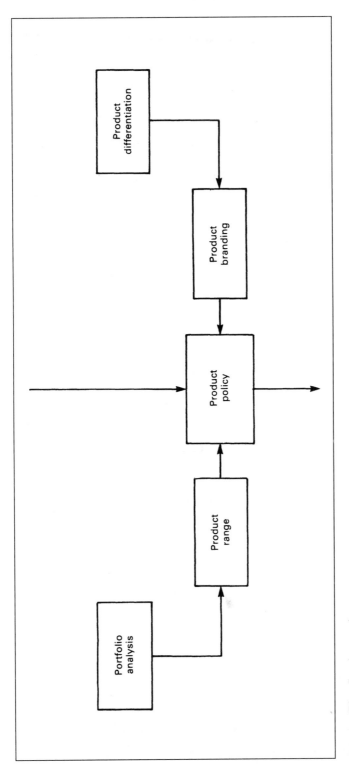

Figure 70 Product policy

very well-publicized approach to definition of the business we are in, that the next quantum leap in personal transportation, whatever it is, will find those organizations running airlines left behind, just as the shipping lines were left behind twenty or thirty years ago. Organizations seem to find it impossible to separate the product from the benefits which the products deliver and, as a result, we see a constant and steady decline in yesterday's organizations. They are simply left behind as consumer requirements are met by new organizations with different solutions to the same problems.

If, then, we move from the idea of the product as a physical entity to the product as a system or package of benefits, this helps us understand what constitutes the product and what the product does. I find the most

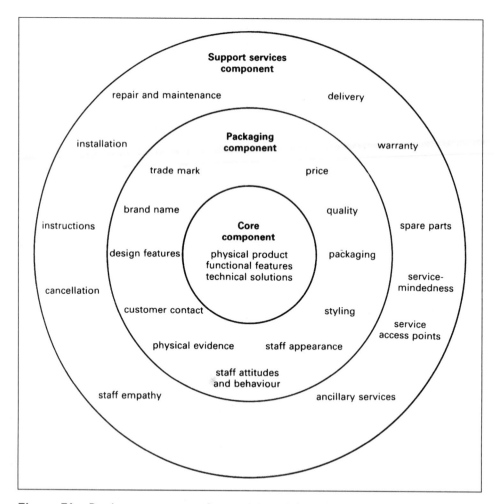

Figure 71   Product components *Source:* Adapted from Kotler P., *Marketing Management* (Prentice Hall, Englewood Cliffs, N.J., 1984)

useful way of considering this multi-faceted aspect of the product is to divide the product into its three broad component parts. Any product, be it service or a manufacturer of physical product can be seen as being broken into three quite distinct parts (see Figure 71). The most helpful way of approaching this concept of the product is through worked examples, the motor car provides a useful illustration of a physical product and an insurance policy of a service product.

The core component

The core component refers to the physical product and the functional features. In our example of the motor car this would be the body shell, a wheel on each corner with an engine of X cc that actually gets you from A to B in a certain fashion.

In terms of a service product, an insurance policy, the core component would include the technical expertise and 'know-how' which resides within the organization and allows the investor to be sure that money invested today will grow and will generate the future financial benefits expected.

The packaging component

The packaging component would add elements such as the trade mark, the brand name, certain design features including moulding, style, and colour. It would also include elements such as price (an important packaging component in that it links strongly to quality). Naturally, as soon as we take the core component of the car and add a trade mark such as Ford, Citroen or Volkswagen and then add brand names such as Granada, or Polo, the entire nature of the product will change in the eyes of the customer. A whole collection of attitudes, both positive and negative, will begin to be associated with the core component.

For the service product, trade mark, brand names and design features are equally important in the customer's choice. Additional elements such as customer contact, staff attitudes and staff appearance are all clues to the specific nature of the core component which most customers are unable to judge technically for themselves.

The support services component

The support services component would include repair and maintenance, installation, instructions, delivery terms, and spare parts. When the customer is considering the purchase of a major item such as a motor car, there are questions that need to be answered, for example, how reliable is the product? Is it likely to break down? What are the service charges? How fast will the service and repair be carried out? What guarantees and maintenance contracts are available? Elements of the support services component are becoming more and more important as product differentiators.

In terms of service products, we should be concerned with additional aspects such as service access points, staff discretion – always very important when dealing with financial service products. As one insurance company looks (or seems to look) much like another, staff empathy and other related services offered can become important differentiators.

To emphasize the point yet again (as if I really needed to), there is no doubt at all that the core component, the physical product, functional features or the technical know-how, actually has to work. This is after all the basic promise of your organization: that your product (core component) will deliver the benefits required of it. This, of course, was not always the case but, since the advent of Japanese motor cars which, once they are put on the road, actually work with a minimum of trouble, customer expectations have been raised.

What is most telling, however, is that most organizations I talk to, estimate that about eighty per cent of their total organization's effort goes into making sure that the core component works. If we look at the problem from the customer's point of view, it is fairly obvious that, in most situations, eighty per cent of the customer choice is made up from a consideration of the outer two rings, the support services component and the packaging component. Often this is because customers are not technically capable of assessing the core component.

The division of the organization's effort between the core and the support/packaging components is a strategic marketing decision and

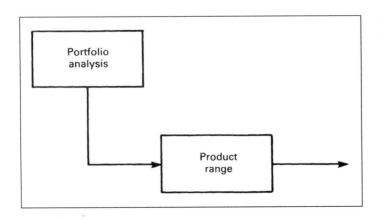

Figure 72
Portfolio analysis

needs to be considered very carefully. Now, I am certainly not suggesting that any organization should completely shift its effort from eighty
per cent core component twenty per cent support services plus packaging to twenty per cent core component eighty per cent the rest – this
would clearly be unreasonable. But there does appear to be a shift of
emphasis needed, certainly in most of the organizations I have come
across, and more attention should be paid to the support services and
packaging components. This is, after all, the primary point of interest of
our customers. In the service sector, it is the only area which is tangible!

Portfolio analysis and product decisions

This is another area of product policy where the strategic level decisions
need to be made before passing down to tactical marketers for implementation. Since marketing strategy is primarily concerned with longer
term marketing activity, it will need to cast some thought to the likely
product range developments that the organization will need to satisfy
future market demand.

Product range width and depth decisions will largely be driven by
business and marketing strategies – decisions already made about how
the organization is to operate in its marketplace (see Figure 72). The
differentiated organization will need to concentrate on extending the
product range width to support its claim to be an industry-wide player.
The focused organization, on the other hand, will probably need to
market a more narrow range of products, but, within its segments should
be able to offer a deeper range, in other words, more product variance in
the same category than its competitors. The product range enables the
organization to differentiate itself and its marketing effort from its prime
competitors and, therefore, to reinforce its selected strategic market
position and image.

Another strategic product decision is the development of the product
portfolio underneath the organization's management. Portfolio analysis,
dealing as it does with the future, is a fairly difficult task. However, there
are a number of concepts which have been developed over previous years
which may help us in this area. Firstly, the Boston or BCG matrix suggests
that the organization's products can be divided into four broad categories
(see Figure 73).

In simple terms, the BCG argument is that cash cows should be milked
for all available funds, these funds should then be channelled into the
question mark products in the hope of turning these into stars which
then turn into cash cows. Dogs, they suggest, should be removed from

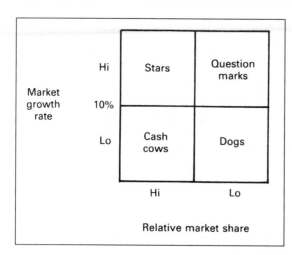

Figure 73 The Boston or BCG matrix. *Source:* The Boston Consulting Group

the product range as they do little or nothing for the organizational image or its long-term future. From a portfolio point of view, the Boston matrix may help an organization to classify its current product range and identify changes required for the future. Too many products falling into the 'dog' category could spell trouble. Likewise, too many 'cash cows' may mean a cash rich position now but little or no future sales potential. The problem arises, however, in how to classify the existing products.

Another concept which can be useful in some circumstances is the product life cycle (PLC) (see Figure 74). Most marketers are conversant

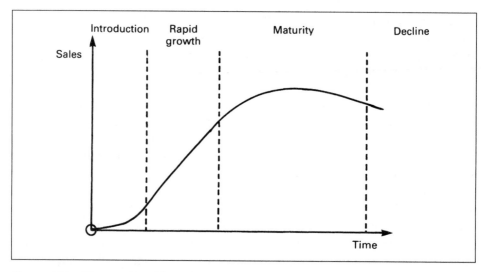

Figure 74 The product life cycle

with the concept of the PLC which states that any product will pass through a predictable path from introduction through growth through maturity into eventual decline. The underlying idea is that you should ensure that you have a reasonably balanced portfolio of products through the various stages. You want neither all of your products in the introduction and growth stage, nor even less all of your products in the decline stage. You should attempt to have a reasonable balanced portfolio to ensure that enough new products are coming through to replace the older products as they fall off the end of the life cycle. Not all commentators believe that the PLC is a valid concept so you should be careful how far you pursue this particular theory within your organization.

The third suggestion of portfolio analysis comes from Peter Drucker who suggested that most organizations' products fall into one of the following categories:

- tomorrow's breadwinners;
- today's breadwinners;
- products with potential if something drastic is done;
- yesterday's breadwinners;
- the 'also-rans'; and
- the failures.

Again, the idea is to try and make sure that the organization's product portfolio is balanced, ideally a mixture of 'today's breadwinners' and 'tomorrow's breadwinners'. If the portfolio is overloaded with 'yesterday's breadwinners', 'also-rans' and 'failures', you could be looking at serious troubles for the future.

Although these concepts and others (look for ADL, GEC/McKinsey, Johnson and Scholes for example) are to be found in all marketing texts and their use is widely attempted by marketers, you should be wary on relying too much from the theories of this nature for detailed planning of the future. For example the BCG matrix was generally held to be applicable by most organizations until Hanson not only started buying a large number of 'dog' industries but then started showing everybody how you could still make money out of these businesses. Portfolio analysis models can be considered useful memory joggers and useful concepts to be used in planning future product development but, as with all such models, accurate measurement is extremely difficult. Identifying current positions is the first hurdle, predicting future market movements is the second. Decisions based solely on mathematical analyses of this nature are unlikely to stand the pressure of an irrational marketplace.

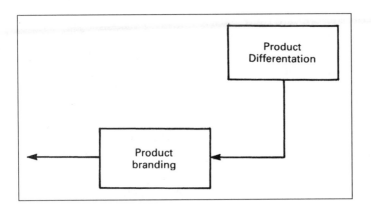

Figure 75
Product
differentiation

Product differentiation and branding

There is little doubt that, nowadays, profitability is directly linked with the organization's ability to successfully differentiate and brand its products and/or services. (See Figure 75.) Since profit is the ultimate measure of marketing objectives and the organization's marketing activity, the question of differentiation and product branding must remain a strictly strategic decision. If we look at the sorts of products and services which are now differentiated, appearing to possess a sense of uniqueness, and compare this to the more commodity images of twenty or thirty years ago, the whole area of product differentiation must be counted as one of marketing's success stories.

From a marketing strategy point of view, there are two important questions – how to differentiate and how to achieve consistancy. There are a number of ways in which products and services can be differentiated from the competition, but beware the appearance of production orientation when a choice has to be made. The key to successful differentiation lies, not inside the organization, but in the marketplace. It may sound heretical, or even dishonest, but the 'unique' positionings that work are not always based on true differences – but they are always based on what customers perceive to be true differences. It is the important job of marketing strategy to identify possible gaps in today's and tomorrow's marketplace, and then to identify differentiated positions that are credible in the eyes of the organization's customers.

The second strategic task is ensuring that the differentiated image and positioning of products and/or services is consistent with the organization's business and marketing objectives. It is especially important that the various differentiated positions of the organization's product/service range appear to be consistent first, among themselves, second, with the organization's target image in the marketplace, and third, with the organization's long-term strategic intentions.

Brands and branding have also become more important over the past ten to twenty years, to such a point that larger organizations are looking at ways of including the value of their brands onto the balance sheet. Many organizations have started to recognize that the value represented by their brands may outweigh the assets value appearing on the balance sheet. The takeover battle between Nestlé and Rowntree in the late 1980s was certainly not fought for the control of a small number of UK-based manufacturing plants – it was a battle for control over a small number of extremely important global confectionery brands such as Kit-Kat and Polo mints.

Brands, like any other major asset owned by the organization, need constant attention, investment and managing. This is certainly a strategic activity to be carried out over the longer term for major returns. A brand's development is very much a long-term activity and the strategic development of a brand should never be put at risk by short-term profit, volume demands or other tactical activity of this nature. The marketing strategy should identify its critical brands and should also clearly plan the strategic development of these brands so that the marketing tacticians can orchestrate their shorter term activity planning within an overall context and established guidelines of the longer term growth of the brand.

Chapter 10

The rest of the mix

'All men can see the tactics whereby I conquer, but what none can see is the strategy out of which victory is evolved.'

Sun Tzu, 500 BC

While product policy is obviously central to the development of marketing strategy, and the market–product match critical to the organization's success, the whole mix needs to be carefully, systematically and creatively designed so that the target market sees only a seamless presentation (see Figure 76).

Pricing policy

I always find it fascinating to see how little time is spent on pricing policy decisions relative to the other three or six major elements – depending on which marketing mix format you happen to be following. This relative disregard for the importance for pricing policy is even more surprising when we realize that pricing is the only source of revenue and potential profits. All the other elements of the marketing mix are costs! (See Figure 77.)

Since the success of the organization in achieving its marketing objectives is measured on a profit basis, pricing policy must be under strict strategic control. Pricing is certainly not the last activity of the mix to be considered, nor is it something which can be quickly solved on the back of an envelope on the way to a meeting with the advertising agency.

Most organizations find the pricing policy a difficult area to manage. More often than not, this is because insufficient research has been carried

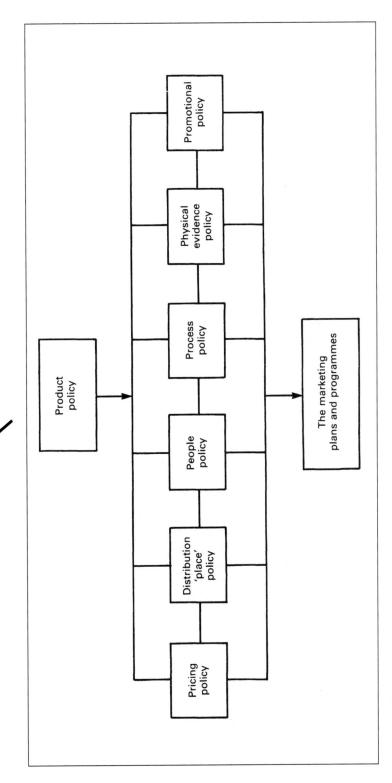

Figure 76 The rest of the mix

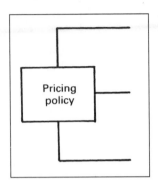

Figure 77 Pricing policy

out in the marketplace to find out the important parameters on pricing – the right price levels and the real flexibility open to the organization in its pricing decisions. Often an organization is more than happy to spend a hundred thousand dollars or pounds on researching its new product concepts, but is loathe to spend one per cent of that on researching the different customer perceptions to various price levels.

There are a number of factors which will probably influence your organization's pricing policy, factors such as the competitors' price, the position of the product in the lifecycle, company positioning policy, perceived level of differentiation and perceived value, and so on. One factor which, of course, should not have any influence on the pricing policy is the internal production cost of the product/service. Cost does not inform the organization about what price it should charge, that is the job of the marketplace. Cost only informs the organization about the level of profits it will make from its sale.

The most common mistakes in pricing policy can easily be identified. First, organizations tend to be too cost oriented in the pricing. Second, price is often not revised enough to capitalize on market changes. Third, price is too often set independently of the rest of the marketing mix rather than as an intrinsic element of the market positioning strategy. Fourth, price is often not varied enough for different product items and different market segments.

The critical element in strategic pricing is to strike the elusive balance between the organization's need for profit and the market's desire to pay the right price for the right product.

Distribution 'place' policy

Distribution or 'place' policy is another area where the marketing function can spend lots of time for ultimately very little return. (See Figure 78.) Distribution is a major question for most organizations – manufacturers are

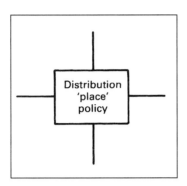

Figure 78 Distribution 'place' policy

concerned with how to distribute and deliver product to the customers and service providers are concerned with the location of service points and customer accessibility. While the basic marketing question behind distribution policy is quite simple – where would our customers expect to find our products or service? – most distribution channels tend to have grown historically to their present configuration. There are two strategic questions to be answered before the distribution problem can be passed on.

First, the distribution system should be assessed on a regular basis. If the organization were starting afresh, with a clean sheet of paper, what kind of distribution system or network would be required to meet our marketing objectives? Then, how would this ideal system compare with the system we currently have? Are there changes that the marketing tacticians need to look at here?

The second strategic task is to ensure that the distribution policy matches, as far as possible, the needs of the overall marketing effort. With the shift of power, in some industry sectors, from the producer to the distribution channel manager, we are starting to see entire marketing strategies being modified to ensure adequate product/service coverage. Such modifications, while they may produce short-term market advantage, also produce a marketing strategy which is distribution-led rather than market-led.

People policy

There are two aspects to the 'people' element of the mix which have a strategic dimension:

- service personnel – of interest to both manufacturers and service providers; and
- customers – of more interest in this context to the service sector.

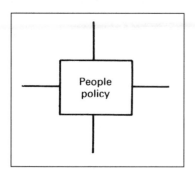

Figure 79   People policy

In the 1990s, as more and more competitive activity shifts from the tangible to the intangible, then the selection, recruitment, motivation and training of the right service personnel becomes more important to all organizations. As technology becomes more widely available, so differentiation based on the product's 'core component' becomes more difficult. The 'packaging' and 'support services' components are becoming the modern arenas for competition. Service levels are becoming critical. (See Figure 79.)

The customer's perception of service quality will be made up from a number of fairly different and diverse factors:

- the attitudes of staff;
- internal relations;
- the observable behaviour of staff;
- the level of service-mindedness in the organization;
- the consistency of appearance of staff;
- the accessibility of people;
- customer–customer contacts,
  . . . and so on.

It is an inevitable trend that as the use of advanced technology becomes more and more widespread, the physical or tangible component of each organization's product offer will tend more and more towards a common standard. In other words, there is really not very much to choose between a motor car produced by Ford, Vauxhall, Volkswagen or Renault. They all take advantage of the same level of technical competence, they all tend to bring in the same advanced features over a limited period of time, they all obviously seem to use the same wind tunnels and the 'jelly-mould' design of the modern motor car seems to be a standard feature. The physical components of more and more manufactured products are tending towards a standard. Most competitive activity, therefore, is tending to concentrate on the intangible aspects of products such as reflected status, fashion and, of course, the all important customer service. As more products, especially consumer durables, tend towards a common standard, differential levels of after sales service, maintenance, repair etc., become the only factors on which the customer is able to differentiate between and make an informed selection from the products on offer.

In the service sector, the words 'customer service' are even more important. As there exists no standardized physical product capable of carrying the organization's image into the marketplace, customer service is all that the organization has to offer.

The importance of customer service

Customer service programmes have experienced a boom in the 1980s, much of the work stimulated by the reported success of British Airways' 'Putting People First' programme.

I should state at this point that I have nothing against customer service programmes per se, it would be very difficult to be negative about customer service programmes since all they are really preaching is the marketing concept. And, if we need to re-package the idea in order to get the marketing concept through to the people in the organization that really matter, then the ends certainly justify the means. The problem with customer service programmes lies, not in the programmes themselves, but with the senior managers who initiate the programmes in their organizations. Customer service programmes, while extremely valuable in any organization, are not, and can never be, the panacea to all ills and problems. So before you rush off and spend large amounts of your hard-earned money on developing and running a customer service programme, there are two important questions you should ask yourself:

- Assuming that we have recognized that changes/improvements need to be made to our marketing, are we supporting the changes in customer service levels by the appropriate changes in the other areas of the marketing mix?
- Have we set appropriate service level objectives?

Customer service as part of the marketing mix

From our discussions on the marketing mix so far, it should be evident that no single element of the mix can, or should ever be expected to, solve all the problems of the organization and satisfy all needs of its target market alone. This is also the case for customer service. Even the much vaunted 'Putting People First' exercise carried out at British Airways was not simply a programme in making people smile. The changes in customer service were accompanied by quite significant changes in the product policy, in pricing, distribution (routings and service outlets), in all other elements of the marketing mix. The programme was also accompanied by significant redundancies which always focuses peoples' minds.

Satisfying customers needs is a more complicated business than just making sure that your service personnel smile more. Too many organizations approach the customer service aspects of the marketing mix as a 'have a nice day' exercise, and seem to think that its execution can be seen as an independent element of the marketing mix. This cannot be so. To be effective, any customer service programme must be fully integrated into the overall marketing mix. If the effort is to be successful, in marketplace terms, then any changes need to be accompanied by the relevant changes in product, pricing, promotion activity to produce a better overall marketing package that meets customer needs and expectations.

Customer service objective

The biggest trouble with bandwagons is that people tend to jump on them without quite understanding where they are going. Customer service programmes in the 1980s is an extremely good example of a modern-day bandwagon. As a number of leading organizations, in a wide variety of industries, have become more customer oriented, they are starting to deliver improved and enhanced levels of customer service. This has led generally to an increased level of expectation among customers throughout all sectors. Organizations that have been slower to respond to this new trend have started to see the number of complaints about their service levels increase, as a result the customer service crusade has started to build momentum.

The one big problem with customer service programmes is that they are expensive. They are expensive to set up, they are expensive to run through an entire organization and it is also very expensive to maintain the changes in place after the initial programmes have been completed. A marketing investment in customer services is not, of itself, a bad thing – any investment, however, needs to be measured against what it is trying to do. In too many cases, customer services programmes are set up in organizations without a clear understanding of what they are trying to achieve. Responses from organizations such as 'to be the best provider of customer service in our business' or 'to be the Marks & Spencer of our particular business' are really not the most appropriate objectives to be working to. Customer service levels and, possibly, customer service programmes, need to be seen as an integral element of the marketing mix.

It is the job of marketing strategy to highlight any possible shortfall that the organization has in this area but then also to determine the 'appropriate' level of customer service to which the organization should aspire. The customer service level must be 'right' given the organization's market objective, market strategy, strategic market position and differentiated position relative to competition.

Even 'flavour of the month' activities like customer service programmes must be integrated into the overall marketing effort. Additional (often significant) investment to establish your organization as the highest provider of customer service may not be 'a good thing'. If, due to your established market position, your customers would not expect particularly high levels of customer service, expensive customer service programmes do little more than waste hard-earned marketing resource. In the longer term it could even be detrimental to your business as your customers may start to resent the additional cost of service levels which they perceive to be inappropriate for an organization with your established market position.

Process policy

Process policy is all about production and operations management. (See Figure 80.) Operations management is not just concerned with manufacturing organizations producing physical products, although the former labelling of the area as production management did tend to give it this emphasis. Increasingly, service organizations are discovering that operations management ideas are now an essential input to their control of costs, systems improvements and levels of customer service. If we define operations as the means by which resource inputs are combined, reformed, transformed or separated to create useful outputs (i.e. benefits) then we can start

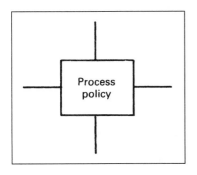

Figure 80   Process policy

to see the application of operations management as a concept in service as well as physical product organizations. Unfortunately, marketing texts rarely discuss operations management in any detail. The usual view expressed is that marketing management and operational management need to work together if customer needs are to be satisfied. We have already looked at the strategic interface between marketing and operations and at some of the areas in which the two functions must work together if the organization is to achieve success in its marketplace.

While, in an organization which markets a physical product, it is easy to see the important role played by production/operations management, this vital link is often less clear in the service sector. Nevertheless, a significant component of any service product, from the customer's point of view, is how the process of service delivery actually functions. The service operations systems which make it possible for a customer to leave a car for service, to pick up a hire car at the airport, to withdraw cash from a bank with little effort – all these systems will have advantages over competitive systems which do not run on time, impose excessive demands on customers, or do not deliver what they promise. This brief description of the operations management system in a service organization will also apply to those organizations who produce and market manufactured goods, since, as well as a physical production system, there is also a parallel service production system which is needed to deliver the important customer service elements of the product.

There are two aspects to the 'process' element of the mix which have a strategic dimension:

- degree of customer contact; and
- quality control standards.

Degree of contact

The managers responsible for the efficient and effective running of the operations management function in the organization will be working, quite properly, to a set of pre-determined performance criteria. These criteria are normally concentrated in areas such as output and costing – internal measures. The marketing strategy, on the other hand, has as its primary focus the customer and the marketplace.

Bringing these two foci of attention together, the point at which a seamless partnership needs to be fused is where the customer comes into contact with the production system.

Any production/operations system can be seen as a series of inter-related operations or jobs which ultimately end in the creation of either a product or a service, but in any case a package of benefits which the target customer will want to purchase. Since the managers responsible for operations will be motivated by internal, structured performance measures, they will concentrate on allocating resource to those areas of the operations process which are more delicate or more important in an operation sense. First line resource will be dedicated to ensuring that these 'critical' points in the production process work most efficiently and that the production flow is smooth and uninterrupted. The marketer, on the other hand, will, or should, be more concerned in ensuring that the operations process works cleanly and efficiently at those points where there is direct customer contact. Naturally enough, these points of high customer contact may not necessarily be the most critical point in terms of technical production flow.

This is best explained through an example. Let us imagine that (like me) you drive a car but have only a sparse knowledge about mechanics and servicing. Let us also imagine that (unlike me) you have an upmarket company car provided by a garage that likes to pride itself on its after-sales service. The first two times that you put the car in for a service it comes back with some minor defects cured without you even asking and has even been cleaned, inside and out. On the third service, however, the car comes back as dirty as it went in. Being a marketer, and a gentleman, you say nothing but start wondering, if the garage can be inconsistent when it comes to valeting the car, what are they doing with the mechanics? Are they cutting corners over things that really matter? Can you still trust them? Is it time to start looking for another garage? In all probability, the service manager was faced with a sick mechanic on the day and decided to maintain quality on the 'important' (technical) jobs and sacrifice the 'unimportant frills'. Sadly, by doing what he thought was the right thing, he may have lost a profitable customer.

It is specifically at these points of high customer contact that the 'process' element of the marketing mix needs to be managed most carefully. The customer should be able to see an overall logic and consistency to the organization's operations. At high contact points in the operations process, the organization should be asking itself whether the steps in the process are arranged in a logical manner from the customer's point of view. We should also be asking ourselves whether these steps are all necessary or whether any steps can be eliminated, combined or, at least, balanced. Finally, we should be asking ourselves whether the high contact steps in the operations process are employing the 'right' level of automation. In operations, there is always a trade-off between people and systems. Automation may remove the high-cost element (people) but may, at the same time, produce problems in staff motivation. More dangerously, customers faced with more and more technology can become dissatisfied – be careful that automation is not introduced at the expense of personal service.

Quality control standards

Quality control standards can, and should be set for service operations in the same way as for manufacturing. Service quality standards may, however, be more qualitative than the quantitative standards set in manufacturing. As we have already seen, there is an area of potential conflict between operations management and marketing management when it comes to agreeing and setting quality standards. Standards should always be driven by the marketplace (represented in the organization by marketing) and should not be set by internal production-led benchmarks or, even more dangerously, by what we are able to achieve.

The process element of the marketing mix is, increasingly, an essential ingredient in the organization's battle in the marketplace. These aspects of the organization's activity are far too important to ignore and must be integrated into the overall marketing mix at a strategic level if the organization is to appear logical in market and marketing terms.

Physical evidence policy

Physical evidence policy, like people policy and process policy, is one of the additional three elements introduced into the marketing mix by Booms and Bitner in 1981. (See Figure 81.) We have already seen that more and more physical products are being differentiated by their intangible rather than tangible aspects. Physical evidence policy, as an element of the mix, is becoming more important for all organizations. However,

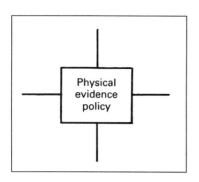

Figure 81   Physical evidence policy

the emphasis which needs to be placed on the physical evidence differs for services and manufactured products. To explain the difference, I will deal with each sector separately.

Physical evidence policy in the service sector

Physical evidence is the term Booms and Bitner use to describe the various tangible elements which the organization uses to facilitate the purchase and consumption of an intangible service product. For example, admission tickets to a theatre or a concert, cheque books and credit cards for banking services, aeroplanes used by airlines and the cars used by car rental organizations. While these physical aspects of the service product may, or may not have any intrinsic worth in themselves, they are essential to the delivery of the service product. More importantly, physical evidence of this type can be used to create the 'environment' or 'atmosphere' in which a service is bought or performed, and can help shape customer perceptions of the service.

Customers tend to form impressions of a service organization partly through physical evidence such as buildings, furnishings, lay-outs, and goods associated with the service, like carrier bags, tickets and brochures – how else, apart from grasping at these clues, are we to assess the suitability of a hotel, airline or bank before we agree to buy the service offered? Unfortunately, many service marketers neglect this aspect of service design and often fail to recognize the various forms of evidence that they can actually control. Classifying them as below-the-line publicity items, many marketers fail to see the strategic importance of such physical evidence and its place in the marketing mix.

Not only do people form images of various service organizations based on an array of physical evidence, but management of the evidence is essential to ensure that the image projected conforms to the image which the organization desires and is set down in the business strategy. Service organizations with competing service products may also use physical evidence to differentiate their service products in the marketplace and give their products some competitive advantage. While, in some respects, managing physical evidence may be seen as optional by some manufacturers, it is essential for organizations in the service sector.

Senior marketers in service industries do not have the option not to manage the physical evidence. In the absence of the active management of this element of the mix, the physical evidence will still communicate to the customer, but in an uncoordinated and chaotic fashion, result – a confused customer – and a confused customer is just what marketing is trying to avoid.

Physical evidence policy for physical products

Unlike the service sector, the apparent problem in manufacturing at the moment is not that the physical evidence aspects are not being managed, but that overall control and consistency of the physical evidence is lacking. Many of the individual elements of the physical evidence policy are currently covered and managed under elements of the original four Ps marketing mix. Packaging design comes under the product mix, store location, accessibility, merchandising, in-store display, point-of-sale material, brochures, leaflets and below-the-line support all come under the headings of either place or promotion.

The change which I am suggesting at this point may, to many organizations, appear to be cosmetic – that the various elements above, most of which are being managed already, should be brought under the new heading of physical evidence in the mix. This change is, however, far from just cosmetic and is certainly not included simply to confuse, much less to enlarge and expand the role of the marketing function.

The key to successful marketing strategy is, as I have argued ceaselessly, controlled implementation. At the forefront of the marketing function, it is the role of marketing strategy to ensure that the overall mix has a degree of consistency and logic which will appeal to the target marketplace. The management of the physical evidence aspects of the mix for manufactured products is going to be more and more important as we move into the 1990s. Manufactured products are already, and will continue to be, purchased more for the intangible promises which they offer than their physical attributes. Since successful marketing in this area of intangibles will depend more and more on the effective management of the physical evidence aspects of the product, then it is imperative that the organization brings these various elements under a common, standard banner.

The most important task is for the various elements of the physical evidence to appear to be logical and consistent to the customer. The product packaging and design, the point-of-sale support material, the selection and location of the intermediary or service access point etc., should all appear to be completely consistent and support the organization's target market image and position. It is more important that the elements that come together in front of the customer appear to be consistent than that the brochures are consistent with the above-the-line advertising, that the product packaging is consistent with other elements of the product mix, that the distribution outlet is consistent with the distribution policy. Obviously, if it can be seen as consistent from every angle (also known as the holy grail), then we have done our job properly. Unfortunately, this is not always possible.

By moving the various elements under the single banner of physical evidence policy, there is more chance that these important aspects of the marketing mix will be managed properly, that is from the customer's point of view.

Promotional policy

Promotion is defined as the whole array of methods and procedures by which the organization communicates with its target market. Physical evidence also has a strong communication effect in the marketplace as does price (a strong communicator of product quality and differentiation). Personal selling is also traditionally included in the promotional element of the mix since it is essentially a communication function in the same way as other below-the-line activities. (See Figure 82.)

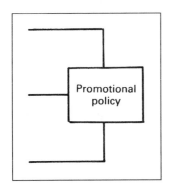

Figure 82   Promotional policy

I have placed promotion as the last element of the marketing mix since it should be the final activity to be planned within the marketing strategy. It is the final activity because no promotion can really take place (or promotional objectives and plans laid) until decisions have been made on the rest of the mix, and the organization knows what the product is on offer, the target market to be addressed, the price levels to be set, the distribution channels to be used and so on.

I will cover the promotional aspects of the mix in a very short form. This is for two reasons, first, there is more written on advertising and promotion in the marketing literature than in any other area, probably because it is one of the more interesting and glamourous areas. Second, we find that, in marketing, people are always expert at two jobs – their own and the advertising agency's.

What can promotion do?

Since promotion is the primary communications element of the mix, the objectives that can be set for promotional activity must be of the communications nature. In other words, promotion, including personal selling, cannot actually sell the products and/or service on its own. Therefore, any objectives which include sales targets cannot be dedicated solely to promotional activity. The achievement of sales targets will be dependent on many other factors as well as promotion.

At marketing-strategy level, it is as well to understand exactly what promotion can do for your organization. It is commonly accepted that promotional activity can achieve five broad objectives:

- to build awareness and interest in the product and the organization;
- to differentiate the product and the organization from competititors;
- to communicate and portray the benefits of the product;
- to build and maintain the overall image and reputation of the organization; and
- to persuade customers to buy or to use the product.

The promotion process

Strategically, the entire promotional activity can be seen, very simply, as a set of six broad steps (see Figure 83).

While everybody gets really involved in discussing the subjective merits of this or that advertisement or the advisability of using this or that colour on the packaging, it is essential that the marketing strategy remains above the tactical fray. An understanding of this simple six-stage process can help to remind us what we are trying to do with promotion.

Promotional objectives

These objectives should be couched in communication terms and should be passed down from marketing strategy. They are an intregal part of the marketing mix and relate to the marketing objectives and business strategy.

The target audience

Promotion must start with an understanding of who we are trying to contact. We need to understand who these people are, where they are to be found, what motivates them, what de-motivates them, what their needs and problems are, before we can tackle any structured promotional activity.

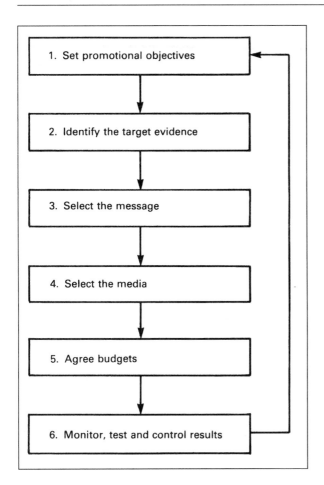

Figure 83 The promotion process

The message flow diagram contains:

1. Set promotional objectives
2. Identify the target evidence
3. Select the message
4. Select the media
5. Agree budgets
6. Monitor, test and control results

The message

Marketing strategy must state clearly and unambiguously the precise message that we wish to communicate to the given target audience. Twenty six different messages may be interesting but they will be impossible to communicate. We should look for simple messages such as 'Buy product x' or 'Product x is different because ...'. Don't be concerned about being too simplistic and straightforward – the communications experts will be able to deal with (and complicate) any raw material you give them.

The media

Once you have decided on the audience to whom the message will be addressed, and the message we need to communicate, then, and only then, can we start to work out the ideal form of media through which this message should be communicated. The media at your disposal, depending on your country of operation, may include:

- Above-the-line:
    newspapers and magazines
    trade and professional press
    television
    radio
    cinema
- Below-the-line:
    exhibitions
    direct mail
    point-of-sale
    packaging
    sales promotion
    personal selling
- Indirect:
    company image
    the product/service
    pricing
    word of mouth

Budgets

Advertising and promotion is one of the best ways of wasting money known to any organization. Budgets must be clearly agreed and settled in advance of any promotional activity, and everyone in the organization must know where the budgets came from, how they were devised and how they will be used. On the other hand, cutting pre-agreed promotional budgets at the first sign of adverse market conditions is not good business practice either.

Testing and control

Every promotional plan requires a short statement which explains, succinctly, how the investment in advertising and promotion will generate a return for the organization – and how this return will be measured. It is especially important that the measurement of the advertising and promotional effectiveness and how the activity is going to be tested and controlled, is clearly understood before any activity takes place. It is also important that any sub-contractors such as advertising agencies, PR agencies and sales promotions agencies understand the parameters by which their work and their contribution to the organization's marketing effort will be measured.

The strategic mix – conclusions

From a marketing strategy point of view, the marketing mix, as we have seen, is the primary means by which we convert strategic marketing

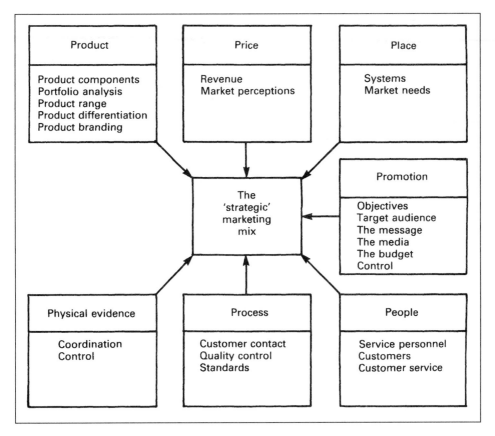

Figure 84 The strategic marketing mix

planning down to day-to-day marketing tactics and operations. I have concentrated, during this very brief review of the marketing mix, on the critical role of marketing strategy in ensuring the consistency and logical linking between the elements of marketing mix such that the target marketplace receives the full benefit of a perfectly co-ordinated marketing activity.

The key strategic issues of the marketing mix were identified as shown in Figure 84. It is always difficult to separate cleanly the activities which are strategic from those which are tactical. The biggest problem, however, arises in organizations which think and act in a predominantly tactical mode at the expense of strategy. Unfortunately, these are the organizations that confuse good marketing with being responsive and reactive to changes in the marketplace. There is a fine balance to be made between remaining flexible and reactive and being inefficient. That difference is encapsulated within the distinction between strategy and tactics.

Returning right to the very early pages of this book, we defined strategy as a long-term activity which is not changed every week. Strategy means knowing where you are going and broadly how you are going to get there. An organization will achieve nothing if it changes its strategy on a regular basis.

Tactics, on the other hand, are all about change. They are about remaining responsive to the requirements of the marketplace and responding to tactical changes in competitive situations and stances. Tactics, described elsewhere as manoeuvres on the field of battle, are themselves all about change – without the strategy to guide them, change for changes sake can be as inefficient and as harmful as no change at all.

The last link in the marketing strategy process comes in the guise of the marketing plan.

Chapter 11

Marketing plans

'Do not repeat the tactics which have gained you one victory, but let your methods be regulated by the infinite variety of circumstances.'

Sun Tzu, 500 BC

The process of marketing planning and marketing plans has been described at some length and in some detail in a number of specific and specialized marketing texts, so I shall not repeat their efforts here.

From the marketing strategy point of view, the marketing planning process fills in the gap between the strategic process and specific, market-based activities. We have seen that the marketing strategy process is concerned with taking various elements of internal and external data, turning these into information and blending these pieces of information into a strategic marketing mix.

The strategic marketing mix can also be seen as a set of inter-related sub-objectives which are passed down to the relevant section of the marketing function to be turned into detailed operational plans. It is these later detailed plans, when combined, which form the basis of the organization's marketing plans.

While, as I have said, I have no intention of turning this into yet another long book on detailed aspects of marketing tactics, there is one final aspect which marketing strategy must bring to the marketing plans – an effective and functioning control system.

The marketing process described so far depicts marketing objectives and marketing strategy as translating the business strategy into market-based terms. The marketing strategy is then translated into a strategic marketing mix which is in turn operationalized through a series of detailed marketing tactics, activities and programmes. Of course, the process will only be deemed an ultimate success if the organization is able to generate profits through satisfying customer needs (see Figure 85).

Up to this point, you will probably have seen the entire process as one of analytical thinking and (hopefully) intelligent planning. We have

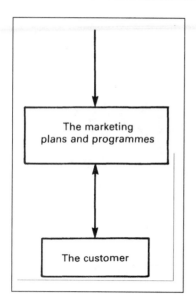

Figure 85 Marketing plans

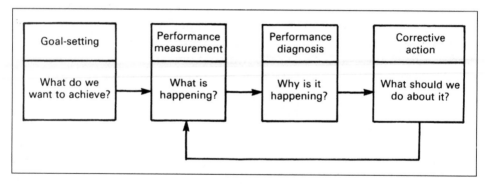

Figure 86 The control process. *Source:* Kotler P., *Marketing Management* (Prentice Hall, Englewood Cliffs, N.J., 1984).

nothing, so far, to prove to us that our thinking and planning has been along the right lines. The only true test of strategic planning is market-place response. Naturally, most of our effort so far has been to minimize the possibility of marketplace rejection by making sure that the analysis is, both qualitatively and quantitatively, as accurate as possible – but, the final verdict always lies with the customer.

A marketing control system is essential if the organization, and its business and marketing strategy, is to be validated by real, unbiased market response. As the organization's marketing strategy is turned into marketing plans and programmes which result in marketplace activity, we need to create a fast, reliable and accurate feed-back system to allow amendments and changes to be made – and early enough to make a difference! (See Figure 86.)

Marketing control systems

Typically, a section on control systems in the marketing plan (if it appears at all) is included as the very last section. This is an unfortunate sequence of events since it tends to undervalue the role of the control system in translating plan into action. Essentially, the control system will detail the controls that will be applied to monitor the progress of the marketing plans and their success (or otherwise) in achieving the marketing objectives.

Often, marketing control systems, where they exist at all, tend to be spelled out in budgets and budgeting terms. Product, pricing, distribution and other objectives will have been broken down, on a monthly basis, and transformed into a set of targets. These subsidiary targets, as we have already seen, are merely surrogates for profit and profitability. Few control systems even mention profitability let alone relate profitability to the various marketing activities. It is always better to involve the operating management in real life profitability so that everybody has a very clear idea of what the organization is out to achieve and how their activity will play a major part in the broader business strategy.

The ideal control system will also contain some element of contingency planning. A contingency plan is an outline plan for additional or alternate activity which management would initiate if specific correctional activity were required. The idea behind contingency planning is to encourage marketers to think forward through some of the difficulties which might arise in the marketplace. It encourages managers to pre-plan in case (albeit extremely unlikely!) the marketing strategy and plans do not operate like clockwork.

Because of the fundamental inter-connectedness of the various elements of the marketing mix and the other functions in the organization, contingency planning of this sort should not be restricted purely to marketing activity. The effects of such contingency plans on other areas of the organization, human resource, finance and operations, must not only be communicated to other functions, but their active help in developing contingency plans must be sought. If this is not done, then contingency planning is purely an exercise to keep the marketing strategy team quiet – it should be much more than that if it is to be taken seriously.

The last comment to be made on marketing control systems is the use to which they are put. Like targeting and forecasting, if control systems are put in place merely to act as a stick for recalcitrant or under-performing marketers, much of the positive potential of the control system will be wasted. Control systems should be seen as an method of improving performance, not a way of identifying and punishing under-achievers. Some organizations even prohibit the development of marketing control systems in their marketing plan in the belief that this is defeatist thinking and that it will of itself produce marketing plans that are bound to fail. Frankly, it is very difficult to know how to respond to this type of organization, apart from saying that it is completely wrong. This thinking is symptomatic of an organization that believes marketing is a science that can be practised and controlled according to well understood rules. Unfortunately (or fortunately?), the marketplace will remain unpredictable. Marketing control systems and contingency planning are essential tools. Never leave home without them.

To bring the subject back to strategy, I leave you with one final quote from the ancients:

'Our plans miscarry because they have no aim. When a man does not know what harbour he is aiming for, no wind is in the right direction.'

Seneca

There's really nothing new is there?

Further reading to Part Three

Cowell D., *The Marketing of Services*, 2nd revised edition (Butterworth-Heinemann, Oxford, 1991).

Part Four

How do we make it happen?

Planning is important but, without implementation, it is a pointless and expensive exercise which will probably take the organization backwards rather than forward.

Over the past ten or twenty years, academic books, business schools and boardrooms have been alive with questions about what the company should or must do. We have already seen the grandiose scale of some of the schemes and theories which have been postulated to aid with our corporate, business and marketing planning. Mintzberg, among others, has been railing against this overly intellectual exercise for years, now with some success.

There are reasons for the reigning preference for planning over doing but this is not the place for such a discussion. Nevertheless, the future belongs to those companies who do rather than just think and above all to those who are able to think and then do!

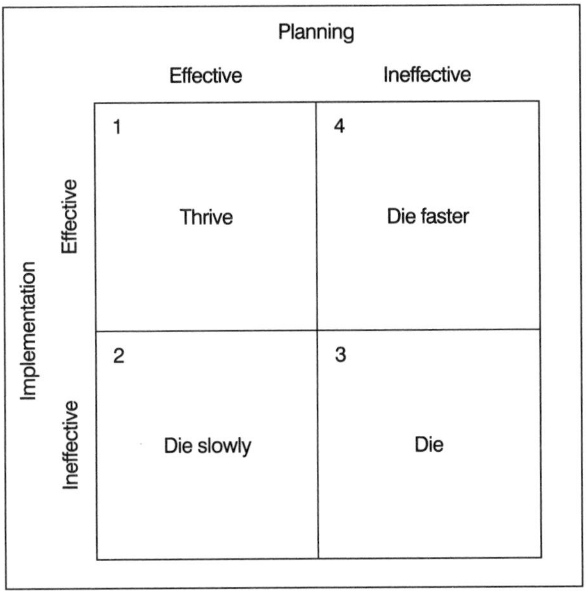

| | Planning | |
	Effective	Ineffective
Implementation — Effective	1 — Thrive	4 — Die faster
Implementation — Ineffective	2 — Die slowly	3 — Die

Figure 87 Planning and implementation

We have spent a lot of time in this book looking at the concepts that will support the 'right' sort of marketing strategy, so now we know what we should be doing. This emphasis is important since the right (and wrong) plans can still have a disproportionate effect on the organization's success (and failure). Figure 87 shows the strange relationship between plans and implementation. Boxes 1 and 3 need no explanation. Box 2 shows what can happen when the company has an effective plan but badly implemented. Box 4, interestingly shows that a bad plan (or one highlighting the wrong direction), if well implemented, can kill the company off faster than would have been the case had no planning been carried out!

Once we are sure that the strategy is right, the big question then is how do we make sure that it gets done?

There are a number of steps in the chain to implementation, this part will consider them in sequence. The main steps are:

- strategy evaluation and appraisal;
- identifying barriers to implementation;
- identifying drivers for change;
- using the system.

Chapter 12

Strategy evaluation and appraisal

'The means and forms which strategy uses are in fact so simple, so well known by their constant repetition that it only appears ridiculous to sound common sense when it hears critics so frequently speaking of them with high-blown emphasis.'

Clausewitz, 1820

Which strategy is best?

The primary consideration here is the evaluation of alternative strategic options open to the organization. We have already seen the number of different routes that the strategist might consider in his or her planning. Once you have uncovered all the options, how do you decide which is the best way to go? The chance of successful implementation is greatly increased if we choose the right strategy in the first place.

Considering both broad business and marketing strategies as well as more detailed marketing programmes, the marketer is faced with two separate but related problems:

1 What choice criteria should be used?
2 How can we evaluate alternative options that appear to be open to the organization?

Short or long term?

Before considering the best way to evaluate marketing strategy, it is probably wise to think about where we started this journey. What do we mean by strategy? If strategy is about marshalling the gross resource of the organization to match the needs of the marketplace and achieve the business objective, this cannot be a short-term activity. Every organization is complex and any change takes time to accomplish. Strategic decisions, such as the general choosing his battleground, will have long-term implications. Strategic decisions, such as which business area to enter cannot be reversed at a moment's notice – momentum has to be built up over a planned period of time.

The choice of evaluation methods is critical because quickly they can become the *raison d'être* for the organization's activities – it always amazes me how few managers are capable (or even wish) to keep a hand on the strategic issues that confront their organization, it seems tactical operations are always safer! We have to be careful that the evaluation methods are aimed at assessing how well the intended strategies will achieve set objectives (difficult to measure) and not how well they will meet current sales or revenue targets (easier to measure).

If marketing strategy is about the long-term success of the organization (by this stage it should be a rhetorical question!), its success or failure must be measured by procedures that take into account this long-term view. A practical evaluation system should note any short-term set-backs in the plan but more importantly, should be capable of setting these within a long-term context.

Financial versus non-financial measurement

In marketing and business texts generally there is surprisingly little discussion over the difference between those measures which assess efficiency and those which assess effectiveness. Efficiency is defined as 'doing things right' and effectiveness is defined as 'doing the right things'.

Efficiency measures are by far and away the most common in business and tend to evaluate, often on an ongoing basis, the efficiency or precision with which actions are carried out by the organization – mostly internal. When we look at effectiveness measures – and these are much less common – we will be looking at how well the organization is doing the right things. In other words, how well the organization is meeting its paying customers' needs.

Figure 88 shows just how important the differentiation of these measures can be.

For the rare organizations who manage to be both effective and efficient, that is they are efficient in their operations and also are delivering what their customers want, the future looks very rosy. For those

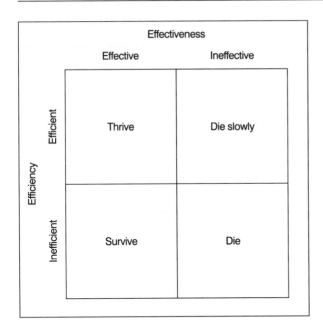

Figure 88 Efficiency and effectiveness

organizations who are neither effective nor efficient then it is just a matter of time. In the middle, however, the situation is quite interesting. It is clear that organizations can become more and more efficient, leaner and leaner in their operations but if they still fail to supply to the market what the market wants and needs it is only a matter of time before they are supplanted by eager competition. On the other hand as long as an organization continues to supply what the market wants the demand remains rather buoyant. They may not be very efficient in their operations and the way they supply the marketplace but they are likely to survive.

More worryingly, however, for organizations is that the majority of measures that are used to evaluate and appraise strategy tend to be of the efficiency rather than of the effectiveness nature.

The majority of financial and accountant driven measures also fall into this category. While, of course, there must be a point of inefficiency beyond which no organization can survive, efficiency of itself is no guarantee of the organization's survival. Unless the organization delivers what the market wants it will die – albeit slowly.

The answer, as in most strategic issues, is one of striking the elusive balance between these two apparently opposing forces. An organization's survival over the long term depends upon it being both effective and efficient. We should be searching out the evaluation and appraisal measures that allow us to pursue both these goals simultaneously.

Financial measures

The more usual measures of evaluation under this heading will include:

- profit;
- profitability;
- shareholder return;
- cash flow/liquidity;
- share price;
- earnings per share;
- return on net assets;
- return on sales.

Most of these traditional financial measures concentrate on profit and it goes without saying that profit is essential to the long-term survival of any business no matter what size or shape. However, as Levitt said: 'profit is a requisite not a purpose of business'. Profit is essential to any business but is not the only reason why we are here. Also, far more importantly, evaluation and appraisal processes which rely exclusively on profitability can overshadow the fact that the only way we make profits is by satisfying customers!

The laws of physics apply to all activities. Short-term returns above the average often have to be paid for in the long term. You might recognize the following UK companies who regularly produced profits at an average level three times higher than their international counterparts during the 1980s:

- Coloroll;
- Polly Peck;
- Maxwell Corporation;
- Mountleigh Properties;
- Ratners;
- Burton;
- BCCI.

You might well ask 'where are they now?'. Strangely enough the city and investors never do when the next crop of 'high rollers' come along – human nature I suppose.

Equally important, if somewhat shorter term, liquidity/cash-flow evaluation is essential. Lack of long-term profitability is not a major reason for the demise of business but cash-flow problems can even eliminate companies with a rising order book. Despite everything we have said about strategy being longer term the one thing we have to bear in mind is short-term cash flow. Without this there is no longer term.

Non-financial measures

The non-financial measures of performance tend to measure the effectiveness rather than the efficiency side of the equation although not exclusively so. Non-financial measures may include:

- market share;
- growth;
- competitive advantage;
- competitive position;
- sales volume;
- market penetration levels;
- new product development;
- customer satisfaction;
- customer franchise;
- market image and awareness levels.

Two things should be readily apparent from a review of the above list. First, that any one of these measures taken in isolation is unlikely to be sufficient to guarantee the long-term survival and development of the organization. Secondly, implicit (although more often than not unstated) is that growth is always a good thing. The growth aspect to strategy is very much a development of the heydays of the 1970s and remains largely unquestioned in most texts.

Certainly the organization must develop if it is to continue to adapt and remain in touch with its marketplace. But growth? Growth of what? Growth can be a good and healthy influence but if pursued for its own sake can lead to problems. Sales maximization and volume growth can often lead to serious declines in profitability especially in highly competitive marketplaces. Directed and controlled growth based on a qualified and detailed analysis of the marketplace and potential business opportunities can lead to a flourishing organization. However, as Ed Abbey has noted: 'growth for the sake of growth is the ideology of the cancer cell'.

Multiple criteria

In almost every situation the dependence upon a single criterion for evaluating and appraising strategy is likely to be dangerous. There are two extremely good reasons why we should consider using more than one criterion in our evaluation of strategy. This is because:

1   Organizations behave ineffectively from some points of view if a single
    criterion is used.
2   Organizations fulfil multiple functions and have multiple goals, some of
    which may be in conflict. It would be inappropriate to assess strategies
    purely on the basis of any one criterion.

Organizations and their strategies can best be regarded as living entities.
If they follow their markets they will also need to be dynamic and evolving entities just to be able to survive let alone flourish. Time, if no other
factor, will always act to make certain measures redundant and other
measures important in new situations.

We have also seen from the discussions above that conflicts naturally
arise in the management of any organization. These require that different
performance measures need to be traded off in different situations, for
example:

1   Customers' need for value versus shareholders' need for return.
2   Cost of achieving market share versus need for profitability.
3   Organizations' need of efficiency versus customers' need for service.
4   Production efficiency requirement for long runs versus the markets' need
    for choice.
5   The organization's drive to standardization versus the consumer's need
    for individualism.

The choice of the most appropriate measures for evaluation and appraisal
will depend entirely on the organization's situation and the marketing
strategist's ability to balance internal and external needs.

Choosing the right criterion

How then can we make sure that we are choosing the right criterion
against which to evaluate our longer term marketing strategy? Although
there are no hard and fast rules for this selection the application of simple
common sense can take us a long way forward. The judicious use of some
selective models could also shed light on this problem. For example, if
we consider the well-known product life cycle as a concept it is worthwhile trying to plot our organization position on this cycle. Whether we
consider this cycle applicable for the organization, the industry, the
product or service category or even the particular brand it will help us
to select those criteria which are of most relevance in the situation at
hand.

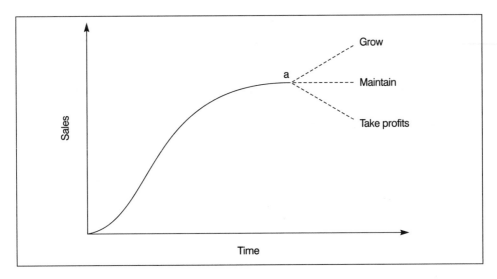

Figure 89   The product life cycle

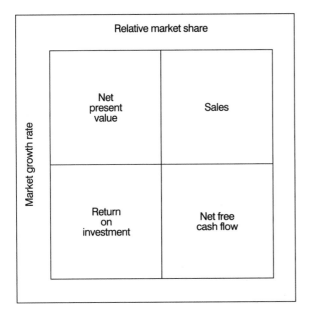

Figure 90   The Boston matrix

From Figure 89 it can be seen clearly that an organization that plots its position at point 'a' and still decides to evaluate its long-term strategy according to either market share growth or maintenance is trying to beat the market trend. Buying market share in a declining market is possible but only at the expense of profitability. Looking beyond the product life cycle model to another popular model, the Boston matrix, we can see that the same form of guidance is also available for those who wish to look (Figure 90).

Although there is much debate about the continuing validity of the Boston matrix, and much care must be taken in its use, it can still be useful for conceptually placing products or businesses in the overall organization's portfolio. Figure 90 shows that different forms of evaluation need to take place depending on the market and business situation of the product or the business considered. For example:

- 'Dog' products or businesses need to be measured according to the net free cash flow that they generate.
- 'Question marks' are best evaluated by the sales volume and revenue that they are able to generate in their particular market situation.
- 'Stars' are best evaluated by an assessment of net present value.
- 'Cash cows' need to be assessed, evaluated and managed to generate the maximum return on investment.

The GEC/McKinsey matrix and other models can also be used, with a little common sense, to ensure that we are measuring strategies within a sensible context of the business conditions that the company faces. The common use of a standard set of criteria to assess any strategic option is both naive and dangerous – of course, that is what analysts do all the time.

What is the best way?

Considering the area of evaluation and appraisal of marketing strategy, the question always arises: 'so what would one of the best marketing organizations be doing?'. Always a difficult question to answer since much depends upon the environment, the industry and the prevailing competitive situation of any particular organization.

However, as far as it is possible to answer such a general question, recent research carried out by the CIM and Cranfield School of Management has identified the following factors as those evidenced by the 'successful marketing company':

1 Start at the top.
2 Involve everyone in the organization in the marketing philosophy.
3 Be prepared for structural change.
4 Use the new structure to feed a 'customer facing strategy'.
5 Review marketing tactics (4Ps). Do they work from the customer's point of view?

6 Accept that change is a way of life.
7 Understand the difference between 'quality systems' and 'quality products and services'.
8 Focus on the customer, not the competition.
9 Look 'end-to-end' not piecemeal, customers expect seamless service.
10 Keep the end user in sight, don't be distracted by the middleman.
11 Measure the success of the marketing approach and be able to demonstrate the link between customer focus and profit.

This review gives good guidance to the types of evaluation criteria that can/should be used to drive practical marketing strategy.

Chapter 13

Identifying barriers to implementation

'... to carry out the plan without being obliged to deviate from it a thousand times by a thousand varying influences, requires, besides great strength of character, great clearness and steadiness of mind'

Clausewitz, 1820

There are many barriers that stand in the way of successful implementation of marketing strategy, some evident, some not so. The barriers fall broadly into three separate categories: external pressures on the organization, internal pressures on the marketing function, and pressures within the marketing function itself. We will consider these three forms of pressure independently.

Environmental barriers

To consider the external pressures on the organization first, these are best described under the traditional PEST or SLEPT headings to describe the environment.

Social factors

Changing demographic and social patterns such as an ageing population, fewer school leavers, and the shift in emphasis from manual to white collar skills will have a major impact on any strategic plans that require implementation over the next five to ten years. British society is also undergoing some level of fundamental change and trends such as ecology, class structure and individualism need to be accounted for in your plans (see Chapter 5). Customers and consumers are also part of the social element of the environment but these are considered in more detail in Chapter 14.

Legal

There are an increasing number of laws that are affecting business activity on a wider and wider scale. Laws now cover employment, pay and price policies, health and safety as well as specific acts to control particular industries such as financial services and telecommunications. Also, as time progresses we can expect more impact on British activity from European Union (EU) based laws.

Economic factors

The past ten years have witnessed an unparalleled level of change in the British economy, and this change is unlikely to slow down. Strategic implementation of plans needs to take into account the changes that are likely to occur in the marketplace and you should consider changes in your own industry such as mergers, joint ventures, share price movement and investment as well as any trade union activities; suppliers' actions and changes to include vertical integration and disintermediation (the disappearance of intermediaries in the process). Distribution channels are also undergoing a radical change in a number of industries and successful implementation will depend upon a good forecasting of likely change in areas such as distribution infrastructure as well as in transportation and channel management and control. Internationalization is a major factor in all economic situations and is likely to affect your customers' perceptions of your offer, and the entire nature of competition. Competition itself is one of the most important factors to forecast in strategic implementation since no marketing strategy ever operates in a vacuum. You should be attempting to analyse not only the direct (own industry) competition but also the important and often more difficult to predict indirect competition from outside your traditional industry base. Competition is expected to increase in all sectors over the next ten years driven primarily by the internationalization of business and the fragmentation of many markets.

Political factors

There is a general trend in most western markets for government to take an increasingly active role in business. Political activities include taxation, lobbying, as well as the ability to pass laws which affect not only your organization's ability to act in a free market but also customers' ability to buy your products or services. In most markets political activities are often aimed at influencing competitive activity. Whatever the intention behind political actions, the result is always some form of restriction over the organization's activities in a marketplace and these restrictions need to be forecasted and attempts made to modify implementation of the strategic plan within this new framework.

Technological factors

Technology generally has had a massive effect over the past ten years and we can expect this influence to continue if not accelerate. Technology has made radical change in manufacturing possible and has been a major catalyst in the recent proliferation of new products and services. A major factor in the development of technology has been its ability to reduce, if not sometimes eliminate, barriers to market entry. The application of modern technology has enabled small- and medium-sized organizations to operate at cost levels previously the exclusive preserve of much larger organizations. Economies of scale are no longer the barriers they used to be.

Internal barriers

As well as external pressures acting upon the organization, there are a number of barriers, internal to the organization, which will also affect its ability to implement its strategic plans successfully. All of these factors act as significant potential blockages to implementing marketing strategy and unless these blockages can be overcome inside the organization the marketer has little choice but to amend the goals and strategy to those which the organization is able to implement.

Leadership

There is little doubt that the ultimate success and implementation of any strategic plan will depend upon the degree to which top management buys in to the process. This is especially evident where the strategic thrust of the plan involves any form of significant change. The organization's leadership may be opposed to objectives of the plan for any number of reasons. For example they may be from non-marketing disciplines, may feel that the need for change is not yet apparent or simply be more comfortable with 'steady state' management style. Whatever the reasons, unless strong leaders are 'bought in' to the vision and strategy completely, little progress is likely to be made.

Organizational culture

There are many forms of organizational culture and, in truth, few of these are customer or market focused. In the organization with a non-market oriented culture, the chances of successfully implementing a truly customer focused strategic marketing plan must be severely limited. Marketing in this type of organization tends to be all about marketing services, often linked or even subservient to the all-important sales function. In the product or production-oriented organization the marketer's role is to provide sales materials, product information and market analysis to support the sales and production functions of the organization.

The market or customer-oriented organization is the only one that sees the marketer's role as that of catalyst and change agent to focus the rest of the organization's activities on the one activity that really matters – the customer. Changing the culture of an organization is never a short-term task. However, as today's markets become more and more competitive, the options are becoming clearer – change the culture or the organization may not survive beyond the medium term.

If the culture will not change in the short to medium term then goals and strategies will need to be amended to something which the organizational culture can assimilate. Looking back to the ideas now current in strategic thinking, organizational culture cannot be ignored or treated as if it does not exist – that has been the reason for the demise of many a good strategic idea. If implementation is what counts then pragmatism must be the order of the day. The strategist can try and work against culture but will not win. Working with the culture means that the whole strategy may not be implemented, and not straight away at that. But it will mean that something happens and it may mean that in a few years the culture will be more accepting of change than now. Patience and sensitivity are required to get things done.

Organization design

In many organizations the existing organization structure is simply not designed to be able to deliver the proposed marketing strategy as is intended. Too many organizations are designed for the convenience and administrative ease of those that work in them rather than being designed in order to deliver satisfaction to customers. It is simply unrealistic to design a customer-focused marketing strategy without spending some time looking at the organization's ability to deliver on the promises that you may be making to your customers. If organizations are so rigid that they cannot be redesigned then your marketing strategy may need to be modified accordingly. 'Re-engineering' or 'Business Process Redesign' initiatives may be successful in this regard but only if they are directed at redesigning the organization in customer terms and not simply aimed at restyling the IT processes, or worse, just saving money in the short term.

When dealing with organizations (culture and design) it is important to consider the 'soft' elements such as style, skills, staffing and shared values as well as the traditional 'hard' values. Remember, an organization is nothing without the people who work inside it.

Functional policies

A subset of organization structure: most functions in an organization (finance, operations, human resources and marketing) tend to grow and produce a number of functional policies and procedures which determine how their part of the organization and their staff manage the day-to-day business. The intended marketing strategy may fall foul of these functional processes and will encounter a blockage on the path to implementation.

The marketing strategy is not just the strategy of the marketing department. The marketing strategy is, or ought to be, the strategy which guides the whole organization's activities relative to the customer. The marketing strategy, therefore, should not be something which is imposed on the other functions but a route and direction which staff and managers from finance, operations and human resources share with other members of the organization. This sense of common ownership will not be created simply by imposing a marketing strategy on them but requires that they are active in the development process. After all, the customer is everyone's responsibility, not just the marketing department's.

Resources

The proposed marketing strategy may require either significant additional resources be allocated to certain functions or even the reappropriation of resource into different areas of the organization. Successful implementation will depend upon these resources either being available for the implementation of the plan or making the appropriate resources available so that the plan can be implemented fully. The potential blockage here is likely to be either in the resources simply not being available or that senior management considers that other causes are more deserving. In any case this could provide a significant blockage to implementation.

Evaluation and control procedures

The lack of appropriate monitoring and evaluation procedures in an organization will be a significant block to the successful implementation of any strategy. It is a truism that what gets measured, gets done. No matter that your long-term marketing strategy is aimed at improving and developing customer satisfaction levels, if the organization is managed and motivated by monthly sales figures – that is what will be achieved.

This potential blockage can be less of a problem than ones outlined above in that you are not necessarily faced with overcoming perception or resource problems. As long as the proper control measures are installed there need be no problems in implementation. Control measures will be considered in more depth below.

Given the scale and complexity of the blockages and pressures upon the marketing function from inside its own organization, the importance of internal marketing starts to become apparent. An integral part of successful strategic implementation, internal marketing involves all the processes necessary to carry the message of the strategic marketing plan inside to the various audiences that comprise the organization. We can see from the list of possible blockages that exist in the organization, that success or failure of strategic marketing can depend upon people and functions inside the organization not only believing the message but putting their weight behind the effort too. Internal marketing means more than just promotions, it means the same as it does in the external environment, the application of the full marketing mix to achieve some predetermined behaviour change. Internal marketing, like external marketing, requires a good understanding of the needs and motivations of the target audiences to be successful. The above review should start to give the marketer a reasonable understanding of where people in the internal organization currently stand and the measures needed to gain their full and willing support for the proposed marketing strategy.

Barriers within the marketing function

Not only are there a number of issues internal to the organization which can act as blockages to developing and implementing quality marketing strategy, there are a number of aspects of the marketing department or function which can also act as potential blockages to the development and implementation of your plans.

Marketing's interface with other functions

Delivering satisfactions to customers may be the responsibility of the marketing function but it is not a job that marketers can carry out on their own. In order to deliver customer satisfactions and thereby improve the organization's position against competition, the entire organization needs to operate as an effective partnership and deliver seamlessly. In order to do this marketing needs to interact positively with other functions within the organization, such as production, purchasing, personnel and finance.

Unfortunately some of these functions may consider that they have competing responsibilities and may not fix the priorities in exactly the same way as marketing. Once again this solution is not in 'telling' other functions what to do but in involving them in the process. The marketing manager must find means of securing better coordination among the various functional subsystems that are not directly under his or her control. This may be achieved by improving communications and inter-organizational understandings about what is in the interest of the organization as a whole. History and the often constant threat of 'downsizing' do not make this an easy process.

The role of marketing/the marketer

The role of the marketer will depend largely upon the organization culture and structure. In the non-market oriented organization marketing tends to be synonymous with 'advertising and promotion'. The marketing manager is often taken on as a necessary (and expensive) evil because the competition seems to be making inroads into the organization's markets by advertising. Other managers in the organization often have little understanding of the marketing concept and don't appreciate their role in satisfying customers. The role of the marketer in the production or product oriented organization is twofold – to give his or her internal customers what they want and, secondly, to act as catalyst for organizational change toward a more customer oriented position.

In the case of a customer or market oriented organization the role of the marketer and the marketing function is quite different. Rather than concentrating on advertising and promotion, the marketer's function is to identify, anticipate and satisfy customer needs profitably. To do this needs much more than a depth knowledge of advertising and promotional methodology and techniques. In this type of organization the marketer's key area of responsibility is to understand the organization's customers and to feed this information back into the organization and other functions so that people may act upon it profitably.

Marketing feedback

How effective a marketer is in his or her job and how well the marketing strategy is implemented will depend on how much, how relevant and how good the information is and how well it is interpreted and acted upon. Information is critical. Information and feedback on a plan's progress is never 100 per cent accurate but it does act to both reduce uncertainty in planning and improves the quality of action. Critically the marketer may not be in complete control of the information sources and the speed at which they are delivering quality information back to the marketing function. A great deal of data is often raised elsewhere in the organization but often not in a form which will provide adequate information for the marketer's use. The marketer has two main flows of data. One from the environment and the other from internal operations. Some, but not all, is likely to be under the marketer's direct control, for the rest, other departments need to understand the importance of quality and timely information flows and internal marketing can help this process.

The final, crucial area of marketing and market feedback is market research. In many organizations some market research is carried out but invariably it is insufficient to meet the organization's needs. Market research should not be regarded as a crutch to support weak decision making but as an essential 'investment' in the marketplace and future prosperity of the organization. Unfortunately many organizations, often product, production or planning oriented do not see the investment aspects of market research but rather consider it as a cost. As competition increases and markets continue to fragment, it is unlikely that investment in market research will decline in the most successful organizations, rather we can expect it to increase as market circumstances become more and more involved.

Chapter 14

Identifying drivers for change

'It may sound strange, but for all who know war in this respect it is a fact beyond doubt, that much more strength of will is required to make an important decision in strategy than in tactics.'

Clausewitz, 1820

Rather than simply paint a completely negative picture, organizations and the current market can be used to support actively the implementation of marketing strategy. The astute marketer should be able to use these drivers for change to enlist help and active cooperation within the organization to implement strategic change.

Customer expectations

Customers in all markets are now starting to demand the 'impossible'. As their needs and wishes are met in very competitive markets such as groceries, consumer goods and motor cars, they see no reason why these expectations should not be met in unrelated fields such as banking, telecommunications and travel. As customer expectations continue to grow so concepts such as 'brand loyalty' and retention appear to be less effective. They are as important as ever but the rules, as imposed by customers, are changing. Customers are becoming less and less loyal to brands and organizations if these fail to provide what is wanted, when it is wanted, at a reasonable price. The explosion of choice in so many markets means that customers do not have to put up with second best – loyalty has to be earned, it is not given as of right.

The astute marketer can use the changes in customer demand (and forecasts of future demand) to drive through changes inside the organization at a rate which internal departments would otherwise consider 'uncomfortable'. Knowledge is always power, in the information age this is as true as ever. The marketer's ability to investigate and understand market changes will be crucial to an organization's survival in the future. Knowing, and being able to communicate this to others inside the organization are, of course, different matters.

Revenue

Revenues and profits are the life blood of any organization. The four or five years of deep recession in the British market in the early 1990s (and slightly lighter variants in other European markets) has meant that many organizations have cut costs dramatically in order to maintain revenue flows and returns to shareholders. The movement out of recession was somewhat slower than normal and organizations also emerged to find even more competition than they had faced in the 1980s. The cost-cutting, always short sighted in times of economic recession, has left many organizations ill-prepared for the more competitive market conditions that now face them.

The only source of continued revenue and profit growth for many organizations is now the marketplace. Customers are the source of all revenues and profits and satisfied customers have now (at last!) started to top the agendas of more and more businesses. The marketer needs to use this trend and to drive through the message that long-term profits do not come from a numbers game (adding more customers at any price) but from a quality game that involves constantly offering customers a solution that meets their needs better than the competition can.

For many businesses and managers, this will be a lesson in how to compete in the new millennium.

Competition

Not only is technology driving down the barriers to entry to many markets. Markets are beginning to fragment in many and devious ways and competition is intensifying in practically every business sector. Not only are existing players fighting to gain and retain customers but also new entrants are often being attracted by more substantial profits than they can gain in their home markets. Brands and products are proliferating and customers are now faced with a greater choice in more markets than they have ever experienced in the past.

The only way through this maze, as we have seen already, is to be able to establish a clear and differentiated image and position in the market in which the business operates and to give customers good, simple and relevant reasons why they should come to them rather than the competition. Effective market positioning is not achieved solely by product quality but requires the deft application of all the elements of strategic marketing. We have already played out all the arguments. The marketer's job is to convince the organization, before it is too late, that customer orientation and quality are the keys to survival and growth. Investment in customers, not more cost cutting is called for. Increased competition must be used as a central driver for change.

Innovation

A byproduct of the increasingly competitive nature of most markets and the application of modern technology, innovation has become the norm in many industry sectors. Innovation for its own sake is unlikely to gain market share or profitably but innovation directed at supplying more relevant products to customers will. In the future, innovation in both product or service delivery and processes and service will be the norm rather than the exception. Unfortunately many organizations tend to find innovation an uncomfortable experience and many prefer the 'steady state' environment to work in. It is unlikely that such environments will prove profitable in the future and the marketer's role now is to use this tide of innovation to get the organization on stream to match, if not to exceed, the competition's offering.

Innovation, like all other potential business saviours is a dangerous path to travel. Simply doing new things is unlikely to be enough and could even be a way of hastening commercial suicide. Much innovation does no more than create more choice and complication in customers' lives – is this really what they want? Innovation that creates more effective solutions to customers' *existing* problems is truly competitive. The marketer's experience and knowledge of customer needs, carefully communicated in the organization, should make the difference between investing in productive innovation and wasting scarce resources by chasing rainbows.

Barriers to the implementation of marketing strategy are big and intimidating. The drivers that can be used to support change are equally imposing. At the end of the day it comes down to people – any organization tends to get the degree of change and success that it wants, and deserves.

Chapter 15

Using the system

'War is a mere continuation of policy by other means'

Clausewitz, 1820

Apart from the self-employed entrepreneur with no staff, everybody is likely to encounter resistance to change. And, moving from product to customer focus which will always be at the core of a real marketing strategy, will encounter more resistance than most changes introduced to an organization. The marketer charged with a great sense of the rightness of the cause is understandable, even laudable. But the resistors of change are also fired with what they believe to be the rightness of their cause and will fight hard against what they believe to be a threat to the future of the business – after all, working this way has got them this far hasn't it? And they are particularly good at doing this sort of business.

Head-to-head conflict may be fun, even gratifying, but will it change the organization into what it must become? Unless you are vested with more power in the organization than anyone else, there is no certainty that you will win the battle on these terms and, if you lose, you could even set back the change process to terminal levels. No, the important thing is to achieve the change, the survival of the organization must come first. The best (and most effective) method of achieving change is to use the systems – not fight them. How can this be done?

Control systems

Planning without control simply means that the organization has a nice, sophisticated document. The control systems are essential to make sure that the organization drives through the content of the plans and achieves its objectives in the marketplace. Control systems will be in place in organizations even if plans are absent. Every organization believes that the achievement of particular things is important for advancement. Controls, explicit or implicit, will always be found.

The nature of control systems

James Bureau in *The Marketing Book* (Baker, 1994) describes the nature of good control systems. They must be driven by the following principles:

- *Formality:* firm rituals that are applied regularly and in a standard manner.
- *Necessity:* should be seen as useful by the organization and not just a ritualistic process.
- *Priority:* be concerned with those elements which the organization needs to control, not with everything capable of control.
- *Veracity:* need to be data based, not based solely on intuition or subjective opinion.
- *Regularity:* as regular as is affordable and useful depending on the activity measured and the dynamics of the market situation.

Using control systems to support marketing strategy

Control systems are many and various and selecting the right method of control will depend very much upon the market that the organization is addressing, the particular goals and objectives that the organization has set itself as well as the particular organization structure, design and culture.

Control systems become the reasons for the organization's existence quite soon after their introduction as managers and staff focus on the achievement of agreed targets. The reasons for the existence of the targets is rarely questioned. In some organizations, the accepted behaviour is to exceed targets not just meet them. There is often no thinking involved, it is just 'the way things are done around here'. Sales (revenue) targets are an obvious example. Often in the belief that sales and marketing people are simple souls who can't deal with the concept of profit, simple sales figures are handed down as quarterly and annual targets to be met. Salespeople too have to pay mortgages and put food on the table and, if that is what they are bonused to do, that is what gets done. If achieving the set sales targets means cutting margins to buy sales or doing deals to meet today's targets at the expense of building relationships that will bear fruit tomorrow, then so be it. This is clearly the fault of those who set targets, not of those who relentlessly achieve targets that should have been set differently in the first place!

Control systems then are a matter of balancing four primary issues.

1   Standard setting.
2   Performance measurement.
3   Reporting results.
4   Taking corrective action (if required).

Setting the standards

This is the role of the planning element of the process. The goals and objectives which fall out of the business and marketing strategy process are then translated into standards which will drive the organization. Ideally the standards will have been set within an understanding of what the organization is currently able to deliver.

Performance measurement and reporting of results

These are the key areas of most control systems. Most discussion then will centre around which performances should be measured and how results should be reported. The measurement activities of the planning achievements can simply be broken down into three broad areas.

1   *Quantity:* How much was achieved? How much should have been achieved?
2   *Quality:* How good was that which was achieved? How good was it meant to be?
3   *Cost:* How much did the achievement cost? How much was it planned to cost?

These basic parameters of the plan can then be quantified through an analysis of one or more or five distinct areas of operation which are:

*   financial analysis;
*   market analysis;
*   sales and distribution analysis;
*   physical resources analysis;
*   human resource analysis.

Audits

One method of assessing strategic marketing effectiveness is by the use of constant and regular marketing audits. The marketing audit (which is described in detail elsewhere) is a robust method of monitoring the successful implementation of marketing strategy, plans and policies. No matter which form of marketing audit is taken, marketing management should ensure that all areas of marketing activity are regularly monitored and their performance measured against pre-set standards which, once achieved, will guarantee the successful implementation of the plan.

Budgets

Budgeting is probably the most common form of control mechanism. Although developed for financial housekeeping and management, budgeting is often applied to marketing implementation as well. There are a number of advantages as well as disadvantages to using the budgeting process. Many budgets tend to be short term, typically based on the annual plan for the achievement of that year's profit and turnover forecasts. Short-term budgeting of this nature is not always the most relevant for the measurement and control of long-term strategy and the strategic marketer should note that short-term deviations from plans may require just short-term tactical alterations but no longer term strategic shifting in direction.

Where the budgeting process is longer term and/or continuous rather than periodic in nature the feedback results may be more relevant to longer term strategic proposals. When dealing with budgets it is vitally important to understand that budgeting is not the same as management. Budgeting is an important aid to management decision making but budgets are always based on estimates rather than reality and are always, at best, someone's idea of how the future will happen. Therefore, when deviations from budgeted figures arise marketing must ask itself not only whether the deviations are significant and require corrective action but also how valid were the original estimates incorporated into the budgeting at the outset.

Variance analysis

Another analysis and control procedure which falls out of the budgeting process is the detailed analysis of the variance (difference between actual and expected results) that arises from the organization's activities.

Variances of a number of different items can be measured and assessed, much will depend upon the key parameters used by the organization to assess its performance overall. Typical variance measures will include sales price variance, sales quantity variance, sales volume variance, profit variance, market size variance, market share variance, etc.

Whatever the method of analysis and evaluation that is deemed the most appropriate, it is important to recognize that analysis on its own is rarely sufficient to monitor and implement strategy properly. As well as identifying the actual variances or differences from expected results, equal attention has to be laid on understanding the reasons for the variance in the first place. Before any corrective action can be taken (if indeed it is required) the reasons for the variance need to be identified. Corrective action needs to be taken against the reasons for the shortfall (or the overrun!) if it is to be effective. At this point additional feedback is required from marketing intelligence and assessment of the external and competitive situation which may give some clue as to the reasons for the deviation from the expected plan. At the very least it needs to be established whether the reasons for the divergence from the plan has been caused by internal problems or external problems.

Taking corrective action

Once the control system has been established and then during the implementation phase of the plan's divergences or deviations from the estimated results have been highlighted the marketer's role is to decide whether corrective action is required and if so how to implement this action in time to bring the plan back on target. The options open to the organization in terms of corrective action fall into a number of separate categories.

Environmental changes

If the reason for the divergence is caused by unpredicted changes in the external environment of the organization the marketer has a number of options open to him or her at this stage. If the environmental factors are deemed to be of short-term nature then a modification in the tactics needed to implement the strategic plan can be considered. If the changes in the external environment or the marketplace are deemed to be fundamental or structural in nature then the marketer may need to revisit the overall strategy and aims and objectives of the plan itself.

Internal problems

If the non-delivery on the estimates of the plan are caused by internal problems the marketer has to decide whether this is a shortfall in performance or is caused by active blockages in other parts or functions of the organization. Corrective action will need to be directed at these points.

Faulty estimating

It may be apparent from a deeper analysis of the variances that the problem lies not in the market or in the organization's ability to deliver but that the original estimates were erroneous. In this case the marketer needs to re-estimate the rate at which the organization will achieve its strategic objectives.

Strategic decisions will have long-term implications and organizational momentum has to be built over a planned period. Constant change produces uncertainty, confusion, misdirection and wastage – not results. Tactics are designed to change on a weekly or even a daily basis in response to changes in the marketplace caused by customer needs or competitor response. Tactical change causes no problems of uncertainty as long as the strategy, the broad overall direction of the organization, remains constant. Control systems which drive regular tactical changes to keep the strategy on course are a positive boon to any organization. On the other hand, if the control systems allow managers, through ignorance or panic, to make constant changes to strategy and direction the organization will end up achieving nothing and going nowhere.

Using control systems to create change

We know from research and experience that people are frightened and threatened by the unknown. And the best thing to do with threats is to destroy them. This should alarm nobody, it is basic human nature and we should not be surprised by its manifestation in the business world. Rather than wishing for what might be, should we not concern ourselves with what is and determine what needs to be done in the 'real world' to achieve the aims we have set ourselves?
  We know that:

I   Performance targets are expected by both managers and staff and, often, the achievement of targets becomes a macho/ego driven issue. Many people seem to thrive on targets and on achieving them. People don't seem to worry too much about where the target or performance measure comes from, nor why it is there, just about its achievement.

2 Strategy and strategic issues and horizons seem to make many staff and managers uncomfortable. The world for most people seems to be made up of what 'I' can do 'now'. Longer term issues tend to be less clear cut and often outside an individual's area of direct control – so best avoided.

So why worry about educating and convincing people that a particular strategic route is better than another? Why worry people talking about issues they do not wish to embrace and that fall outside the areas of 'comfort' that they wish to preserve?

Radical thinking possibly. It certainly goes against many of the 'politically correct' trends in some of today's texts which are taken up with *empowerment* and similar issues. Empowerment is fine and good, but do you have the time? Do people want to be empowered anyway? My experience suggests that there are still large numbers of people who just want to be told what to do and then left alone to get on with it.

If you really want to achieve change where it matters, with the customer, look at changing the control systems as a first step. Many existing control systems have been selected because they use variables which are easy to measure, e.g. sales revenue, defects, telesales contact time, calls per day etc. If what matters to your strategy is customer satisfaction, find a way of measuring it (there are many ways) and simply substitute the new measure for, say, sales revenue targets. Stand back and watch the change take place.

Before you give me all the reasons why this can't be done, let me tell you that I am ready for this too. There is no doubt that it *can* be done, and quickly too. More to the point is how bad do you want to do it?

Marketer's note

Having a marketing strategy is interesting, even commendable, but unless the strategy is implemented its existence is ultimately futile.

Implementation is EVERYTHING.

This is the point at which we must leave behind the theories, constructs and ideologies that make marketing what it is – and that I as well as you find comforting. This is the point at which we decide whether marketing strategy will be any more than an interesting intellectual diversion. This is the point at which this book becomes either a working tool or a bookshelf trophy.

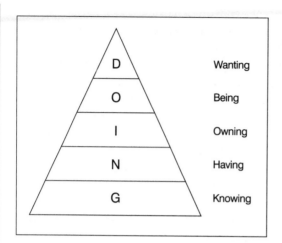

Figure 91   Implementing a marketing strategy

Implementation can be reduced to a number of key aspects as shown in Figure 91.

Implementing marketing strategy will depend on the existence and intensity of the following five items. The more powerfully these individual items exist, the more strategy will be implemented and the more it will be implemented, undiluted. For the more technically minded:

Doing = f(knowing + having + owning + being + wanting)

In more detail:

1 *Knowing*
   This stage depends upon you knowing what needs to be done. Most of the content of this book has been aimed at achieving this objective. Knowing what needs to be done means knowing what customers and other stakeholders want from you and your organization – and the relative importance of each. It also depends upon you knowing what needs to be done compared to what can be done, and how to manage the process from the practical to the necessary over time.

2 *Having*
   This stage depends upon having the skills, capability, capacity and resources to do what needs to be done. If you do not have these things now, you should know how and where to get them and the time required to acquire them. This stage also covers the vision and the 'power' required to achieve the change in the organization. If you haven't got it can it be borrowed?

3 *Owning*
   This stage depends upon the organization, or at least the key implementors, owning the strategy for themselves. A strategy developed in an in-

house ivory tower called the planning department is about as powerful as employing consultants to draw up a plan of action for you. It is not your plan, it is not the company's plan, it is not real, it is not serious, it is not workable – it will not happen. Managers and staff may implement their own strategy, why should they implement somebody else's?

4 *Being*

This stage considers the internal and external environments and their effects on implementation of the strategy. Strategy, and change, are far more likely to be implemented if the organization is:

- market leader
- closely followed by competition
- involved in a price war
- running out of ideas
- desperate.

When an organization is comfortable, even in decay, change will not occur. Sadly, it is the nature of (especially larger) organizations, that decision makers are often the last to be discomforted.

5 *Wanting*

This final stage is more important than all the others – and needs no explanation:

It's not how good you are, it's how bad you want it.

Further reading to Part Four

Baker M., *The Marketing Book*, Oxford (Butterworth-Heinemann, 1994).
Piercy N., *Market-led Strategic Change*, 2nd edition, Oxford (Butterworth-Heinemann, 1997).
von Clausewitz C., *On War* (Wordsworth, 1997).

Part Five

Where next?

Chapter 16

New age marketing?

Since I wrote the original few pages on the likely future of marketing and the possible changes in society that I saw coming at the practising marketer I have been deafened by the absolute silence that my comments provoked. This is obviously a good sign since it means that everybody has been shocked into reflection by the enormity of the predictions – and they are quietly planning their responses to tomorrow's customer needs.

Heartily warmed by this positive response to my first efforts I have decided to respond to this now identified and quantified (if still latent) customer need by reformulating and refining Part Four of the first edition to look further forward again. This time I have chosen to use a single source of reference rather than several so that the interested reader will have an easier job of tracking down the original data and applying the concepts to his or her own organization.

In 1991

I wrote:

> 'Marketing is not a difficult discipline. Or, at least, it shouldn't be. As long as the marketer and his organization continue to listen closely to its customers and continues to provide the customers with what they want then the organization will continue to flourish. When, for whatever reason, the organization stops offering the market what it wants we can expect to witness the flight of customers, business and profits. One simple approach, one simple solution, so why the problem?

Typically the difficulty arises in trying to find out what our customers want in the first place. Finding out what our customers want *should* be a simple and straightforward task – unfortunately this is not the case. In ever more competitive and crowded marketplaces organizations are continuing to search for that elusive 'niche' or unique market position which will afford them a defensible profit haven. So the question moves from finding out simply what our customers want to finding out what our customers *exactly* want from the organization. And, of course, while our customers would find it very easy to choose exactly the right product from a competitive range, it just doesn't seem to be quite as easy to describe in detail something that they want but have never had – anyway you're the producer – isn't this your job? Not only do customers sometimes find it difficult to describe what their needs are currently, but lengthy lead times in many industries require that organizations find out what customers are going to want one, two, five or even ten years away. None of these problems are new. These are situations which have been confronting the marketer for decades and it's just something that we have learned to manage over the years. However, the past few years have seen even more interesting changes in the marketplace than ever before. Change has suddenly become a major factor in its own right.

Recently change has started to become a major factor in every marketer's life. But change itself is not new. All of human history is a catalogue of change. So why, all of a sudden, is change starting to be written in capital letters? If we look closely it is not the amount or the degree of change which is causing a level of anxiety in most organizations and among many managers, it is the rate of change which seems to be surpassing that level at which most people feel comfortable. We just don't seem to have enough time nowadays to assimilate the last lot of change before we are being asked to change yet again. Of course, nowhere is the rate of change more evident than in the marketplace, the marketer's raw material.

For the marketer, who in order for his organization to survive, needs to understand and be able to predict likely future customer needs, the most worrying aspect of the 1980s is the apparent demise of clear trends in market demand. Along with the demise of the 'mass market' (we all knew where we stood in those days) we are starting to see what looks like the growing co-existence of opposites in almost all areas: as the large global organizations grow in size and importance so the number of small specialist organizations also continues to mushroom. As medical science makes significant leaps and is capable of treating more and more human diseases so alternative medicine and eastern practice become more popular. As technology advances and continues to pervade all areas of modern life so people become more nostalgic and there is an intensified search for simplicity and the 'natural' things in life. We do not have to try and understand this apparently impossible co-existence of opposites, it is in all our lives – we seem to live it easily and quite naturally. But it does make prediction difficult.

Not surprisingly, the more this evident and increasing rate of change affects our marketplace and therefore our organizations, the more we feel threatened by events that we do not understand and cannot control. Most people are afraid of change, staying in their own comfort zone is a natural human reaction. If marketers, like other mortals, were guaranteed that change would be for the better then maybe we might approach it a little more optimistically. Nevertheless, we all tend to be wary. When faced with change which is too fast to deal with, even marketers can be tempted to drop out of the real world and create a stable environment within which to operate. While this may suit the organization, most of which are organized to exist in a stable state, it will not suit the customers for very long.

Before we can work out the best way to deal with this problem we really need to try and understand what is going on. The futurologists, pundits, self-publicists, cranks and prophets of doom all have their own pet theories and it often seems like a situation of 'you pays your money you takes your choice'. Nevertheless, the explanations of the current phenomena tend to fall into two broad camps and ways forward tend to be based on the idea that either this is just another cycle or that this is the end of an era or even the end of history itself as we know it.

No change here then in the past seven years! Change is still pushing organizations and, generally we are getting better at managing it. Some organizations have even appeared that seem to thrive on change, but at the same time seem to have problems dealing with the need to plan for the future. That magic 'balance', as always, seems elusive for us.

Since understanding the reasons for change often plays a key role in dealing with its effects, in 1991 I surmised that the nature of the change about to come through into UK markets (other national markets possibly later) was this time structural rather than just another cycle. A move from 'industrial' to 'post-industrial' society. A frightening concept at the time perhaps but one that is much less daunting when we just live through it.

Chapter 17

Back to the future

The future is where the marketing strategist spends a lot of his or her time. There are four ways to deal with the future:

1 you can ignore it;
2 you can predict it;
3 you can control it;
4 you can respond to it.

The first is popular in many organizations but dangerous, the second and third are the focus of much strategic attention but, in most markets, impossible to achieve fully. The fourth is, like the 'matrix organization', attractive on paper but difficult to make work. Practicality, as always, lies in a flexible compromise between the extremes. In any event no marketer or organization can afford not to look forward. How do we do this?

Collecting data on the future

This is never an easy task. How do you know how good it is? The only thing anyone can guarantee about looking forward is that we will be wrong – the question is: how wrong?

The people writing about the future are as many and as various as their reasons for doing so. They range from, at one extreme, ordinary research organizations masquerading as 'forecasters' but offering little more than straight-line extrapolations from the current data, to, at the other extreme, individuals who seem to inhabit a future world and have trouble relating to today's realities. Separating out the charlatans from the commentators is no easy task, especially since none of it can be tested (until it's too late). For the interested reader, the following writers are worthy of some time:

- Charles Handy;
- Aberdene and Naisbit;
- Faith Popcorn;
- and of course, Nostradamus!

A book on marketing strategy should be dedicated to that task – marketing strategy. As I have said more than once, the foundation of solid marketing strategy is not skills or techniques but knowledge and understanding of customer needs and wants. Tomorrow's marketing strategy will only be as good as our ability to understand and plan for our customers' needs and wants in the future. As Faith Popcorn (1991) says: 'Predicting the future is the easy part. It's knowing what to do with it that counts.'

For this edition's view into the future I have decided to take a different approach. I have decided to focus on a single source which collects data in depth (2000+ interviews), regularly (yearly), has done so for a long period (over twenty years) and can be compared to other international data similarly collected. The data I will be using is based on 'values theory' which itself has a long history and a respected theoretical base. The data is collected commercially in the UK by Synergy Consulting and is used here with their kind permission.

Values analysis attempts to classify people's dominant values and motivations. Personal values drive everything from the way we think to the way we behave. When grossed up to a national level, values – attitudes, aspirations and motivations – can be used to explain societal behaviour patterns. These values represent a mindset which creates the terms of reference against which people make sense of their world. Because values are constantly (if only subconsciously) referred to, they are used as a basis for making and reinforcing decisions, actions and approaches to life. While major events such as divorce, redundancy and death will undoubtedly affect the balance, values will also define an individual's response to such events.

Synergy Consulting use the outputs of the data analysis to support clients in areas such as market segmentation and targeting. Synergy have been using their own segmentation into 'Social Value Groups' (SVG) for many years. Here, however, I shall be considering the latest (1997) data to identify broad tendencies in the UK population as a whole and what these moves mean for the future and for marketing in particular.

Where has Britain been?

1998 sees Britain continuing its transition from a hierarchical consumer/industrial patriarchy to a more open, diverse, slightly more feminized information transforming culture.

Feel free to take the time to re-read that last bit. ...

What other commentators and pundits have called the move from industrial to 'post-industrial' or even 'post-modern' society has been showing up in carefully collected research data for a number of years. Where it will lead and what it will look like when we get there nobody seems to know. No society has yet completed the journey. This is obviously the excitement of living in changing times.

The 'transition from a hierarchical consumer/industrial patriarchy to a more open, diverse, slightly more feminized information transforming culture' can probably be explained more clearly by looking at the past twenty years' changes in the population broken down by the three classifications most used by marketers to describe society: sex, age and socioeconomic groups.

Sex

Women have become more central to the promotion of core society values as those values have become more emotion-driven. Male values have become more marginalized.

Men are more pragmatic and judge life more on 'rational' grounds and less on emotions, they also don't feel the need to belong to any group and therefore espouse individualism.

Women on the whole are more family oriented than men and are more at ease with the complexity of today's modern world, they don't feel as threatened by it and are more likely to see opportunities and to try new behaviours.

Age

The generation gap, first noted in the 1960s is still there but now between the under 45s and the over 55s. The first generation of baby boomers, the 45–55 age group most typifies the status quo in Britain. The under 35s are significantly different to the rest of the population.

In a shorthand form, British society can be said to consist of three parts: The under 45s represent change, the over 55s represent resistance to change and the 45–55s represent the generation gap.

Socio-economic groups (SEG)

This has effectively become a non-differentiating segmentation tool with the passage of time. The data shows little differentiation in values between the major SEGs, with two exceptions.

ABs have a more diverse range of values than any other SEG. This is largely a function of extended education and the material ability to change their behaviours. This gives them the opportunity to try new ideas and subsequently examine their existing value set.

Es have a wider range of values than any group except AB. This is because SEG classification automatically puts retired people into E category. Forty-nine per cent of Es are over 65.

What are the key trends for the future of British society?

There are a number of key social trends that can be identified within the British population. Naturally some trends are more marked among certain groups than others – that is what market segmentation is all about. More importantly we can separate the trends which are 'leading' societal change and those which are 'resisting' change. An review of the leading trends makes stimulating reading.

Searching for continuity

As change continues, and indeed gathers pace, there is an understanding that identity is a transitory phenomenon – people are aware that the person/'I' who reacted to a stimulus in the past is not the same person/'I' reacting to the stimulus now. There is a growing need to understand the continuity between the transitory identities.

Empathetic individualism

This is a new form of individualism in British and western culture and it is a manifestation of the changing core values of post-industrial culture. Empathetic individualism refers to the trend towards individuals who are able to understand and empathize with the individuality of others with no submersion or loss of identity to their own individual position.

Caring holism

Today the more 'feminine' values are firmly at the core of British values – empathy, aesthetics, creativity. Two other values combine to create this leading trend, connectedness and spiritual awareness. The result is an understanding that the further along the road of life we travel, the more today's confusions will clear away and life will become clearer. This ability to transcend some of today's confusions, not by ignoring but by contextualizing them is key to caring holism.

The Tao generation

This is the most important and leading edge set of values trends in Britain today. This trend creates a person who has a range of key motivations in their approach to life, among these will be:

1   I am who I am. The empathetic individual trying to understand their own caring holism.
2   Life is what it is. Life is messy and full of emotions and intuitions. Life is (probably) part of something larger but not through established religion.
3   Both are constantly changing. Living with and embracing change is key to this trend. Life is understood to be about personal growth, of understanding and of having an effect on the greater whole.
4   Enjoy. The sense of freedom felt in the ever changing complexity of life creates a potential for a sense of enjoyment not felt in earlier times. This sense of potential joy is firmly based firmly on individuality, independence and self awareness. At an even deeper level, it is felt that life is basically 'safe' and that, just as fear was learned, so too can enjoyment be learned, if people can holistically experience themselves and their world as it 'is'.

The new and the now

The driving force to experience anything new, and especially different. This desire for experience is not a conceptual construct, it is a motivator for action. There is never enough time to do all the things that want to be done, consequently, life becomes a series of largely unplanned often chaotic 'doings'. This chaos is, however, very enjoyable, and in many ways liberating since trying new things changes perceptions of 'risk'.

Using complexity

The new world is not chaotic, there is an innate order to it. Although this order is not hierarchical, sequential or rigid in any sense (the Tao generation). Thinking about the world in new or different ways doesn't create answers – just stimuli. This desire for stimuli creates a sense of excitement in even the most mundane situations and creates 'opportunities' for breaking the boundaries of tradition as the world becomes less certain but more knowable.

Excitement and pleasure

A desire to extend the life of the five senses and a mind that complexifies all perceptions creates a world view of opportunities, for pleasure. The drive to know and understand life creates a frisson of excitement when the right behavioural path is selected. This trend explains the number of innovators in so many markets, life is not only about enjoyment and fun, it is about truly taking chances and gaining pleasure.

Rage

There is a downside to the optimistic risk in the experiencing of the new and now and the payoff in pleasure that comes from this behaviour. Sometimes the risks are not sufficiently taken or the outcome of the behaviour does not meet the expectations. In either case, the reaction is likely to be one of blame and anger – don't just get mad, get even. The social/excitement edge to the trend means that social unrest is exciting. An urban riot means the rules are set aside for a while and new behaviours are possible, the payoff is emotional thrill and the opportunity is pleasure.

The key linkage among all these leading trends is rather one of 'fluidity'. Society members riding these trends are capable of changed behaviours without a lot of outside pressure. In fact it tends to be their own internal dynamics or orientations that drives their behaviours. All aspects of behaviour are capable of quite rapid change, the key word is 'capable', they don't necessarily change rapidly they are just capable of it.

Such an appetite for change among the leading trends is not surprising given the often traumatic changes forced on society over the past decade. Society has responded, not by resisting change or by sinking into nostalgia, but by embracing change and learning to love it. And, of course, wanting more.

Naturally, there are large numbers in British society who actively resist these changes and we have not discussed these restraining trends here. We know from past analysis that the leading trends in society will be restrained by other forces, even to some extent contained for a short while. Inexorably though, these leading trends are becoming the core values of tomorrow's society.

Who is currently espousing these leading trends? It is not, as one might think, the young on their own. They are held across society although there are (*not* strongly marked) tendencies towards the:

- under 50s;
- SEG AB/CI;
- East Midlands and East Anglia;
- Well educated.

It's all very interesting ...

But why bother? Here I am wondering how to make this quarter's sales figures and .... But marketing strategy is like that. It forces us to take some time off from the day-to-day routine and to check that we are moving in the right direction – to check that we are moving at all! Our customers are not just a resource that will always be there to take the output from the factory, they are more important than that. If for no other reason than to plan what the factory needs to be producing next year we need to know where the customer is going. This is when the future becomes important today. What then will these leading trends produce in the way of customers? And before some of you turn off, remember that these trends will affect both industrial/business-to-business customers as well as consumer markets.

It's been said before, but let's say it again – the customer is the business. The customer (and his or her needs and wants) must drive the organization, its marketing strategy and its market activity. The idea that an organization drives its marketplace is an idea whose time has gone and, if not abandoned quickly, will take the organization with it.

Also, apart from commodity suppliers, organizations will survive more and more by offering differentiated products and services to identified market segments. As competition increases, the future can only belong to those providers who offer the 'right' product or service (hygiene factor) as well as a sense of identity and involvement in the brand that meets the customers' broader emotional needs (motivator).

Relationships and involvement don't just rise like Excaliber from the lake, they have to be based on a deep understanding of the target customer's life, needs, wants and aspirations. And these, as we have seen, have already changed and are still changing.

And tomorrow's customer?

Will be something 'new'. Tomorrow's customer will not be a replication of the past but will be whatever a post-industrial customer will be. Without looking too deeply into the crystal ball, we can already see some important pointers:

Customer traits

Inner-driven

Customers will be more driven by what happens inside themselves than what happens around them. Less driven by fads and fashion unless they feel it is right for them and what they want to be. Life will also be a voyage of discovery and experience so customers will change over time and will 'grow' as individuals.

Marketing implications

Fashionability and relying on the herd instinct for sales will be less successful. Organizations will have to invest more in really understanding what customers want and what is motivating them – shallow understandings will likely cause more harm than good. Customers will be looking for products and services which both support their voyage of self-discovery and reinforce the sense of personal 'being' at different stages. 'Loyalty' will depend on products, services and producing-organizations being seen as – and acting as – central to the customer's life. Peripheral products and services will be easily discarded when it is time 'to move on'.

Multi-individualistic

Individualism will continue to grow and, as customers become more secure with their individuality they will experiment with other forms. The rise of the 'multi-faceted individual' will produce customers who are quite different individuals in different circumstances.

Segmentation models created in the 1970s and 1980s will finally break down as will the old models of consumer behaviour. Successful companies will be those who are able to use empathy and intuition to map customer progress. Customers will create new patterns of behaviour and will expect producers to follow them, they will not conform to what business would like them to do.

Interconnected

As life becomes more complicated, 'chaotic' and interesting, so customers will get better at connecting the previously unconnected facets of their lives.

Much more than 'lifestyle' marketing, customers will get better at understanding, trying and creating their own lifestyles through individual connections. Previously unconnected relationships will be made between brands and organizations as new relationships are created to deal with the new realities. Individuality and uniqueness of brands and organizations will facilitate this new sense of 'mix and match'.

Pleasure seeking

Hedonism always implies lack of responsibility and maturity. Future customers will rewrite the definitions in this area. It's not only OK to have fun – it is necessary. Previous generations believed that life was a serious business and look where it got them! Tomorrow's customer will expect to enjoy life and expect organizations to help them in this.

Fun, pleasure and optimism are good. There will be two big markets for the future – products and services aimed at helping customers to have fun and products and services to take the drudgery out of life to give them more time to do what they were put in this world to do. Before you all jump to materialistic conclusions this does not mean having to earn and spend more money. The advertising agents (bless them) have already noted the appearance of a new consumer group, the HAPPIs (Happy on a Part-time Income) who are happy to scale down their previously materialistic lifestyles to one which gives more time. Maybe all marketers should beware of projecting their aspirations on to their customers!

Deconstructed

Customers are already rewriting the rules – and some organizations have noticed. The post-industrial society is still a society waiting to be defined, today's customers are defining it. To do this they have had to throw away the rule book which constrained past behaviour and look for ways (and ends) which make the future possible. Society's institutions such as 'work', 'family' and 'class' have already been completely redrawn so that they can function into the next millennium.

Throw out the old models, they won't work in the future. It is finally time to move away from the economic concepts about price and rational searches for maximum economic value. It is time for the emotions to start playing their role in understanding customer needs and motivations. It is time for producing-organizations to use emotions and intuition in product and service delivery too. Where there are no rules or history to guide us we have no choice anyway. Marketers may, in the future, be described as the blind feeling their way with the aid of a white cane. Nothing wrong with that. Make sure you have a good cane – and you develop your senses to tell you whether you have arrived at a kerb or a brick wall before you hit it!

Unforgiving

No longer the passive customer who will consume the mass-produced product put in front of them (and be happy for it) without question. No more. Today's customers are already baring their teeth, tomorrow's customers will get even.

Customers will be extremely tolerant of honest mistakes, especially of organizations who, like them, are experimenting with the future and trying to get it right. They will not give any latitude to those organizations who are simply paying lip-service to the new future. Tomorrow's customer will be looking for partners not simply providers. Organizations who are not part of the customer's solution are part of the problem. Tomorrow's customer has no time for problems, there are only opportunities.

What is a marketer to do?

Look, listen and LEARN.

The lessons are already there – for those with eyes to see. Society has changed mightily over the past decade and the change process is irreversible. The post-industrial society will come about although its final form is still unclear. The question every marketer should be asking is: 'Do I want to be a part of it?'

For those individuals who do not want to be part of the future – and there will be many – they need not panic unduly, there will be a market for the old products, delivered in the old ways for the foreseeable future. This market will not now grow but, like the old washing powders, it will contract gently until a small profitable 'rump' remains. As long as managers don't panic about the decline and try to play Canute by turning the unturnable tide of change, the decline should be quiet and stately.

For those who want to be part of the future and of growth the lessons are clear, grow and develop with the market. Work with your customers to create tomorrow together. Don't worry that you don't know all the answers, tomorrow's customers won't expect you to. What they will expect is organizations to work with them to create the new society – together. They may be willing to trust you, are you willing to trust them?

Further reading to Part Five

Popcorn F., *The Popcorn Report* (Doubleday, 1991).
For further information contact:
Synergy Consulting, 5th Floor, Bilton House, 54–58 Uxbridge Road, London W5 2TL, England.

Index